EULOGISTS FOR FREEDOM

Our ANCESTORS   Our ANOREXIA

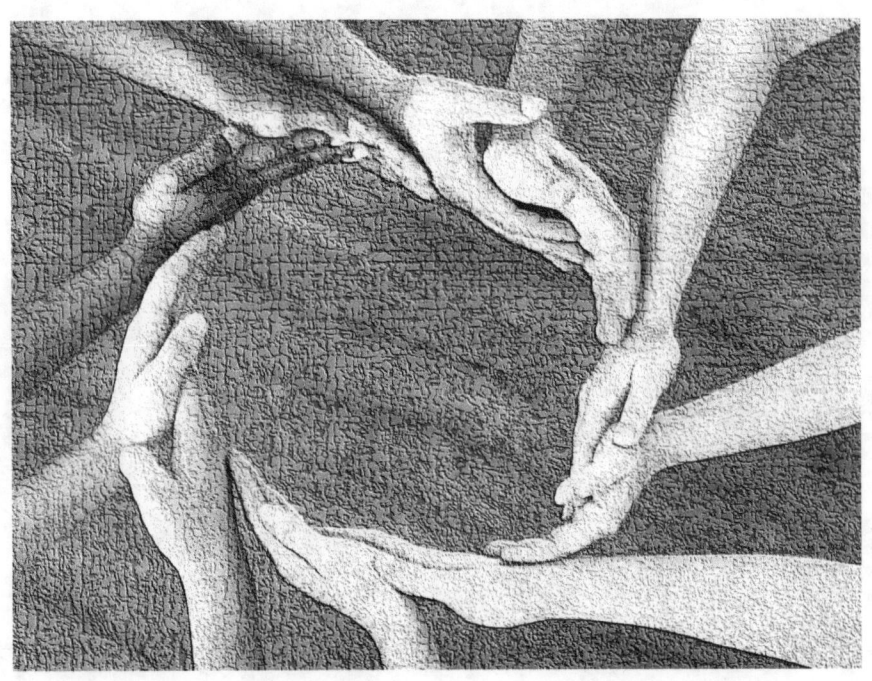

BERNARD F NORMAN   &   LUCY B G TAN

Chapbook Press

Schuler Books
2660 28th Street SE
Grand Rapids, MI 49512
(616) 942-7330
www.schulerbooks.com

Eulogists for Freedom

ISBN 13: 9781957169200

Library of Congress Control Number: 2022917293

eBook ISBN: 9781957169224

Printed in the United States by Chapbook Press.

CONTENTS

INTRODUCTION

Just for a moment imagine yourself at a far-away place, a very long time ago. Nothing is familiar, only that the ground is beneath your feet and the sky is above your head. Much of human history as you know it has not yet happened. You have no communication or time keeping devices, and your legs are your only mode of transportation. Mysteriously, this book is one of the few things you do have. It is not a re-write of human history. That would be ridiculously pretentious on our part. But as you read it consider yourself being on a journey without many of your usual preconceptions. You will read about some particular people that many of us think we know enough about already as our contemporaries, and that some-how they are also very different. But as the story un-folds we learn that these persons perhaps represent things meaningful for us all. Much of the story features recent deliberations. But we start in the distant past, and return there occasionally, to remind us of the past when trying to make sense of things in the present.

Qafzeh Cave, predating Nazareth in Israel, around 95000 years ago. A small clan of adults and children left the dry ravine and began their somber ascent. Stronger members helped others maneuver over snags of small rocks and protruding roots. Slowly but surely the whole group reached one end and then the other of a gently slopped terrace. Its bed of fallen rocks and pervading silt had been infinitesimally liberated from the mountain above. Some clan members rested under the shade of a carob tree that traced close to the cliff face. A singular sentry for the entrance to the cave. Its dried pods and seeds scattered on the ground. Their measure not yet realized. Other group members stood and surveyed the distant precipices which had been inaugurated too from deeply faulted ground. And of the surrounding valleys whose watersheds stretched to the awaiting coast. The broad vista of woodlands and yellow terrain, with big blue sky, but hazy horizon.

Some children flittered near the mouth of the cave, daring each other to be the first entrant. But none ventured in. After only a short while though the group

1

was called to gather again and begin its entry into the cave. The younger children's eyes popped with awe as they entered and looked around the widening chamber. A few glanced backward and were assured by the daylight radiating at the cave mouth. They all then wanted to rush and touch the walls and to reach up and pretend their fingers could brush the ceiling. But they resisted, taking their cues from the older children who appeared to have been there before. The group then passed through a slight narrowing into a second chamber. They all again settled into silence. The two who had led the procession, from the ravine and into the cave, lowered to the ground a platform of animal skin stretched taught across cedar saplings. The oldest of the clan pulled away loose animal skins to reveal a lifeless adolescent body. As he lifted the body the willowy neck fell back over his scarred but muscular arm and revealed again the deep gash on the young and rounded head. The elder crouched again and gently laid the body in a shallow pit. He moved the motionless legs and arms to the same side. He then repositioned some deer antlers already clasped by the awfully wooden hands. Before standing he held his shell necklace close to his chest to prevent it from snagging on the antlers. Another elder opened a small pouch and with her two grizzled fingers pinched some red powder and sprinkled it over the body. She held the pouch out for others to sprinkle some too. The shuffling of their feet was the only sound. Some in the clan took moments to stand and observe the small grave, while others studied the darkness in the nooks and crannies above them.

Westminster Abbey, London, England, September 6, 1997. Ascending sounds of Elton John's solo voice and piano reached the vaulted ceiling, like the productions of predecessors, but were on this occasion transmitted simultaneously to the world. Musical notes and lyrics bathed the ears and hearts of the solemn congregation, attended from afar and close in. "Goodbye England's rose, From a country lost without your soul, Who'll miss the wings of your compassion, More than you'll ever know". (1). A message of gravity recognized by applause firstly from outer places and then ratified by inside congregants. A fine preamble to a brother's eulogy on the private and public parallels his sister travailed. Followed by a Lord Archbishop with his Primate ring on hand he held out as he prayed God-speed and eternity for all of whom had passed and those still present. Then the funerary casket, with royal standard, a son's written note and white wreaths atop, was hoisted to shoulders by red dressed bearers. Their march through streams of stained-glass light seemed an achingly slow strobe down the long aisle. A minute's silence taken at the immense doorway and around the world was then repealed by bells tolling in the towers aside. The cortege then slowly proceeded down the cold stepped masonry. Grief again plain to see as the casket was lowered into the awaiting hearse. As the motorized cavalcade departed it passed by mounds of floral tributes and mourners by the thousands who crowded at sides of city streets. Many witnesses at windows, roof tops or viewing massive video-screens in London city parks, or in their own homes all around the world. Still others watched from bridges and over-passes as the motorcade carried the deceased princess to her resting place on a tiny island in an ornamental lake.

From caves to cathedrals, the places and practices of funerary ritual have be-come more ornate. But our core rituals of respect, when interring or cremating our dead for practical reasons, have remained universal for untold millennia. As has the offering of food as part of ceremonial observance. Like yeonpo-tang (soup) in Korea, rakia (fruit brandy) and soda bread in the Balkans, koliva (boiled wheat) in Greece and Russia, arvels (sweet cake) in England, and at least far back to refrigerium (refreshment) in ancient Rome. Eulogizing our dead is to recall their achievements in the life span they had available and the intense person-al value they had meant for us. But eulogies can also remind us that our own personal freedom for life's endeavors is mortally time limited. The younger the loved one is at death the more salient the reminder. After funerals, or memori-als, we rapidly return to our everyday activities and self-comforting distractions. We do this obviously for good reasons of normality for ourselves and especially the bereaved family, but we continue to exercise our freedom with barely any further thought.

Freedom. 自由. Sloboda. Haere Noa. Vrijheid. Zivou. Huriya. Liberte`. Uhuru. Ominira. Fahafahana. If freedom was somehow quantifiable then undoubtedly it would be assigned hefty weight and prominent position in a humanities equiv-alent to chemistry's periodic table. However, do we recognize freedom when we have it? Or do we know it better when we or others don't have it? We often think about freedom mostly in terms of when it is lost or threatened. Wars are supposedly fought in freedom's name by selfless soldiers yet are fraught with persecution and catastrophic loss of homes, livelihoods, friends and family members. Weather, geological, and pandemic disasters can also unfold huge misery. Such extreme tragedy for other people seems to make our own freedom clear.

We, and undoubtedly most others too, feel humbly disturbed when we hear of persons past and present who have suffered the loss of freedom. Disturbed by reflecting on the multitudes of people who have been trafficked and enslaved during the centuries of human existence; and of the terror experienced by the millions in the Nazi death camps and Stalin's gulags of the 1930's through 1950's; the thousands of Cambodians in Pol Pot's S-21 from 1975 through 1979; the Rwanda genocide of 1994; and the annihilation of Yazidis by Islamic State of Iraq and the Levant that began in 2014; and troubled by what can happen to individuals, such as remembering how Margaret Wilson of Wigtown, Scotland 1685, at age 18 years, on the basis of her neighbors accusations, and facing death one way or another, suffered drowning in the rising tide for her "refusing to swear the Oath of Abjuration and hear the curates" (2); the attempted assassination of Malala Yousafzai, of Pakistan, in October 2012 in retribution for her activism for female education; the imprisonment of Aleksandr Solzhenitsyn in Soviet gulags from 1945-1953; the 1967 to 1973 captivity and torture of John McCain during the American-Vietnam War; of Nelson Mandela on Robben Island, South Africa, 1964-1982; of Mikis Theodorakis imprisoned by a military junta in Greece, 1967-1974; of Tagni Rahmani and Narges Mohammadi in Iran, numerous times since 1999, and so many other selfless advocates for human rights over the centuries; and the secret suffering of countless persons who still today continue to be victims of abuse by other people.

If we are fortunate to live in a place where our vote counts, we still rush back from mailboxes or polling booths to our busy lives. Even then we still rarely think about freedom. That is until we might surprise ourselves with barely disguised indignation that we think another car driver is impeding our free and speedy passage. What should we make of our indignation? Where the heck did that come from? Then on another day we might empathize and donate to fundraising for victims of a tsunami at a very distant country from our own. But where should we look to learn more on how we experience freedom in relation to each other in closer proximity and lucky to live in the absence of shared extreme life events? There are indeed some people who could help us understand freedom

4

from this subtlety of a psychosocial perspective. Informative as these people are, they don't have to be as exalted like Confucius (Kong Zhongni), Galileo Galilei, Marie Curie (Maria Sklodowska), Mohandas Gandhi, Mother Teresa (Anjeze Bojaxhiu), or any other famous person. Nor are they necessarily all of the same religious, political, social, ethnic, cultural, or of many other groups. They instead are helpful because of how their experience may be a reflection for all of us but manifested more clearly by them. For that they can legitimately be called beacons.

These beacons are, however, still described in clinical and social narrative terms as having an eating disorder (ED), such as anorexia nervosa, bulimia nervosa, or binge eating disorder. An example of let the obvious symptoms or behavior determine the labels that persist as a dominant understanding of what they represent about the person. Which infers that these people are greatly different from their same age peers, and the rest of us too. There can be, of course, life threatening circumstances for some persons who have an ED, for which careful treatment is needed. However, there has always been a hint or two that we all have more to learn for ourselves from persons who experience an ED. And although we, as in the authors, both have had lengthy and busy clinical and com-munity professional experience of persons with an ED and other persons with a wide range of mental health concerns, we have reached that point of wanting to review our own level and limits of knowledge and understanding. And with being fortunate to have more personal time now, we can dive deeper into the surrounding sources of knowledge to explore what hints we think we got along the way and what we didn't sufficiently understand. This review, we think, will possibly reveal more about freedom and how that applies psychosocially for those of us already fortunate to not have our freedom under immediate threat from authoritarianism, war or other sudden social chaos and catastrophes.

To borrow a theme from the Celestine Prophecy by James Redfield (1993), it is in coincidences rather than the planned or expected from which we may learn the most about ourselves. It could be re-stated that it is by chance or by taking a different perspective, rather than with what we set out to discover or by hold-ing on too tightly to our ideas, that we learn more about other things and other people, and so ourselves. We may see a person with excessive thinness and almost automatically categorize them in our private thoughts as being anorexic, who has eating problems with possible fatal consequences, having succumbed to social pressure to be thin. What we typically not do is ask the question of what there is to learn from them and in a way that does not categorize them as being so very different from ourselves.

As we worked on this book, we each had to reassess some of our own preconceptions about EDs. We did not set out to refute the 'nature' (genetic, biological, physiological) or favor the 'nurture' (social environment, learning) arguments for explaining complex human behavior of an individual person. In doing so we had to sometimes take a view of being more like students of learning than professional experts. We had to remind ourselves that persons who have EDs can often be seen as social 'misfits' while 'ill', and that instead they might somehow represent a social purpose, perhaps even evolutionarily important. It helped us to be aware of reductionism in our own thinking, and in that of others. To be more carefully attuned to how the repetition of ideas become the basis of accepted common knowledge but over time can be inefficiently non-adaptive paradigms. Recognizing how Thomas Kuhn had back in 1962 warned of how prevailing paradigms persist too long without sufficient review in many spheres of science and human endeavor. So, before we dive into the review about EDs we firstly invite you to read about reductionism in the next chapter. Some of the examples we wrote to illustrate reductionism also fortuitously provided information and concepts we thought worthy of a bit more preparation before carrying them over to the chapters which discuss EDs in more depth. So, we plead for your patience in first reading the chapter on reductionism.

As you continue reading, please do keep in mind that this writing is a philosophical exploration and not intended as a guide to the assessment or treatment for persons considered to have an 'eating disorder'. If you are looking for information on direct care and treatment, there are many resources available online. It may be important to firstly narrow your search to resources that are in your local area. Although we may not personally know you, we do think of you, like everyone, as a fellow human whose life is of great value. So do take good care of yourself. If you need help to preserve your life do at least reach out to your primary health care provider or emergency medical services. It can take time to figure out, in partnership with you, what further assessment, treatment and support you might require.

There is a lot to cover in our review in subsequent chapters about current knowledge on EDs. In our attempt to keep the review from being too convoluted some of it may come across as unintentionally blunt. So please consider not taking any judgment about you or others from what is written. Especially that which uses clinical and diagnostic language as default terms so to better cross reference information from various sources. To explore the complex concepts involved in this philosophical review we also had to take an almost 'forensic inquisitive' approach. We had to be observant for pieces of information from sources not previously identified as associated with EDs and from those directly associated but which had not recognized the possible significance of some things they themselves reported.

By the end of reading this book you may have some good ideas for better labels that convey more than just the obvious behaviors of EDs. Some readers may consider that the descriptions about eating, and body image and bodily function are not relevant to them. But do read on because it is how beacons view themselves and experience the world which is relevant for us all. Remember too, all of us have a common interwoven ancestral history that makes us more the same than different from each other, and we are still evolving together; likely then making life's experience by these beacons ours as well.

To repeat-

when the discourse is cowardly

limited to a single, autonomous object

-treated as if an unrelated thing-

knowledge flees

and the understanding turns its back

in shame;

then how could it face

the all-fearful, immense machine,

whose terrible unendurable weight

- if not supported in its own center-

would crush the back of Atlas

or flatten Hercules,

who could not judge that labor

more prodigious than investigating Nature?

[excerpt from EL SUEÑO (The Dream) by

Sor Juana Inés de la Cruz (1651-1695),

translated by John Campion, 1983]. (3)

FOOD FOR THOUGHT

You may notice Sayer or Jaden is increasingly shying away from food. They could be your child, sibling, parent, friend, lover, or yourself. You may experience the subtle pangs of fear for when a loved one's basic survival seems under threat. Your first instinct may be to suggest they "will feel better" if they did eat something. They reel back even further and may not yet understand much of what they are experiencing. They have perhaps unwittingly shifted some discomfort and instead see it represented in food, eating and changes in their body. You both feel at a great loss about how to talk about food before this survival chasm becomes any wider.

You may begin to search for quick and understandable reasons for this 'threat' to their or your own survival. However, consider for a moment the relative ease at which you can select and savor food. Then imagine how you may feel, if having never spoken in public, you are asked to address a crowd of thousands and with notice of only a few minutes. Your anticipatory anxiety only approximates that which Sayer or Jaden may experience every day. But this anxiety is only one part of the complex puzzle that envelops a person who may also have a distinctive eating style. So, before we proceed further into exploring how beacons may help us understand freedom, we need to take a brief side journey to look at how we limit our understanding when we try to find quick answers for complex things. That is, reductionism. Lay people do it and scientists have not been immune to it either. This side journey is intended to show examples of how with only a little deeper digging we can see alternative perspectives to that of pre-existing assumptions. Like us, you will possibly not remember some of the detail of what you read. But that does not matter as much as understanding reductionism generally. At the end, of this side journey, we will suggest a simple strategy for how to counter-balance for that of our own reliance on reductionism.

Sometimes reductive reasoning can be helpful and relatable for interpersonal communication. Metaphors and similes have been used to convey abbreviated meaning in probably all languages and cultures for a very long time. We also

9

still use fantastical contrasts to emphasize meaning, such as: *It's raining cats and dogs* for describing unusually heavy rain, and *they have a heart of gold* to suggest a person is consistently generous, or *as tough as nails* to say we think someone is emotionally strong but also possibly very insensitive to other people. A particularly relevant example is the phrase they are *as skinny as a rake*. This seems to imply the observer is overly impressed by the physical appearance of another person and that the thought process of the observer is going to be stuck, for a while at least, rather than moving on to better relate to and understand the person. While metaphors and hyperbole are often useful and easily understood we do need to be careful about relying on these types of tools for our own deeper thinking, understanding of complex human behavior, and communication generally with other people. The same applies to what is called 'black-and-white' or 'all-or-nothing' thinking by which some people tend to take an extreme or catastrophic point of view on themselves, other people, or any subject and can sometimes swap to take the opposing extreme view. Seemingly without the ability to consider in-between points of view. There is already a lot of information on this style of thinking in the psychological literature. For some persons who experience depression, black-and-white thinking manifests with accompanying low mood, low energy, disrupted sleep and appetite, and can be the basis of severe self-criticism and suicide risk. Here, though, we will limit our discussion to be about reductionism.

Here is a topical example of reductionism in a personal interaction: a new guest hesitates while eating at your dining table. Like many other people on 'host alert', one of your go-to thoughts is that they do not like my cooking. But being typically indirect at first you only ask whether the food is too hot or perhaps cold. After they confirm it is neither, you then offer to serve them something different and more to their preference. The conversation may switch then on to whether they have any food allergies you think as the host you should have asked about when you invited them. They confirm that is not the case either, but others around the table then add their lists of allergies into the conversation. But the guest resumes eating and the opportunity to understand their hesitation in eating is lost. It was instead in reaction to another diner's comment triggering in them a fond memory. You can see in this example that the host's reductionism, the guest "does not like my cooking", was also probably associated with

10

being self-critical. By making and following a quick assumption the host inadvertently missed other possible lines of inquiry and understanding. The host possibly could have remarked that they noticed the hesitation and asked the guest if everything was alright. The guest might have then had opportunity to explain they were just remembering something pleasant. So now let's take a trip from an anecdote on interpersonal space to the science of outer space.

When we look up to the night sky, we see stars and some planets, but mostly dark space in between. This dark space is not necessarily just empty but instead contains what is called dark matter. The heralded physicist and cosmologist Stephen Hawking (1942-2018) in his theorizing on dark matter in space may have himself shown our human tendency to be reductive. In his description, of dark matter, he applied what is believed about black holes (large spaces left by collapsed stars in which an intense gravitational force can pull in and prevent the escape of any mass and light too). Hawking theorized that dark matter could be made up of tiny black holes. It should follow then that these tiny black holes would block or distort the light transmitted by stars in their vicinity thousands of times over in only short periods. However, a team of astronomers at the Kavli Institute in Japan, in 2019, observed the nearby Andromeda galaxy and saw only one small flicker of distortion in over seven hours. (4) This appears to refute Hawking's fledgling theory on dark matter. But even geniuses are human and so prone to being reductive via borrowing ideas from what they have already generated and so is familiar to them. And being deceased Hawking did not have the opportunity to reconsider his theory, or that since by other scientists, on this specific subject. (5)

Albert Einstein (1879 – 1955) had too been reductive but was alive and able to change some of his thinking when contrary evidence was pointed out to him. Initially his ideas about the conservation of energy and mass here on earth and in space also included that the universe was static rather than expanding. However, a Belgian priest and physicist named Lemaitre, at around 1927, drew Einstein's attention to work in the USA by Slipher (1912) on 'red shift' (amongst the light of many color frequencies transmitted by stars). The extent of red shift by a star over time is said to represent its movement away from a prior position, which was confirmed by Hubble of the USA in 1929. Einstein had to acknowledge his error and drop his assumption about the universe being static. Alexander Friedman in Russia, in 1922, had independently thought of the universe as expanding and yet also demonstrated that Einstein's Relativity Theory, with some minor computational changes, remained intact. (6) Whew! That was fortunate. All it took was for Einstein to recognize his reductive error and still his main theories remain relevant to this day: for the computation of time and distance for satellites orbiting earth, our landing on the moon and deep space exploration.

Reductionism, by staying within what is familiar rather than putting more effort into understanding something anew or differently, not only occurs with individuals. It can manifest too in groups or organizations. This was evident when the US Navy during World War II was not receptive to accepting some inventions from outside the military. In doing so the US Navy rejected the invention of frequency-hopping that eventually proved to be useful for preventing the jamming of radio-controlled torpedoes. It is noteworthy that the invention, which foreshadowed Blue-Tooth and Wi-Fi technology, was the brainchild of Hedy Lamarr, an Austrian-born US 1930-40's film actress and self-taught inventor, and her pianist friend and music composer, George Antheil. With far less resources than the US military, Lamarr and Antheil not only showed great imagination but designed something that has proven very useful for the transmission of digital age information. The US Navy had also rejected Grace Hopper (nee Murray) based on her being under-weight and too old at age 34. However, she persisted and received an exemption to instead join the US Naval Reserve in 1943. Her expertise in mathematics led to a career of innovating computer language, eventual Commodore rank, and the US Presidential Medal of Freedom posthumously. If the US Navy had then different admission criteria for specific roles, rather than a reduced common set, they may have been able to utilize her much earlier for wartime code breaking.

While on the topic of technology, reductionism can also occur with joining a popular sweeping change before fully realizing the implications for a specialized situation. The US Navy, with its procedures for examining serious incidents, provides us with an example. This time from its investigation into the USS John McCain's collision in 2017 in which ten US sailors died. The US Navy found that the adoption of touchscreens over-complicated the ship's bridge control functions, even for personnel transferred from other ships that had touchscreens as well. Rear Admiral Bill Galanis characterized the finding as being in the "just because you can doesn't mean you should" category. Returning to conventional controls and physical throttles was thought to not only restore greater commonality between its destroyers but also return operations to being more intuitive. (7)

Another example of reductive reasoning can be found in the medical health field where research in 1983 by Australian physician scientists, Barry Marshall and Robin Warren, showed the presence of a bacterium (Helicobacter Pylori) to be a predominant cause of duodenal and stomach ulcers. Prior to that finding the general view was that ulcers were a direct result of stress, a genetic disposition, or poor dietary lifestyle, each of which alone or together over-produced acid that eroded the stomach or duodenal linings. Reportedly, Marshall and Warren were at first ridiculed because many physicians believed bacteria could not survive stomach acid. This is a good example of how a generally held view, even in medicine, appears to be broad and sophisticated when it is instead reductive and remains unchallenged until a new finding requires a change in thinking. From implying someone having personal tendency to stress and lifestyle rather than those factors perhaps playing more of a secondary role, if at all in some cases. And it wasn't as though the medical field did not have much knowledge about bacteria until the 1980s and so could have also listed it as a probable suspect to consider in general practice. To be fair, perhaps one could say that in the absence of a reliable test for a particular bacterium then it would be difficult to diagnose. However, it would seem the absence of a test was instead filled with supposition and reductionism rather than acknowledging the contemporary limits of science and diagnostic practice.

Forty or so years later, examples of further research tell of an even greater complexity involving bacteria and our gastro-intestinal system. Obata and others (2020) have shown that when nerve cells in our gut sense bacteria they activate a gene called AHR which coordinates with other healthy gut tissues for muscle contraction in the colon. Research by Dunn et al. (2020) suggests that the human gut microbiome adapted when our ancestors ventured around the world and encountered new food choices and diseases. Quinn and others (2020) were surprised to find that gut microbes also produce bile from cholesterol and amino acids. This bile mechanism being hidden for "170 years of bile acid research" that presumed it was mostly the liver and enzymes that produced our bile. We guess you could take this to mean, if you are not looking and instead hold

13

on to old ideas you won't find new things for a very long time. Or if the same old methodology is used you may miss vital clues. Which almost happened to Marshall and Warren. They discovered that their hospital laboratory regularly discarded samples due to being thought of as not clinically useful after two days. However, one of their samples was accidentally not discarded which led to the HP bacteria being detected.

The Human Genome Project (HGP), which began in 1990 and completed in 2003, was a stunning achievement of international collaboration in the mapping of the 20,000 or more protein-coding genes in the human genome. (8) The knowledge from the HGP has led to increased fidelity of tests for identifying some cancers, cystic fibrosis, liver disease and other disorders. Concurrent with and since the HGP there has also been the development of gene-editing therapy (e.g., CRISPR) (9) for some types of leukemia, multiple myeloma, hemophilia, sickle cell anemia, and for Leber amaurosis, which causes congenital (present from birth) blindness. One method of gene therapy is the use of a neutralized virus to carry the genetic DNA treatment material to the nucleus of an affected cell and disrupt the replication of the mutant proteins. Victoria Gray of Mississippi, in 2019, was the first pioneering patient in the USA to undergo gene-editing to restore healthy fetal hemoglobin to compensate for her defective adult-hemo-globin sickle cells. Almost eighteen months later she had no severe pain attacks like those before receiving infusion treatment. (10). Such an approach of using a person's individualized genetic and environmental information is called precision medicine. With such great promise of life-changing and life-saving advances from genetic research we might be lulled into being less weary of reductive thinking, let alone biomedical ethics, in such fundamental science.

However, Angela Saini, in her book The Return of Race Science (2019), provides a good example of reductionism in recent post-HGP genetic research. She tells the story of Bruce Lahn and his research published in the prestigious journal Science in 2005. Lahn claimed that a gene variant in humans had emerged as recent as 5800 years ago (c 3800 BCE), that it was more common in people living in Europe, the Middle East, North Africa and parts of East Asia, was likely associated with an increase in brain size and presumably a cognitive advantage, and purportedly supported the founding of the 'first' great civilizations. Lahn's assertions began to fall apart when other genetic researchers pointed out that

14

the gene variant could have appeared within a time range as broad as 500 to 14,100 years ago and therefore not necessarily as neatly coinciding with the 'first' great civilizations. Other researchers also pointed out that the gene variant was likely involved in changes to other human organs as well, which could mean a generalized process was underway and not necessarily anything as specialized as brain size and inferred intellectual advantage. Saini goes on to say that the Canadian psychologist John Philippe Rushton did IQ tests on hundreds of people with and without the gene variant and found no evidence to support Lahn's contention about the association between the gene variant with brain size and intelligence. Saini goes further and cites Martin Yuille, a molecular biologist in the UK, who reportedly said, "If you're going to do an experiment, you have to be reductionistic. You have to look for one of the factors that is associated with a phenomenon, and you're tempted inevitably to try to think of that factor as being a cause, even though you know it is actually (just) an association". So, you are kind of driven to it. As Saini points out too, when so many notable discoveries have already been made, researchers have little choice but drill down to smaller areas of study. To make a name for themselves they need to believe and to get others to believe that what they are studying is significant.

The above example provides a clear message for us going forward into writing and reading about EDs in subsequent chapters. That is, when attempting to understand complex human behavior and physiology, in the here and now or over recent millennia, we might have to keep in mind that the time span behind some of our behavior and physical form may be extensively and broadly ancestral.

For instance, we 'modern' homo sapiens inherited virus-fighting and life-saving genetics from our Neanderthal and Denisovan relatives too. Denisovan hominins are also extinct but had lived in a variety of forest, tundra, mountain and jungle habitats mainly across Asia and Melanesia, so it is thought. The Denisovan gene EPAS1 likely helps Tibetans live in high-altitude environs (11), while a Denisovan gene mutation in Papua New Guineans is potentially linked to malaria resistance. (12). Neanderthal genes are linked to metabolism, growth and sperm formation. (13).

To date most evidence of these ancient genes has been in low numbers of study populations. However, Zeberg et al. (2020), in Europe, conducted a massive study with 450, 000 participants that showed a Neanderthal gene that promotes progesterone related fertility in about a third of women of European decent. Evidence from an extensive genomic study of Icelanders (n=27,000) found genetic traces of Denisovan ancestry in a northern hemisphere Homo Sapiens population. (14). While it is possible those traces originated from Neanderthal descendants of more distant (time and location) Neanderthal-Denisovan interbreeding, they provide some evidence of how Icelanders, and likely most northern hemisphere peoples, are related to currently geographically distant Australian Aboriginals and Papua New Guineans.

Not only did we 'modern' homo sapiens inherit physiological traits from ancient ancestors we may also share symbolic and civilized behaviors with our Neanderthal and Denisovan relatives too. Neanderthals in southern Siberia made stone tools very similar to those made by their Neanderthal contemporaries in distant eastern and central Europe around the same time over 50,000 years ago. Indicating those ancestors were capable of long-distance migration and adaptation, and independent skill development too. (15) Cord making, and so the ability to select preferred tree fiber and spatially organize it into bundles for weaving, was around at least 40,000 years ago. (16) These ancestors also created cave art and used bird feathers and pierced shells with red and yellow ochre, possibly as personal ornaments (17), and perhaps even carved chevron motifs around 51,000 years ago. (18) They may have also used flowers when burying their dead. (19) Our shared practice of interring the dead was around at least 10,000 years ago in Lapo do Santo, Brazil, by homo sapiens who had descended via migrations from Siberia into North and South America (20), and 11000 years ago at Upward Sun River, Alaska (21). Even just the migration story of these people indicates huge feats of exploration and adaptation; let alone the fact they also developed varied and complex civilizations (Mayan c. 2000 BCE) far away and independent from Eurasia. Seemingly like the Nok (c. 1500 BCE-500 AD), in a region of west Africa (currently Nigeria), with their own innovation of iron tools and terracotta figures. (22) The ancient Tiwanaku and Inca civilizations also developed capital urban centers whose residents had a greater heterogeneity of DNA than further away areas; this being akin to modern cities where people of different ancestries are living side by side. (23). And contrary to the impression that ancient American societies were all autocratic chiefdoms, there were some sizeable communities that have evidence of shared civic space and projects with little or no symbols of descendant hierarchy. These communities were gathering and evolving centuries before European contact and indicate that other societies were also attempting democratic-type governance around the same time as republican Rome (509 BCE -27BCE). (23).

The stone monuments at Gobekli Tepe (c. 9130-7370 BCE), in the Southeastern Anatolia region of Turkey, are thought to have been first constructed by hunter-gatherers pre-dating by around 6000 years the 'first' civilization of Mesopotamia (c. 3100 BCE), the earliest Egyptian pyramids (c. 2830-2610 BCE), and Stonehenge (c.3000-2000 BCE). Pottery used by hunter-gathers (c. 5500-4000 BCE) has shown that different groups each had distinct food preferences and culinary practices even in (Baltic) areas where there was a similar availability of resources. (24)

We humans thought we knew a lot at the end of last century. After-all we had eradicated some diseases, landed on the moon, unleashed nuclear energy, and had almost completed mapping the human genome. However, it appears that our ancestral history is becoming a lot richer as we learn even more. At another level, the same could be said about the beacons of this writing. We, with them, are so interwoven that their experience, although theirs is more manifest, is ours too. Bio-ethically, we perhaps need to carefully consider the implications if it becomes possible to genetically 'diagnose' a person as having 'an eating disorder' in their future. How then can they make their own choice whether to undergo genetically changing treatment rather than from pressure akin to the "survival chasm" with loved ones. And by the end of your reading this book you may decide that there are social values represented in persons, who experience EDs, of which we certainly do not want to lose. And perhaps also the need to extend ourselves to understand better and cultivate what we learn from beacons for a better human society.

Ethan Weiss (2020) wrote a short article about his family's lesson from their daughter Ruthie, which provides us here with a glimpse into what beacons can possibly teach us. Ruthie was born with oculocutaneous albinism (OCA) of which impaired vision currently presents life-long disadvantages. What is interesting about the Weiss' story is the father's decision not to easily redirect his medical scientific career to study the genetic cause of OCA but instead with all the family embrace "loving and supporting the child (they) had, and not the one (they) wished for". He especially, it seems, began to see a new perspective on how differences are not just about one person but can be lessons for a better and more considerate humane world. That medical genetic intervention should not be quickly arrived at just because we can versus because we should (for some serious diseases, such as Spinal Muscular Atrophy). (25). And from a community point of view again, while we all can possibly learn generally from the beacons of this writing and for the future, their individual privacy and choices still should remain paramount. (26)

Being reductive by relying on what is familiar occurs also in psychosocial re-search. A particularly relevant example that will be referred to again later, is the Finnish study by Sipila et al. (2017) in which they professed to debunk the idea that parental or adolescent religiosity increases the risk for anorexia nervosa. They could well be correct. However, the problem is they make this quite wide-sweeping conclusion based possibly on a very narrow method. That method being twelve self-report items selected from the Minnesota Multiphasic Personality Inventory (MMPI), a lengthy questionnaire very familiar in the field of psychology. Those twelve items, yes just 12 out of at least 338 total in the MMPI, in themselves might only tap into very general religious ideas and not be specific enough to address aspects such as self-perception and self-worth within a religious framework. Also, there can be so much diversity in religious cultures that we perhaps should be careful not to generalize from just one or few studies on the subject. Sipila et al hinted at this by mentioning they saw some evidence suggestive of some regional differences of the association (i.e., not causation) between religiosity and life-time anorexia nervosa. And this was just in Finland alone. The persons studied were at first 16 years old and then again at most 27 years old. It is also possible to imagine that most people, even older persons, naturally have insufficient insight or feel permitted to be able to express on their own the likely complexity of any religious belief interacting with their eating or not (except for obvious religious observances). The point here is that even in reading psychosocial research one needs to be weary of reductive (familiar to the researcher) methodology, which possibly reflects reductive ideas behind the research or leads to reductive interpretations.

An example of the possible complexity in the interaction between religious be-liefs and our behavior is sometimes evident when it comes to sexuality. No sur-prise there. But wait, the subtly is what is important. Let alone that sexuality, like eating, has a great deal of meaning for everyone of us in how we feel about and sustain our own body and the integrity and safety of our personal being. Joshua Grubbs and colleagues (2020) undertook to study around 3500 participants who self- reported on the presence or absence of religious beliefs and use of sexually oriented media. A second part of the study involved tracking 850 of the same participants every four months over one year. Both parts of the research found the same result. Despite those self-reporting a below average use of sexual media but greater religious belief, the same persons categorized themselves as being addicted to sexual media. Those with less or no religious beliefs and higher or lower use of sexual media were less likely to report they felt addicted. An important distinction Grubbs et al. make is that health professionals and lay people alike need to be careful not to apply the label of addiction before under-standing more about the person's beliefs. In the field of assessment and treat-ment for substance use, addiction is identified if the substance use itself steadily increases (tolerance and dependency) to reach the same altered effects and/ or has had a large and persistent negative effect on a person's daily functioning. This is with such things as quantitative or qualitative loss of relationships, loss of employment or of other socio-economic milestones, and deterioration in self-care, appearance, and physical health. So, it is possible that those participants with religious beliefs in the study by Grubbs et al. were over-rating themselves as having an addiction based upon feeling a conflict between their beliefs and sexual behavior. This over-rating being possibly another example of reductionism by those persons not considering a wider range of information before judging themselves as being addicted versus conflicted.

Now that you have read some examples of reductionism it may be useful for you to practice how you do with considering the following information from the field of substance related addiction and neuroscience. In 1954 researchers James Olds and Peter Milner found that rats would perform behavior, such as pressing a bar and running a maze, to receive bursts of electrical stimulation to specific parts of their brains. It was understandably assumed that the electrical stimulation of those parts of their brain gave the rats pleasure. Over subsequent decades many other researchers have suggested that dopamine, along with opioid peptides, is one of the main naturally occurring chemicals involved in neural communication in these same and other brain regions (e.g., ventral striatum, that sit under the upper large cortex between the front and midway sections of our brain) and so has been characterized as being the brain's pleasure chemical, including for humans. Indeed, much has been written about the relationship between substance use addiction interacting with the same brain regions and dopamine.

Koob and colleagues for some years now have been prominent in the neuroscience of addiction, including dopamine and other neurochemicals and their functions. (27) For the purposes of our book, their explanation can basically be summarized as that the brain and addiction relationship involve motivation to enhance or restore a hedonistic homeostasis (our status quo of feeling nice and stable, so-to-speak) by positive reinforcement (pleasure) and/or removal of negative reinforcement (uncomfortable emotional states). It is sometimes also described as though the dopamine related brain areas repeatedly do not complete their neural transmission, as they should, and so homeostasis and experiencing things as rewarding is difficult to achieve. The use of alcohol or other substances is supposedly involved in attempt to compensate for that repetitively unfinished neural transmission. This is often referred to as the 'reward' theory of addiction. The motivation for 'restoring' homeostasis or experiencing 'reward' is also amplified and complicated by the chemical substance itself and its unpleasant side-effects, especially when use is increased and extended over time (tolerance) for the same homeostasis effects. So, what would you the reader infer from this information? What would you identify to be the primary motivation for persons with addiction to use substances? Please try not to read on until you have taken a few minutes to think about this on your own.

We both can honestly say we each made the presumption that substance use addiction at our human behavioral level is about getting "high" for "kicks" or to ease our "social anxiety", and so makes sense that at our brain level it relates to neural "pleasure" centers and chemicals. This all sounds sensible and most of the above information about Olds and Milner up to that on Koob and colleagues is a fair summary of what you find first appears on an internet search about the brain and addiction. And is what most professionals in the field, including

20

us, have come to believe. But as we all know, internet searches often give you advertisements first to grab your attention and so it takes a deeper search to find what you are looking for. The same can be said about the science of how we as humans develop and function, especially about things that have some social stigma like addiction does. Much of what Koob and colleagues and other researchers interpret about addiction and reducing it to hedonistic homeostasis may be correct, but maybe there's still a long way to go before we can fully accept that their model sufficiently explains the relationship of our brain and addiction. For example, and briefly for the purposes of this book, dopamine is involved in many other aspects of human physical and mental health. Such as Parkinson's Disease (which greatly effects muscle function and motor coordination) and in schizophrenia (of which symptoms include sensory hallucinations and difficulty in maintaining organization of thinking). These serious phenomena, which have a pervasive involvement of the brain and body, can be extensively life altering for an affected person. The treatment of Parkinson's Disease often includes dopamine-based medications to assist neural transmission. And medications to regulate dopamine are used to assist thought organization and lessen hallucinations in schizophrenia. So, it seems then possibly disrespectful, let alone nonsensical, to suggest that dopamine can be so easily characterized as the 'pleasure' neuro-chemical, even if in only some selective parts of the brain.

But let's get more specific. Research by Augier and Heilig (2018), at Linkoping University in Sweden, trained hundreds of rats of various breeds to self-administer alcohol, like prior studies by other researchers. But they included a different approach to mimic real life a little more by offering the rats some sugary water too. Each of their studies got the same results of 15% of the rats consistently selected the alcohol, while the remaining 85% consistently selected the sugary water. These researchers say this 15% represents the same proportion of human drinkers who manifest alcoholism. Auger and Heilig next looked for differences in the genes that were active in the brains of the alcohol-preferring rats compared to the sugar-preferring rats. They found no differences in five of six regions previously thought (e.g., Koob 2016) to be involved in alcoholism. But in the amygdalae of the alcohol-preferring rats they found unusually low activity in many genes linked to Gamma aminobutyric acid (GABA). The amygdala is thought to be involved in the processing of emotions. It sits close to the hippocampus of which memory processing is its specialized function. They are both located in the front section of the temporal lobe, which is sort of mid-way between the occipital lobes (for visual processing) at the rear and the frontal lobes (for organization and judgment) at the front of the upper brain (cortex). GABA is made and released by some neurons to suppress the firing of neighboring neurons. The neurons that release the GABA use an enzyme called GAT3 to take up the GABA for reuse. But in the amygdalae of the alcohol-preferring rats the gene that makes GAT3 is much less active. Consequently, the over-abundance of GABA makes the neighboring neurons abnormally inactive too. Auger and Heilig then took some sugar-preferring rats and reduced the level of the GAT3 enzyme in their amygdalae and found this simple procedure converted those rats into alcohol-preferring rats. They also had some colleagues examine post-mortem tissue samples taken from people who had donated their brains for research. Of those who had had alcoholism they again found no unusual signs in five regions previously suspected but did so in the amygdala and again low levels of GAT3. It is unclear what this all means at the human psychological level. And it is only a guess for now, but it is possible the over-abundance of GABA in over-suppressing neurons hampers the amygdala from processing fear and stress (anxiety), and other emotions. And that use of alcohol, or other substances, is an attempt at alleviating the emotional suppressive effect of GABA. This interpretation fits both the restoration of homeostasis and removal of negative reinforcement (negative emotion) model of addiction just as well as the dopamine/reward theory.

A different series of studies, by Charles Dorison and colleagues (2019), have shown that sadness, more than anger, disgust, fear or other negative emotions, is a more likely trigger for addictive substance use. In one study they found that in a USA national survey that tracked 10,685 people over 20 years, participants identified sadness being associated with their smoking tobacco and relapsing after one or two decades of quitting. In a second study of 425 smokers, participants who watched a sad video and wrote a story of personal loss reported higher cravings than other participants who watched instead a neutral or a disgusting type of video. A third study of 700 persons who smoke, and using the same methodology as the second study, showed that those participants in the sadness condition reported greater difficulty in delaying being able to smoke. In the fourth study of 158 smokers and using similar video watching and self-story methodology, those in the sadness condition showed greater impatience to smoke and smoked at greater volume of consumption of the one and first cigarette measured. These studies by Dorison et al. are a good example of controlled psychological studies and all in relation to a large (n= over 10,000 people) epidemiological and longitudinal (20 years) survey providing a good theoretical and statistical base to derive findings and so avoid reductionism by method and in interpretation of results. Compare this to what we said earlier about the study by Sipila et al. (2017) being reductive in method (only 12 items from the MMPI) and so likely reductive in interpretation. The finding about sadness in addiction by Dorison et al. also fits well with the model of restoring homeostasis and removing negative emotion. And in later chapters you will read about how negative emotion or affect possibly features in EDs too.

There is still a long way to go to figure out where and how the above type of studies by Augier and Heilig, and Dorison et al, will eventually contribute to treatment and public health strategies for substance over-use and prevention. However, they do raise some interesting aspects for this discussion on reductionism. In a way these studies are like the work by Marshall and Warren (1983) and Quinn et al. (2020), cited earlier, in how they upended the prior reductive thinking on stomach ulcers and on the production of bile, respectively. The possibility of a different brain area (amygdale) and neurochemical (GABA) than those previously thought to be involved in alcoholism, and the specificity of sadness to tobacco smoking addiction, do chip away at the dominance of the dopamine/reward theory. Over-reliance on the latter theory is easy to do while certainly most persons (85%) are fortunate enough to enjoy alcohol and other substances for socializing, relaxation, and even some anxiety relief, without becoming addicted. But we commonly use reductionism, familiarity with only our own experience, in attempt to understand what for other persons is unknowingly complex and operating way before we or they even understand and realize it. At this stage of our history who knows enough to confidently say upon waking up in the morning: "hey, my GAT3 is low so I better not drink alcohol today".

Later, in our review of EDs you will notice how this older brain and dopamine/pleasure or 'reward' theory for addiction has been borrowed and applied, as though theoretically solid and unquestionable still recently, in research on EDs. We will remind you when we get there how there are other ways of looking at addiction and the brain and so the 'dopamine-pleasure/reward' model shouldn't be so heavily relied upon to explain the many complexities of addiction or other behavior. It may explain some but not all or many.

Okay. Alright. I can imagine you are thinking "enough already". But relax, take a deep breath and slowly exhale. Yes, literally, breathing is the last example. Consider our breathing, and even that of your pet dog or cat as they lounge in the sunlight. For most of us, fortunate not to have asthma or other airway problems, breathing at the observable level is so binary (in and out), rhythmic and reliably repeatable. The consequence of not breathing is well known. You feel and see your chest gently rise and fall as your diaphragm and lungs follow in concert. This rhythm is so familiar to us at the easy observable level that it seems so very reasonable to assume our whole breathing apparatus down to the specific nervous system (i.e., our brain stem, like the brain stem in other animals) is binary and rhythmic. You can probably remember the many times you have read or heard of the binary function of computers as analogy for many things relating to our brain and behavior. But our breathing may not be as binary as we see it.

Ashad and Feldman (2020), at the University of California, Los Angeles, studied neurons from an area of the brain stem in mice they believe is specifically involved in breathing. What they discovered was that those neurons at first fire at low levels but haphazardly and not in concert at all. They then quickly synchronize to generate the rhythm. It is though each breath we take starts uniquely and is not the same as preceding breaths as we observe them to be. Ashad and Feldman think that the neurons for breathing perform this way so to be flexible in case there is need for a different rhythm responsive to whatever is the physical need for oxygen. Again, there is still a lot more to be researched and verified about these findings about breathing. However, this last example is very instructive because it involves the hallmarks of familiarity involving us all, and for most of the time our being able to use only partial easy observation, until now possibly. This, like for many things, has left us to reductively guess the rest of the story. Only to find out, often after a long time, from new evidence that many of our assumptions through reductionism have been incorrect.

So, hmm, judgments and decision making based on what we think we know, on what is familiar to each of us, can be unreliable some of the time. This being potentially more pertinent when it comes to things that are more complex than we realize. Which are most things really, except perhaps less so about whether you prefer cream in your coffee. To counter our tendency to be reductive we only simply need to say to ourselves: go ahead, but I may need more information and be open about changing my thinking and course of action soon or in the future. And from what we learned during the above discussion, even scientists can be reductive. But good scientists know how to account for this in their research methodology (e.g., n = being a sufficiently large number of persons; control groups and comparative conditions) and/or by giving more than one and possible counter explanations for results. Even Einstein, who built the new concept of Relativity theory upon knowledge of prior scientists, also had to acknowledge error that was reductive. But it all amounts to life and behavior being so complex, yet so very interesting.

You might find as you continue to read that we the authors sometimes also appear to slip into reductionism. We do recognize that is a likelihood. However, our purpose is mostly philosophical, to review our understanding of EDs and be attentive to possible lessons about freedom in its subtle forms amongst all persons. Our intention is not to imply what is written here has unassailable certainty. Instead, it is to raise awareness of needing to challenge some long held paradigms, that are maintained due to reductionism, and with hope that the ideas presented are examined in future research.

EMBODY HOW (PART ONE)

There is a vast range of psychological, socio-environmental, physiological, genetic, cultural, historical and auto-biographical information relating to what are referred to clinically as the eating disorders of Anorexia Nervosa (AN), Bulimia Nervosa (BN), and Binge Eating Disorder (BED). Fortunately, much of it is accessible on the Internet. The range of aspects is so vast though it seems inappropriate for us or anyone to claim they are an expert. So, the apparent order of the following discussion on the diagnostic criteria, physical health consequences, and so on, is not meant to infer any preference for describing the phenomenology of what beacons experience. Instead, this section of chapters are only overviews for the purpose of raising some questions for us to consider in subsequent chapters. They pertain mostly to information derived in Western countries. It will include more detail on psychological therapies, because they have to date shown a greater efficacy for use in treatment, and we will see some emerging signs about freedom. The next section of chapters will contain more on history, etiology, body image, and include non-western cultural aspects. Again, this writing is not intended as a guide to the assessment or treatment for persons considered to have an eating disorder.

DIAGNOSTIC AND CLINICAL CONSIDERATIONS

This is not our preferred starting point but is kind of necessary for our comparative discussion to describe what currently exists as diagnostic and clinical language as it pervades much of what is available in current research and other literature. Again, by the end of reading this book you might come up with alternative descriptions or labels for the human experiences that include different styles of eating. Nor do we want to understate that for some persons there can be life threatening conditions as part of marked changes in food intake and/or frequent purging of food. Again, our intention is to offer ideas that may be worthy of further research for a better understanding of how we could be of help to beacons, and how their experience has lessons for all of us together.

Diagnostics, Health Risks and Prevalence

Based on the American psychiatric Diagnostic and Statistical Manual (DSM) and the World Health Organization's International Classification of Diseases (ICD) medical classification systems (28), Anorexia Nervosa (AN) is used as a clinical diagnosis for a person who has significant weight loss due to severely restricted eating and not instead attributable to an identifiable medical disorder. A clinician would differentially consider and rule out whether the weight loss was instead attributable to cancer, chronic renal failure, cystic fibrosis, Crohn's disease, or other medical disorder, or a consequence of starvation in captivity, or of abuse and neglect by other persons. The severe restriction subtype of AN involves minimal food intake and food with very low-calorie count, a very narrow range of food, skipping meals frequently, and the following of rigid rules (e.g., eating food of one type or color). In the binge and/or purge subtype of AN, a person sometimes manifests the same behavior as in Bulimia Nervosa (BN), in addition to persistent intake restriction. BN is instead diagnosed if a person engages in binge eating (from their own or another person's perspective too) and may follow that sequentially, or compensate for some time later, by self-induced vomiting, over-exercising, use of laxatives, diuretics or enemas, but not necessarily involve significant weight loss. Binge Eating Disorder (BED) involves recurrent episodes of eating excessive quantities of food, sometimes very quickly and to the point of great discomfort, without regularly using compensatory behavior as in BN. What is interesting about the change from the DSM-IV manual (1994) to the DSM V manual (2013) is not so much the small adjustments to diagnostic criteria but the dropping of the word "refusal" in reference to not eating. Instead, the revised manual attempts to focus more on behavioral descriptions than assumptions about intention. The DSM V manual also for the first time gave stronger recognition to BED instead of it being relegated to 'areas under investigation' or 'not otherwise specified'. Both the DSM V and ICD 10 (2015) systems still refer to "fear of becoming fat" as a primary body image concern in their diagnostic criteria for AN, but adjusted criteria to include how some persons do not necessarily have fat phobia. Another diagnosis in DSM V is that of Avoidant Restrictive Food Intake Disorder (ARFID), which was previously known as Selective Eating Disorder. ARFID is like AN, in that it involves limitations in the amounts and types of food consumed, severe weight loss, and physical health consequences. But ARFID apparently does not involve any distress about body shape or size, or fat phobia. Persons who have ARFID reportedly report more about things like gastrointestinal discomfort and disliking the texture of some foods. ARFID is still in the very early stage of being researched and understood. See later chapters for more discussion on body image and fat phobia.

Weight loss in adults is considered concerning if at least 15% below expected weight or moderately serious at a Body Mass Index (BMI) of 16-16.99, severe at BMI 15-15.99 and extreme at BMI less than 15. (BMI= kg weight divided by the square of the body height in m). In children and adolescents, the corresponding criteria is weight being below the 10th BMI-for-age percentile. The earlier in life the onset of AN the more serious the long-term negative consequences for development can be, such as bone density, growth in height, and cerebral maturation. (29) As a consequence of excessive food restriction, binge-eating and purging, the following physiologic complications can occur and when life-threatening need immediate medical intervention:

28

cardiovascular

  (e.g. bradycardia, arrythmias)

metabolic

  (e.g. hypokalaemia, oedema)

gastrointestinal

  (e.g. oesophageal or gastric rupture)

endocrine

  (e.g., amenorrhoea, hypothermia)

musculoskeletal

  (e.g. reduced stature,

    & osteoporosis)

haematological

  (e.g. low white blood cell count,

    & anaemia)

neurological

  (e.g. seizure, &

    reversible cortical atrophy)

dermatological

  (e.g., lanugo hair,

    & carotene pigmentation)

Prevalence data on EDs tend to be based upon persons who have been diagnosed as having AN and/or BN rather than surveys with broad criteria on eating and psychological aspects in the general population. There is some possibility of cultural and gender differences affecting known prevalence rates. In the USA and other western countries, where "fear of fatness" has typically featured in diagnosis, the life-time rates are around 1% for AN, 1.5-2% for BN and 3.5% for BED in women, and 0.3%, 0.5%, and 2.0% in men. However, in Japan and China the rates for AN have been reported as 0.025-0.030% and 0.01% respectively. While clinical status severity of AN for women in Singapore, Iran, Japan and Korea is no less than that found in Western countries. (30). Other confounding aspects are that many persons may not present with all behaviors or symptoms (e.g., amenorrhea) all at once, or for long enough, to qualify for the diagnosis of AN or BN instead. Most prevalence data show onset for AN and BN to be typically in adolescence or young adulthood. However, some persons experience crossover from AN to BN, or the reverse, and for each person at different stages of their life. Reportedly, men make up only 5% to 10% of known AN or BN cases. (29)

Although, some preliminary evidence from China indicates that in the early 30's age range there may be a greater loss of life-productivity and life- expectancy and actual mortality impact for men than women among those who experience BN compared to the teen years where it is mostly women with AN who have this loss. (Li et al., 2021). In a later chapter we revisit this aspect of loss of productive life and how we unexpectedly came across some other preliminary findings in relation to some Western countries.

Emotional, Physical and Sexual Abuse

Among persons who receive mental health assessment and care many have also been victims of emotional, physical and sexual abuse. Persons with EDs are no exception. An extensive review by Linda Smolak and Sarah Murnen (2002), of Ohio, USA, provides us some understanding about how a history of abuse relates to the manifestation of an ED. They conducted a two-part meta-analysis of fifty-three studies, found through a literature search, that pertained to the relationship of childhood sexual abuse (CSA) and a person having an eating disorder (ED). In a meta-analysis the reviewers justify aligning the independent studies in terms of methods used and to combine the numbers of participants across the studies to raise what is called the statistical power behind results (i.e., literally means if the number of participants is too low in a sole study it is considered not appropriate to think the findings are significant and can be applied to a broader population of people). Smolak and Murnen divided the studies into two general categories. One contained thirty studies in each of which the researchers looked at the incidence of EDs for persons selected because of having a history of CSA compared to other persons without CSA. The total number of participants in this first category was 13,145. Some studies reported that a significant number of participants had a history of EDs, whereas other studies said there were no statistically significant differences among their participants. Only 14 of the 30 studies reported information on actual percentage of EDs among their participants. About 40% of the CSA group versus 20% of the non-CSA group had an ED. The second category of twenty-three studies had each selected their primary participants because they firstly qualified as having an ED (mostly bulimia) and compared them to controls without ED, then looked for the incidence of CSA.

The total number of participants in this second category was 28,159. Many more (20) of the 23 studies in this category reported on percentages of participants, such that 26% of the ED and 13% of the non-ED groups reported having had experienced CSA. One factor, among many discussed by Smolak and Murnen, was that conducting an analysis combining all 53 studies was complicated due to the definition of EDs in the first category was more inclusive than the exclusive diagnostic criteria used by studies in the second category. Remembering that the DSM broadened the definition of ED to include BED more recently in 2013 raises the question of whether more persons with history of CSA would be found in further studies who firstly select participants based on having a more broadly diagnosed ED.

What seems to also remain unclear is whether the 60% of persons in the first category, selected for having a history of CSA, who did not manifest an ED suggests that CSA on its own may not be a definite precursor to having an ED. They may be associated, with CSA amplifying the possibility of a person manifesting an ED, but not necessarily etiologically the same. This distinction seems to be also apparent in self-narratives of which we will review in a later chapter. Overall, though, it seems a take-away message from the review by Smolak and Murnen is that there is a notable number of persons with EDs who also have a history of CSA and for whom appropriate supports need to be available. These supports do not reside in just therapy, a therapist, or sole treatment center or hospital alone. It most often requires community-based peer advocates and emotionally safe places to support recovery. (31)

Medications and In-Patient Treatment

Treatment of EDs with medications, except selective serotonin reuptake inhibitors (SSRIs) for BN, are generally considered ineffective. (32) If other mental health aspects are also present, such as depression, then use of other medications might be indicated if, say, Cognitive-Behavioral Therapy (CBT) has not been effective for a person. Agras et al. at the University of Stanford (1994) in a one-year follow-up study showed that treatment of BN with an antidepressant (desimpramine) alone was inferior to CBT alone and further inferior to combined treatment. Subsequent research into combined treatment has had many limitations and so has not found much to add. (33) We will discuss CBT more fully in the next chapter on psychological therapies. A 2004 study by Perez, Joiner and Lewinshon cautions clinicians to also assess for dysthymia, a subtler and sometimes more persistent form of depression possibly masked by bulimia, which interacts with a person's perfectionism and chronic low self-esteem, each amplifying the other.

For more discussion on the rational and efficacy of medications for treating eating disorders, see the Practice Guideline for the Treatment of Patients with Eating Disorders, Third Edition, American Psychiatric Association (APA) June 2006/2010. The overall impression given is that medications are considered to have low efficacy for directly treating AN, BN and BED but can be helpful for some few other mental health factors (e.g., depression or anxiety) the person may experience concurrent with the ED. The APA review also reports concerns about the diminished tolerance of some medications for some persons with extreme low weight. The same APA review discussed how a few anti-psychotic medications in low doses, specifically Olanzapine and Haloperidol, have been reported to be directly helpful for ED factors in AN. But this information is so far only based on a small set of studies (each n = no greater than 20), ranging from 2001 to 2005, with no larger controlled studies. And by 2015 Marzola et al., of the University of Turin and University of Western Brittany, describe the body of evidence on medication management in AN is in dismal condition. They themselves conducted a study of 75 clients, treated in hospital between 2012 to 2014, who were equally divided into groups receiving SSRIs and either aripiprazole or olanzapine in addition to SSRIs. These researchers reported that upon discharge all groups were significantly improved on all measures for anxiety, depression and eating disorder behaviors. They noted that aripiprazole showed the greatest effectiveness in reducing eating-related preoccupations and rituals. However, their participant sample size of 75 is still quite small and especially so when divided into groups for comparison. By 2020 Kan et al., of King's College London, also found by literature review that twenty-one studies, all published in English, and which examined the use of antipsychotics in AN, the number of participants in each was still very low, with most below 100 each. And this despite that 11 of the studies had used a random control model and four studies combined analyses from previous research. So, it remains inconclusive whether antipsychotics are effective in the treatment of AN. And of the studies that do exist, they tend to focus on restoration of weight or BMI and no other aspects, such as eating-related preoccupations, rituals, and a client's underestimation of their emaciated state, that perhaps persons with AN need therapeutic assistance with over longer durations before expectation of rapid weight recovery. The actual focus of the review by Kan et al. was to examine what was behind why some participants (n=62) dropped out of such studies using antipsychotics in weight restoration focused treatment. Weight gain was mentioned only once, with suicidal ideation for three persons, while most participants voluntarily withdrew and/or opted for a different treatment approach or dropped from any follow-up contact with the researchers. But still, also inconclusive given the low number of participants who dropped out across many studies. The pool of studies that Kan et all drew from ranged from years 1982 to 2019 and so seems to still underscore what Mazola et al. (2015) suggested about a dearth of large inter-center or international coordinated studies on the use of medications in the treatment of AN.

Sometimes hospital in-patient treatment is used for purpose of supervising eating/food intake to reduce the risk of severe physical ill-health. (34). There continues to be debate on how rapidly re-feeding and weight restoration can be undertaken (35), and debate on whether to include AN, when severe, under legal definitions of mental illness to confirm the use of involuntary care (e.g., use of nasogastric feeding tube). (36) Some of this debate is likely driven by the core clinical ethic and responsibility for preserving life being confronted by the perplexing circumstances of a person starving when food is easily available to them.

Post-hospitalization follow-up treatment sometimes includes Family-based therapy, particularly for younger persons still living in the parental home, to maintain food intake, weight restoration, and social reintegration. This type of therapy is discussed a little further in the next chapter on psychological therapies.

Follow-up studies have shown that relapse into severe AN is frequent, with around 40% of persons with AN showing good treatment outcome, 25% moderate outcome but 30% poor treatment outcome. The 10-year mortality rate in AN is around 5%, which is more than ten times other causes of death for persons in the adolescent to young adult age group. Sullivan, Bulik et al. (1998) did a follow-up study of 70 New Zealand (NZ) women (at mean age 32.4) who had been diagnosed with AN (mean age 16.9) and had been through inpatient weight restoration on average about 12 years before the study. They found that 10 percent of the women (n= 7) continued to meet the full DSM diagnostic criteria. The remaining 90 percent (n= 63) did not meet full DSM criteria but still maintained a low BMI and based on their self-report on questionnaires there was a high rate of depression, alcohol dependence, and anxiety disorders. The participants also self-reported perfectionism and cognitive restraint over-eating were still salient. We will further discuss perfectionism and cognitive restraint in later chapters. Sullivan et al also said their results were generally consistent with around 50 similar preceding studies. Sullivan and Bulik are American clinicians and researchers who returned to the USA after being in Christchurch, NZ, for some years. They have since been involved in research into the genetics and metabolism in EDs about which we will review later. Follow-up studies in the USA show good treatment outcome after five years for 50% of persons diagnosed with BN, while about 20% continue to meet the diagnostic criteria. Because BED is a recently accepted diagnosis in DSM V there may be less outcome data. From what is available it appears 50% to 80% of persons have good post-treatment outcome. (37).

PSYCHOLOGICAL THERAPIES

Not a lot has changed about the treatment for EDs for at least three decades now. The psychological approaches of Cognitive Behavioral Therapy (CBT) and Interpersonal Therapy (IPT) are still reported to have the best available evidence as treatment effective for AN, BN and BED. (37) And multiple surveys of people who have had treatment for an eating disorder indicate that psychological therapies are rated above medical and weight restoration interventions as the most helpful. This positive rating is interesting given the characterization made about how EDs include a person's deep sense of control over their eating and body. (37) And it is sensible to also say that for every one of us control over our own body and personal space is a foundation of our personal freedom at and away from home. So, we think it worthwhile to focus on reviewing the psychological therapies of CBT and IPT, more so than other treatments used with EDS, in beginning our endeavor to better understand freedom in its more subtle form.

Generally psychological therapies involve talking and relating so to assist a person to better understand themselves and their world. In CBT the client learns to identify and change their own unhelpful cognitive interpretations (e.g., thinking negatively about one's appearance and capabilities) and related behaviors (e.g., avoiding or not speaking in certain social situations). They might keep a brief structured diary so to firstly raise their awareness of the almost automatic occurrence of self-negative thinking. It is as though we habitually default to negative thinking rather than positive thinking a lot of the time. The purpose is to increase the experience of positive cognitions with positive emotional regulation and thus raise self-confidence to attempt situations previously avoided. Success at managing old type or new situations is supposed to further solidify self-confidence.

In IPT there is less focus on the therapist training the client initially in self-assessment and practice of cognition change and more on the client reporting back on directly trying changes in relating to others and in typical life activities, with some progression to more challenging situations. Both CBT and IPT are meant to be brief and immediately applied, as in weeks or longer, so not like psychoanalysis of an undefined duration.

Dialectal Behaviour Therapy (DBT) was initially developed for the treatment of borderline personality disorder (BPD) by first using it with college students. (38) DBT consistently conveys the message that doing the work of therapy is important because "your life is worth living". DBT firstly involves problem-solving to identify and reduce behaviours (e.g., getting over-involved in something and forgetting appointments, e.g., substance over use coinciding with appointment times) and barriers (e.g., unreliable transport) that may interfere with regularly attending weekly therapy. It also addresses self-injury and suicidal behaviour early on so to establish clear understanding that the client will contact the therapist, or an emergency service, to preserve their own life. DBT also includes four modules of learning mindfulness, skills for distress tolerance, emotion regulation, and interpersonal effectiveness. These are usually learned in a group with other clients facilitated by a skills trainer. The individual sessions with the therapist review progress in learning and applying the skills and discussing ways to interrupt the chain of events and behaviours that can lead to self-harm or suicidal thoughts or actions. The trainer and therapist redirect a client to use and review skills rather than over-focus discussion on self-harm or suicide. The trainer and therapist themselves usually attend a consultation team with other DBT practitioners to do mindfulness, peer review their work they are doing with clients, hone their own skills, and for each to maintain empathy and being non-judgmental in ongoing interactions with clients.

BPD as a diagnostic label could be taken as being pejorative in that it unintentionally infers the whole person is somehow disordered. But the real intention of DBT, and most therapies, is to assist a person to discover/rediscover their strengths, interests, truly supportive relationships, self-worth and many other things to have a better quality of life. And when you read the diagnostic criteria there are likely many of us that could say we identify with at least one aspect having occurred in our own life at least once. However, it is the range, degree and duration of the things identified that suggest the BPD that most of us are fortunate not to experience. So, diagnostically speaking, BPD is recognized as including self-harm (e.g., cutting or burning), other self-destructive behaviour (e.g., binge drinking periods, or risking STDs and HIV from numerous unprotected sexual encounters), risk for suicide, a long-term pattern of contentious and disrupted relationships (e.g., family, romantic, school, or at jobs) fear of abandonment by others (e.g., even when a therapist is just on vacation), an expressed sense of emptiness, most often low self-worth and under-estimation of ability, but occasionally, in some cases, an inflated sense of abilities and status (e.g., when attempting to defend from the perception or reality of being under judgment), and seemingly being over-reactive where most other persons would not be to the same or similar events or interpersonal situations. Some persons who experience BPD can also experience AN, BN, BED and/or substance overuse and depression. (39)

Behavioral Therapy interventions tend to use things that people find pleasurable (e.g., special tasty food, a favorite movie, book, music, game, toy, or tokens that can be exchanged for any of the former) in an arrangement usually agreed upon by the client, and/or their guardian. The arrangement involves trying to reduce behavior that is agreed upon as being problematic (e.g., a child's bed wetting) by rewarding the person with a pleasurable item when they don't exhibit the problem behavior, or exhibit an alternative behavior instead (e.g., going for longer each night without wetting; or waking and going to the bathroom).

Behavioral interventions are used in hospital inpatient and residential treatment settings for persons who have EDs. For example, a client may receive points for each occasion of consuming a prescribed amount of food and/or for not undertaking compensatory behavior (e.g., over-exercising their legs even though in a hospital bed). The accumulated points can then be exchanged for, say, having friends visit and watch a movie together. Reaching increasing weight goals might then be rewarded by similar activities outside of the inpatient unit.

Family-based therapy (FBT) for EDs is kind of an extension of behavior therapy with the additional aspect of where the parents manage the food intake, weight restoration goals, and encouragement of their child to do activities other than being preoccupied with food, weight reduction, or physical appearance. The idea is to re-empower the parents over the dominance of the ED illness and to maintain the child in their home environment rather than provide lengthy treatment in a hospital or residential setting. This type of therapy is also known as the Maudsley (hospital) model, which was developed in the UK in the 1980's by Christopher Dare and colleagues. They recognized the need to move away from assuming family dynamics were part of the cause behind EDs and instead enlist the family as the core of the treatment team. By 1997 their five-year follow-up study of 80 persons post-hospital care showed sustained improvement, in weight restoration, menstruation, and absence of bulimic symptoms, for clients whose AN or BN had begun before age 19 and/or were still in early stages of AN or BN and had undergone one year of FBT. Those clients who were older and had longer duration of AN or BN did better with what the researchers described as supportive individual therapy. (Eisler, Dare et al., 1997). Other researchers have since shown similar favorable results. (Rienecke, 2017). We won't cover any more about these behavioral and family therapies and will instead focus our discussion a little more on CBT and IPT. As that seems sufficient for discovering our first hint toward our main discussion about freedom.

Christopher Fairburn was an early practitioner and researcher in using CBT and IPT for the treatment of eating disorders in adults. He and his colleagues, back in 1993, had reported on a one-year follow-up study of 75 participants with BN which showed a 95% reduction of bulimic episodes at 12 months for both IPT and CBT. IPT fared better than CBT, and CBT fared better than Behaviour Therapy (which focuses more directly on changes in eating and retaining food eaten). The authors concluded "there is a need to reconsider current accounts of the maintenance of bulimia nervosa in light of our finding that the disorder can be successfully treated without addressing the disturbed eating habits and attitudes" (p.427). Then in 2000, Agras, Fairburn and colleagues repeated that study across different treatment sites with 220 participants who had BN and again randomised to either 19 sessions of CBT or IPT over twenty weeks and re-evaluated after one year. This time they found CBT was superior to IPT.

In a study by Green and others (2017) at Cornell College and University of Iowa, forty-seven college undergraduate age women with subclinical and clinical symptoms of eating disorder were randomly assigned to either an assessment only group or to a group in which each participant received assessment and what the authors called dissonance-based therapy. The four weeks of therapy taught the participants to criticize media images that depict beauty in terms of thinness and to counter societal messages about self-worth being based upon appearance. The study found that for the participants assigned to the therapy there were significant changes in their eating disorder symptoms and reduced cardiac risk monitored by ECG at baseline, at completion of therapy and at two-month follow-up. Although the study authors did not call their therapy CBT, the inclusion of re-evaluating messages adopted as self-cognitions and hence positively refocus self-worth are strategies akin to CBT.

Mathisen et al. (2020) of Norway reported on their research of 164 participants diagnosed with either BN or BED, aged 18-40, who were randomly assigned to a physical therapy and dietary therapy (PED-t) group or a CBT group. Only 112 completed the 12 weeks of therapy, with more dropping out of the CBT group. The researchers followed-up participants post-therapy for 6, 12 and 24 months. They found equal long-term effects of reduced remission rates, alleviation of eating disorder symptoms, and improvements in quality of life (measured by a questionnaire). The authors did note that both types of therapy included "normalizing eating patterns, correcting basic self-regulatory processes and reducing idealized aesthetic evaluations of self-worth". It could be said, though, that the two groups were more similar than not since both contained CBT type strategies and that many participants in either group did not take up physical exercise of a type generally recommended for health maintenance versus compensatory muscle damaging exercise or under-exercising.

Other studies that do not directly address EDs still show the effectiveness of CBT for emotional (affective) and physical body aspects somewhat reflective of what also happens in part in EDs. For example, Steiger et al. (2016), at the University of Zurich, demonstrated with a magnetic resonance imaging (MRI) study of thirty-three participants, with diagnosis of social anxiety disorder (SAD), sustained changes and interconnectedness, like that existing already for control participants without SAD, in brain areas thought to be involved in self-control and processing of emotions after ten weeks of cognitive behavioral group therapy.

A 2020 study by Goldstein and colleagues of King's College London, showed how CBT was effective in helping persons with dissociative seizures. Persons with dissociative seizures have often been ignored or disbelieved by physicians because the seizures or fainting are not accompanied by currently discernible epileptic brain activity (e.g., via EEG: electroencephalography). The researchers assigned 368 persons, with dissociative seizures from various treatment centers across Great Britain, into either a group which received regular medical care or another group in which they also received CBT. Outcome was followed up at six months and again at 12 months. Those persons who participated in CBT reported the greatest number of consecutive seizure-free days in the first 6 months post-treatment. But there was no clear difference found between the groups by 12 months. However, for those who received CBT both they and their physicians reported a greater change in resumption of usual daily and pleasurable life activities and satisfaction with treatment. It possibly remains for further research to determine whether the CBT directly treated an underlying neurological, emotional or combined bases to the seizures or instead helped the persons affected experience an improved quality of life despite having seizures. We will very shortly discuss some other aspects of the experience in therapy, not just the mode of therapy itself, being a possible factor for positive outcomes.

Partly due to the overlap sometimes of AN, BN or BED with BPD and some clinicians and researchers equating food restriction or purging with self-harm in BPD, it seems reasonable to consider Dialectical Behaviour Therapy (DBT) would be useful in the treatment of an eating disorder. Lenz and colleagues (2014) undertook a meta-analysis of eight independent studies by other researchers from 2000 to 2011 who looked mostly at the effectiveness of DBT for BN or BED in mostly 20-week treatment programs (1-2 sessions per week), but one study with therapy for a year. Lenz and colleagues reported that by combining the eight studies they found significant results for DBT being effective for reducing the number of binge episodes at end of treatment. In this analysis by Lenz et al there was a combined total of around three hundred participants but across the eight studies the numbers varied quite substantially from only 8 -11, 24-32 to 40-44 participants and only one at 101 participants. If any of the eight studies had sufficient statistical power on their own, it presumably would be that one.

Upon taking a closer look at that study by Safer and her colleagues (2010) they did find that among their participants with BED who completed 12 weeks of weekly DBT, compared to controls who had a different type of group therapy,

64% experienced an abstinence in binge episodes whereas only 36% of the control group did so. What is interesting though is that this difference between the study groups disappeared at just 3- and 6-months follow-up and by a year the abstinence (from binging) rates were 64% and 56% respectively. So, things continued to improve for the control participants even outside of therapy. Safer et al. also reported that there was little or no differences between the DBT group and control participants for sustained emotional regulation at 12-month follow-up. In fact, the control group showed a slightly better outcome on two of the five psychological self-rating scales and the DBT participants on the other three scales used in the study. The authors noted this as interesting because training in emotional regulation is supposed to be one hallmark of DBT in distinguishing it from other therapies. The therapy used for the control participants was called an active comparison group therapy in which there is less use of a structured format like that in typical DBT. Instead, it was based more on a person-centred (Rogerian) approach in which the therapist uses unconditional positive regard and purposeful empathic listening to more subtly guide a client to discover their inbuilt sense of growth and fulfilment. In other words, it is a bit more like interpersonal psychotherapy (IPT) than cognitive behavioural therapy (CBT) or dialectical behaviour therapy (DBT).

Ah. Wait a minute. What did I just read? You might say and then wonder. Is what operating to be of support toward a good outcome of therapy not just the type of therapy but possibly the quality of the experience with the therapist? A good question. Thank you. So, let's look at that a bit. Unfortunately, there is not a lot of research on this question in direct regard to AN, BN or BED.

However, Tobias Six and Ernst Koster (2014), of the University of Gent, found and reviewed twenty-three studies from 2001 to 2013 relating to this question, but without doing a statistical meta-analysis. The studies reviewed did not include any that specifically addressed AN, BN or BED but the overall finding is still interesting. Twenty two of the 23 studies all indicated how it was the facilitative interpersonal skills (FIS) of a therapist and not age, gender, ethnicity, experience, education, or preferred therapy orientation, which make for good outcomes. This seems to relate well to what Safer et al. (2010) found with using more of a Rogerian person-centred approach in a control therapy group having as good an outcome as the DBT group which had been the intended focus of their study.

Six and Koster (2014) did not include Safer et al. (2010), and neither set of researchers' reference any of the same studies. This FIS finding alludes back to what Fairburn et al. (1993) mentioned about beneficial outcome of treatment when not focusing on the eating or purging behaviour. Thereby, less imposition, even unintentional, of control by a therapist over a client's behaviour. The client instead potentially experiencing therapy as though they are more like an ally with at least equal control over the process in the therapy office which transfers better to when they are on their own. The latter being the goal anyway. Getting a hint? The more control we each have over our own process sounds like a subtle example of freedom to us. And in later chapters you will read how this same theme of process (accommodating, facilitative, non-judging, vs. not) possibly plays out for individual persons in their wider social context, not just in the small-scale situation of therapy.

EMBODY HOW (PART TWO)

All of a sudden my heart is drawn.

Toward this plum tree by the lawn.

If I were free to pick my bloom or grass,

If I were free to choose to live or die,

I would resign to fate without a sigh.

偶然间心似缱，梅树边。这般花花草草由人恋，生生死死

随人愿，便酸酸楚楚无人怨。

(Excerpt from The Peony Pavilion, by Tang Xianzu, 1598

translation by Wang Rongpei, 1996. (40)).

"What's in a name?

That which we call a rose by any other name

would smell as sweet"

(*Excerpt from Romeo and Juliet, by William Shakespeare*.1597).

CULTURE AND BODY IMAGE

William Shakespeare, of England, and Tang Xianzu, of China, each wrote about the tragic romance of young lovers. Both playwrights died in 1616. At worlds apart, but contemporaries alike, is remarkable. Hamlet was the first of Shakespeare's plays to be published in Chinese, but not until 1922. The Peony Pavilion, by Tang, was not published complete in English until 1939. (40) The tragedy of Romeo and Juliet's misreckoned suicides over forbidden betrothal reunites in grief their previously warring families of Verona. In The Peony Pavilion, Du Liniang dreams of passionate love with a young scholar, Liu Mengmei, whom she has never met. When Du Liniang awakens she is so consumed with pining for Liu, and while painting her self-portrait, she wastes away and dies. Being filled with passion still she returns as a ghost to find Liu near her shrine, after having seen her portrait. After he reciprocates her passion, she declares being a ghost. Liu exhumes her remains with which Du Liniang reintegrates. After Liu passes his official examination, they reveal their secret marriage which is then sanctioned by imperial decree. A happier ending.

When published Tang's play became popular among seventeenth century Chinese readers. Some historians have remarked that many women readers intensely identified with Du Liniang, as though her transcendence over death in the play helped her transcendence from fictional status. Legends sprang forth of how an actress playing Du Liniang had died on stage, and of some young female readers being so infatuated they themselves wasted away. Some women readers wrote their own commentaries about the play, from which literary historians have offered various interpretations for its intense appeal. Such as, the play represented a young woman circumventing social constraints over marriage arrangement, a young woman being a literary protagonist for the first time, it pioneered an exposition of women's passion and sexuality, and the darker allure of women dying young, and the exquisite pleasure and pain produced in con-templating those deaths. (41).

Intense interest in stories that exalt women as the main protagonists has re-curred, albeit four hundred years later, in 2020 China with television shows. A valid cynical view might be that television producers are tapping into a growing market of financially independent women. However, the interest itself is demon-strated by how there were 1 billion views between just May 18 and June 1, 2020, of a 24-episode show titled The Romance of Tiger and Rose by Chen Xiao Qian, a previously less known female screenwriter. The story is set as though in a historical matriarch society in which men are not allowed to study or hold official positions. The main character is a Princess who is retained in the story, after being initially scripted to die in the third episode, and who kidnaps a crown prince from an enemy city to be her husband. The prince thinks he has his own agenda, except he falls in love with his kidnapper. Kind of a Stockholm Syndrome twist to the Peony Pavilion. Elaine Yau, of the South China Morning Post (June 23, 2020) gives four other examples of an increased interest in shows on Chinese television depicting women as main characters. For instance, a show, titled Older Sisters Who Brave The Winds And Waves, features 30 Chinese female stars in their 30s to 50s who compete for a spot on a five-member pop group. It attract-ed 370 million views in just the first three days on air.

Unfortunately, the barriers of language and politics between China and other countries has intensified and persisted since the 1950s. These barriers, and the Cultural Revolution (1966-1976) in China, have likely limited the availability of translatable information on what history there may be of extreme fasting in China, and that which is aside of brief religious observances and literary as-sociated myths. However, researchers from Hong Kong (HK) in the 1990's had suggested that the semi- autonomous region is historically both an approximate example of a non-westernized and non-communist Chinese culture and a culture in transition. A transition that until recently had been leaning westward but now apparently being directed toward Communist China.

Lee (1991), of the Prince of Wales Hospital, HK, described the commonalities among 16 young Chinese women with AN and amenorrhea, as having come from lower socio-economic backgrounds, each maintaining low weight through rigid management of low food intake. Only few used bulimic methods, and few had depression. While there were multiple possible personal factors associated with the etiology of the anorexia there was no pre-existing obesity, and little pressure to pursue thinness for attractiveness. Instead of manifesting an intense fear of obesity and associated body image, they more commonly attributed low food intake to abdominal bloating. Lee, Ho & Hsu, L.K.G. (1993) reported on 70 female Chinese in HK, among whom 41 (58.6%) did not exhibit any fear of fatness but instead explained their emaciation being due to intestinal bloating, having no appetite or hunger, or simply eating less. The authors suggested that their observations, of some Chinese persons with AN expressing fat-phobia while many others do not, demonstrated the recent (20th Century) Westernizing of some of Hong Kong society, but that AN itself is not a Western, fat-phobic, high economic class, culture-bound phenomenon. These reports by Lee and colleagues may have been what instigated the eventual changes in the DSM V, including the addition of the ARFID diagnosis. By early this 21st Century there was some evidence out of China that Westernizing factors had been permeating the expression of EDs, including for male Chinese. Tong, Miao, Hsu et al. (2005), of the University of Science and Technology, Wuhan, and Tufts-New England Medical Center, USA, reported on five male persons (4 with AN and 1 with BN) in central China all of whom attributed fear of fatness to their food restriction or bulimic purging.

A similar impression of an apparently low prevalence of EDs in India has instead begun to also show a history of EDs without fat-phobia pre-existing Western-ized attributions. Vaidyanathan, Kuppili, Menon (2019) conducted a search for studies on EDs and found that in India there were only 24 case studies, and from 1989 to 2017 only 13 demographic type studies involving high school, medical or nursing school student groupings, and only two studies related to persons in clinical care. The authors acknowledged there is not a lot of information. But of that available on presentations of EDs in India, there generally is a lack of concern about body fat or shape. They also found no reports of BED and only five reports of BN, with only two females having concerns of weight and body image, and one male and two other females having no such concerns. Most cases were of AN without bulimia, were adolescent females, most belonging to the Hindu religion, and came from middle or upper socio-economic background.

The authors referenced contrasting evidence of EDs in females of Indian descent and the Sikh religion, but living in the United Kingdom, who had attributed body weight and shape concerns to having been teased by peers about the same things.

The earliest case study Vaidyanathan et al. referenced, by Jha and Awadhia (1967), illustrates some longevity in the existence of EDs in India and of a woman who did not attribute her severe restriction of food and water intake, which reportedly begun at age 40, to body shape concerns. When first seen by a clinician at age 42 she expressed the need for restriction to help sharpen her memory so to recover a mislaid handkerchief. Additionally, her first episode of severe food restriction two years earlier followed an attempted suicide, itself precipitated by her concerns over her husband's reaction to hearing about another man having shown unsuccessful advance to her in the past, and he was returning to visit their area. Her memory was assessed as being intact and it was reported there were no signs of mental health illness. The woman came from an upper socio-economic background and was married at age 15 years.

Whether this Indian woman's explanations, or those by other persons also without fat-phobia, for her food and water restriction may not make sense to some of us does not give us license to impose our own explanation. And that is what has conceivably happened for some time in Western culture with over-generalizing about fat phobia and associated social pressure about shape and appearance being a dominant explanation for all persons' experiences of ED. Seem familiar? Sound like reductionism on a rather large scale? Remind you of what Rear Admiral Bill Galanis, US Navy, said about "just because you can doesn't mean you should"? He was referring to joining a popular sweeping change to touchscreens before fully realizing the implications for a specialized situation and the sad loss of ten US sailors in the collision involving the USS John McCain in 2017. And for those people without fat-phobia concerns associated with their eating style, has this reductionism taken away their meaning and our understanding. Our beacons' stories are important and may get inadvertently discounted by our reductive interpretations including those from narrow methodology and data sets. We will illustrate this a little further. Please bear with the lengthy explanation as it helps to again show how other possibly just as relevant information gets lost through researchers being reductionistic.

Korn, Vocks et al. (2020), of the Universities of Lubeck and Osnabruck, and Harvard Medical School, proposed that persons with AN but no expressed phobia of fat may be under-reporting in direct discussion. So, the researchers employed a supposedly indirect method of having participants make preference ratings of life profile descriptions, itemized and intermixed, about relationships, belonging, intimacy, hobbies, school or work, and shape and weight. The participants were instructed to make their ratings based on what they wished for most, not on their current circumstances. The sixty-six German female participants ranged in age from 15 years old to 58. Thirty had AN with concerns of fat phobia (AN-FP), there were 29 control participants without AN, but only 7 with AN who had not self-expressed a phobia of fat (AN-NFP). Contrary to the researchers' expectations, each AN group rated items about appearance and shape at about the same level as those without AN. However, those with AN-FP rated concern about weight maintenance vs. gain weight more so than those without AN. Those with AN-NFP rated it even higher. Korn et al. interpreted these findings to represent those persons with AN-NFP possibly have worse insight and really do have some fat phobia. However, the researchers inadequately explained the disconnect between the higher concern about weight contrasting with there being no difference, between all those with AN and those without, in terms of appearance and body shape. An alternative interpretation is that those with AN-FP and AN-NFP can equally identify with commonalities in their peer culture, just that those commonalities do not necessarily relate to all their particular restriction of food. It's not as though persons with AN are from a different planet. They likely have a lot in common with their peers in interests in music, fashion, social media, etc. What Korn et al. did not offer sufficiently well enough was an alternative explanation based on the other differences they found between participants with AN and the controls without AN. For example, the participants with AN-NFP rated 'success at school or work' their highest preference overall compared to those without AN, and even higher than the 'shape' and 'weight' related factors. The authors latterly only mention that this possibly represents a higher sense of perfectionism in the participants with AN-NFP. Participants with AN-NFP also showed preference for being in a stable intimate relationship, whereas controls without AN gave greater preference to other life domains. Which is also interesting because only 8 of the 37 participants with AN were in a romantic relationship at the time of the study, compared to 21 of the 29 participants without

AN. Another contrast finding was that participants with AN-NFP showed lesser preference for having rewarding relationships with friends and family than did the controls without AN. So, it seems that Korn et al. got stuck on interpreting their own findings through mostly the familiar lens of fat phobia and body shape attractiveness and so insufficiently thought about food restriction in AN being more closely associated with other factors too or instead. After-all, the participants with AN-NFP clearly indicated how things relating to school and work performance and intimate vs. family/friend relationships had greater importance for them. These performance expectations also probably play a part in there being more persons with ED among competitive male and female athletes than in the general population (APA guidelines 2006/2010). Let alone the fact that the weight, if you can excuse the phrase in this context, of the cultural evidence outside of the United States and Western world helped effect the dropping the fear of becoming fat criterion as necessary for the diagnosis of AN in the American DSM V of 2013. So why couldn't that also apply in Western countries. Which takes us back full circle to an example like that of the Indian woman of 1967, but this time from the USA.

Davis and Nguyen (2014), of the University of Florida, reported the story of a woman who entered treatment again for AN at age 66, after 12 previous occasions from age 30. She first manifested AN in 1961 at age 13 while living in a Catholic convent while studying to become a nun, a place at which there were no mirrors and no pressure to be 'attractively' thin. She reported that rather than restricting her diet to be thin or attractive, she restricted her diet to be closer to God in hopes of becoming a saint. The woman said she had a happy childhood home life, but was shy, anxious, and ritualistic, with few close friends, was not underweight nor had concerns about weight, had no exposure nor use of alcohol or substances, and had no experience of abuse. There were no similar concerns among her siblings or parents. She described herself as the "little helper" at home and with the nuns at school and then the convent. When she was 21 years old, she was asked to leave the convent by her supervisors who had become very concerned about her extreme fasting and low body weight. She still had no knowledge of sexual intercourse and reproductive health. She became a nurse and was married at age 25. She could not conceive so she and her husband adopted children. Throughout her adolescent and adult life her

BMI had always been extremely low. She had some associated physical health effects, such as osteoporosis, but otherwise had no severe instances of ill health. Which remained the case one year after the hospital and day-treatment she last received at age 66. During this last treatment she reported for the first time having some fear of fatness and a desire to be thin, and that not all of this was religious based. It remained though that her social history had not exposed her to typical peer pressures, nor did she relate thinness to social attractiveness.

Although Davis and Nguyen did not state so, it is possible that their client adopted some of the non-religious fat phobia from exposure through the multiple admissions to treatment settings during which time societal and peer pressure about attractiveness was a theme often 'taught' in psychoeducation. And as we discussed above about the study by Korn et al. (2020), the researchers were surprised that most of their participants with AN rated body shape and appearance at a similar level as controls without AN, but rated concerns about weight gain higher than controls. This apparent disconnect suggests that while persons with AN can equally identify with things in their surrounding culture that does not necessarily mean their restriction of food intake and their self-measure via weight is not to do with other things instead or in combination. Remember the study by Mathisen, Rosenvinge et al. of Norway (2020) and their 164 participants diagnosed with either BN or BED, aged 18-40. Many of the participants, even those randomly assigned to the physical therapy and dietary therapy (PED-t) group vs. CBT group, did not take up the physical exercise ('taught') as generally recommended for health maintenance versus compensatory muscle damaging exercise or under-exercising. Even this disconnect may seem surprising but then again not, if you do not rely on one narrow lens and assume that in EDs over-exercise is just an extension of the goal of physical fitness for attractiveness. It could be for something(s) else instead or in combination.

Remember the study by Sipila et al. (2017) of Finland, and how they professed to debunk the idea that parental or adolescent religiosity increases the risk for anorexia nervosa? The problem was they made this quite wide-sweeping conclusion based possibly on a very narrow method. That method being twelve self-report items selected from the Minnesota Multiphasic Personality Inventory (MMPI), a test very familiar in the psychological field. Those 12 items only really pertain to shared practices and do not in any way sufficiently tap into the kind of personalized beliefs as seen in the above case examples from India and the USA. Although you could split hairs and say Sipila et al were referring only to practice and not beliefs. But that could mean they studied the wrong aspect. And with concerns about body shape and fat phobia no longer a necessary diagnostic criterion for AN, this does allow for a reconsideration of older historical information that was previously treated as though minimally relevant to 'modern' AN. Before the late 1800's examples of extreme food restriction with some religious tones were referred to as anorexia mirabilis.

Davis and Nguyen (2014) provide a good and sufficient summary of that history. Here are those highlights: i) between 700 – 900 A.D.: St. Wilgefortis, princess of Portugal, had vowed virginity and service to God. A suitor, arranged by her father, withdrew his offer of marriage after the princess in protest prayed she would lose her beauty, took no nourishment and grew hair (lanugo) all over her body. The father had her crucified as punishment (and possibly rationalized her behavior as a sign of possession by evil). ii) Saint Catherine of Siena (1347-1380) began lengthy meditations, reportedly cut her hair, forced herself to vomit the little food she infrequently ingested, and flagellated herself in imitation of Christ's passion. She began doing so after her family tried to marry her off to her deceased sister's husband. She died at the age of 32 from malnutrition. iii) they cite Bell's (1985) historical report that between the 13th and 17th century, mostly in southern Europe, there were 181 cases of holy fasting and numerous examples of women fasting to point of death. It was thought that they had direct communication with God in addition to this being a means of avoiding arranged marriages and childbirth. iv) through 17th and 18th centuries many "miraculous maids" died of starvation, and while mostly from poor families, drew the attention of clergymen, physicians and civil magistrates trying to investigate the phenomenon. v) AN, as our Westernized culture has 'known' it these past 150 years, was first described simultaneously by Leseque in France and Gull in England in 1873. They described young women who had "delirious conviction that they cannot or ought not to eat" [7]. This being well prior to mass media and cultural pressures to diet and the perception that thin is beautiful. The diagnosis of AN in the 19th century did not appear to include body image disturbance or fear of being fat. It is as though the 20th and 21st Centuries' versions of EDs borrowed and added on the social-cultural changes about body-image and fat phobia, rather than those changes being the dominant etiology of EDs. And that adoption of fat phobia provided, please excuse the phrase, another layer of self and other distraction from personal and social psychological issues.

Let's look at another example, this time around from this 21st Century and within the geographical bounds of the USA but for persons who do not usually have the exposure to media about social pressure for thinness. Platte et al. (2000) of the Universities of Trier (Germany) and Pennsylvania (USA), studied 50 men and 56 women, with an age range of 14-67 years, in an Amish community of the USA. They asked each participant to rate satisfaction or dissatisfaction of their actual BMI compared to their ideal BMI. They also checked each person's accuracy in rating their body size by comparison with the accuracy of their relatives' own ratings. The researchers found that older persons and persons with obesity of both genders manifested body dissatisfaction. Older women, and men with obesity, also overestimated their body size. For those members of the community, their body dissatisfaction and inaccuracy might be a function of recognizing and accepting loss of agility as the body changes or ages. Young persons and persons of normal weight of both genders showed no body dissatisfaction or inaccuracy in their perception of their body size. One might conclude that this may be in part due to those people having not been exposed to the outside media and social pressure for thinness. However, if one accepts there must be exposure to media and social pressure in order to manifest ED related behavior, such as food intake restriction, then it should follow that EDs would not occur in an Amish community.

Remember though what Korn et al. (2020) inadvertently discovered about how their participants with AN rated body shape and appearance with no greater importance than controls without AN? Well, that disconnect, or uncoupling might be a better expression, is indirectly shown in another study of an Amish community in the USA. Cassady et al. (2005) reported about 5 girls, ranging in age from 9 to 13 years, each of whom had remained in bed for at least three weeks due to extreme physical weakness not explained by medical causes. Because this type of phenomena is instead psychologically derived, they are referred to as being psychogenic or conversion disorder. Four of the girls presented with neck weakness and could not lift their heads. All five restricted their food intake and had severe weight loss. The researchers report that they could not identify any precipitating causes for each girl other than some social conflict going on in the community at that same time. This report by Cassady et al. preceded the 2013 change in adjusting the fat phobia criterion for AN in the DSM V. The researchers might not have considered what they observed as being also on a continuum of eating disorder phenomena. Regardless, the possible connection of the girls' food intake restriction and severe weight loss to ongoing social/interpersonal or personal conflict is reminiscent of the case examples from India and the USA discussed above, and of the evidence in general from studies of persons not influenced by Westernized culture but who still manifest AN.

If one takes this observation of social conflict or stressful precipitants then we might see some commonality between what have to date been considered separate psychiatric disorders, especially by the APA's DSM system. It might help us understand that while in some non-western cultures there may be less so-called incidence of eating disorders, persons there may instead manifest different responses to similar social stress precipitants. Adityanjee et al. (1989) of the All-India Institute of Medical Sciences, provided three case examples that help illustrate this notion. All three persons (one male age 15, two females ages 15 & 16) were not related or known to each other. They had each presented, for intermittent and brief periods, as though convinced they were someone else, spoke and acted in ways uncharacteristic for them, and identified unrelated persons as being their family versus their actual family members. When they reverted to their usual identity and behavior, they had amnesia of their starkly contrasting identity and behavior and had a sense of lost time. In Western psychiatry, including the DSM system, such presentation might be diagnosed as multiple personality disorder as it was also by the authors. Interestingly, the authors reported what were the psychosocial stressors for each case. The boy had been scolded for having a love affair with a neighborhood girl, there was significant rivalry among his siblings, and he had difficulties with his studies. The 15-year-old girl had four occasions in the prior year of the conversion symptom of 'blindness' just as scholastic tests were coming up at school, specifically a change from instruction having changed from mainly Hindu to being predominantly in English. The presenting changes in her identity and behavior occurred just before final examinations. She too had been scolded for romantic interest in a neighborhood boy. The 16-year-old girl had, in the days preceding her marked changes in identity and behavior, had been reprimanded by her three older sisters for her romantic involvement with a neighborhood boy of whom they did not approve. They also blamed her for the boyfriend fighting with other boys over them teasing the girl with sexually toned taunts. The older sisters financially supported the family and were themselves unmarried.

The social stressors involving family disapproval of the romances in each of the three cases above is close to what occurred in the case reported by Jha and Awadhia (1967) and reviewed earlier. In that case, the woman had restricted food and water intake following an attempted suicide purportedly in anticipation of her husband's reaction to a past suitor of hers revisiting the area. This theme of intra-family conflict over romantic desires versus family arranged marriage occurred too in some of the historical European cases of eating disorders as summarized by Davis and Nguyen (2014). Another thing in common among these three Indian adolescent cases is that in their longer standing characteristic behavior and identity they are each described as being sociable, attention seeking and highly ambitious. This ambition is possibly like what Korn et al. (2020) under-stated about the participants in their study (with AN-NFP) who rated 'success at school or work' their highest preference overall compared to those without AN, and even higher than 'shape' and 'weight' and 'family/friend relationships' related factors.

Adityanjee et al. (1989) acknowledge that multiple personality disorder is rarely seen in Indian psychiatric clinics but did say that possession syndrome is more frequently seen, including in other South Asian countries. In possession syndrome the person involved behaves as if a religious deity or the spirit of a dead relative has taken over his or her mind and body. The manifest possession behavior can also be episodic. Keshavan et al. (1989), of the Western Psychiatric Institute and Clinic, Pittsburgh (USA), and the National Institute of Mental Health and Neurosciences, India, also provided three case examples out of 209 clients who self-referred for their clinic and study conducted in the Bidar district of India. The authors stated that most of the persons seen had manifested conversion disorder (108), somatization disorder (30), or anxiety disorder (29) in conjunction with their belief of being possessed. Somatization disorder involves a

54

person becoming so overly focused on bodily symptoms it increasingly interferes with their day-to-day functioning. Many family members also believed their relative was possessed. Again, the three case examples each had some intra-family conflict occurring concurrent with the 'possession' of which the authors stated represented what was seen across many of the 209 clients.

The first case was a Muslim girl (18 years old) who had periods of unconsciousness, during which she would sometimes scream and utter incomprehensible words, and unusual limb movements. These 'possessions' began three years earlier when she became engaged to a distant cousin whom she did not want to marry and would worsen whenever he visited. Eventually the cousin married someone else after the girl's family could not afford the dowry and agree upon an earlier wedding date. The girl's 'possessions' became less frequent. The second case was of a 13-year-old Hindu girl who had episodes of altered sensorium and vague fear which lasted six months. During these episodes she would throw off her bangles and toe rings (symbols of marriage) and her clothes. These 'possession' episodes had begun after her marriage to a wealthier but older man to whom she did not want to marry. She had attained menarche just one month before marriage, had little understanding about sexuality and was frightened by the first experience of intercourse. Her family insisted that neighbors had put a spell on their daughter out of jealousy over the marriage and refused to accept the psychiatrist's alternative explanation about the girl's stress over the marriage itself. The third case was of a 70-year-old widow who had manifested episodes lasting 3-6 months of talking and laughing to herself and of hearing voices. This had begun at least two decades earlier following the death of her husband, her inheriting their large property and her brother-in-law legally contesting for a share of the land. When seen by the psychiatric researchers they also noted she had persecutory delusions, formal thought disorder, and incongruent affect. She declined treatment with psychiatric medication. Both she and her son, a physicist, believed the brother-in-law had put a spell on her. She agreed to see her local physician and wanted to also see a local faith healer. Out of the 209 clients in the study eight others were also considered by the clinician researchers to have schizophrenia. However, although in this study by Keshavan et al. (1989) many of the clients may have had underlying psychological or psychiatric aspects already existing, the involvement too of intra-family conflict based upon cultural expectations seems to have played a part in the actual manifestation of unusual behavior. And for the sake of maintaining family equilibrium and avoiding embarrassment it seems belief in possession became an acceptable rationalization.

Suicide too appears to remain a very sad consequence of not having the freedom to even just discuss emotional discomfort openly in some family and cultural confines. Stunningly, Indian men make up 25% and more remarkably Indian women, aged 15 to 39 years, make up 36% of the known global suicide rate. And Indian housewives, recorded since 1997 at 20 to 25 thousand per year, make up 50% of that rate for Indian women. Some observers suggest that the 30% rate of spousal violence self-reported by women in a nation-wide survey is possibly behind the higher suicide rate for women. Additionally, though, and like the case examples discussed above, a 2021 commentary by psychologist Usha Verma Srivastava infers that behind both the violence and suicide rate is that: "(M)ost girls are married off as soon as they turn eighteen…… to (marital in-law conditions in which they spend the) entire day at home, cooking and cleaning and doing household chores. All sorts of restrictions are placed on her, she has little personal freedom and rarely has access to any money of her own…. Her education and dreams no longer matter, and her ambition begins to extinguish slowly, and despair and disappointment set in, and the mere existence become torture." (42).

The above case examples from India may seem old, but that too may be an advantage before any Westernizing effects and interpretations might have complicated our understanding of the circumstances. However, here is a more recent case example which again illustrates some of the same things discussed above. Tanja Ahlin (2018), from the University of Amsterdam, was in northern India in 2011 doing an internship at an NGO (non-governmental organization) working on a project related to health and female empowerment. While there she befriended a pharmacist who entrusted Ahlin to visit with her and her family on many occasions. Ahlin described how the woman likely had minimal exposure to western social influences because in her region of India any television of Western origin was over-shadowed by local productions. The woman's favorite soap-opera was from Bollywood and reflected many Hindu values rather than

Western ones. The woman herself did not know how to operate a computer, did not have a smart-phone, and did not use social media. The woman at first attributed her severe low weight to possibly having typhoid or pneumonia, both of which were eventually ruled out along with other medical causes. During her new friendship with Ahlin she remembered that she had in fact began reducing her eating and weight at age 20, while a student living in a dormitory. This had preceded any of the persistent physical weakness, she had interpreted as being due to typhoid or pneumonia, by around 5 years. She did not remember why she began reducing her eating, except that she felt uneasy sharing food with unknown people in the canteen. She had not intended to lose as much weight as she had, but she could not control it anymore. She admired an earlier photograph of herself before she lost significant weight and did not express any fear of becoming fat or gaining weight. In discussion with her sisters about each expecting to be in an arranged marriage the woman said, "I am sick, so I'm safe". However, on another occasion the woman remarked how her greatest concerns were her assumptions about the financial burden on her family for her education, affecting the opportunities for her younger siblings, and about if she could ever repay her family financially or in kind. This concern had begun at the same time as first reducing her eating and losing weight and had persisted since. It reached such intensity she often felt she should not have been born. Here again we possibly see the theme of fulfilling ambition through education (to become a pharmacist), like the participants with AN-NFP in Korn et al.'s (2020) study. However, for this woman the fulfillment of ambition coincided with her feeling guilt for thinking of herself as standing apart from her family and causing them harm, financially and socially. The woman, in apparent contrast though, also acknowledged that her parents had tried to dispel her of such concerns and had continued to encourage her education and independence despite this not being the norm for females in their culture.

In another case from India, Srivivasa et al. (2015) describe a case of a 25-year-old woman who they diagnosed as having AN with bulimia. She came from an upper social class Hindu family and had high school education to around age 15. She had been married for 5 years, was a "homemaker", and resided with her husband's family in urban Bangalore. The authors reported that the woman's AN and bulimic behavior had first manifest around two years previously, precipitated by her husband's criticism of her weight. Either her husband or another relative had reportedly described her as having been "dull and inactive most of the time since her marriage (but was) able to carry out her activities of daily living adequately". The psychiatrist authors said it was difficult to establish rapport and the woman was initially uncooperative. Eventually she herself described symptoms of possible depression, being over concerned about physical appearance inspired by skinny models as pointed out by her husband. It seemed the primary purpose of the authors was to alert other physicians to the signs and presentation of AN, giving the purportedly low prevalence and lack of medical practitioner familiarity with EDs in India. The woman was admitted as an inpatient, and treatment followed a similar course to that used in Western country medical services. Except it is not reported whether her treatment also included a behavioral restriction vs. reward system used for controlling her food intake and avoiding bulimic strategies. She was prescribed Cyproheptadine (an antihistamine sometimes also used for migraine or control of vomiting) and "low dose" Olanzapine (an atypical antipsychotic). She also received "insight-oriented psychotherapy" and CBT. The medications and therapy treatments continued on an outpatient basis in which she was seen every two weeks. There was some relapse after one year, at which time she continued with the psychotherapy only. At the end of two years her symptoms of AN and bulimia had reportedly remitted, and she had maintained a 25 kg increase over her pre-treatment weight. Although not reported by the authors, some of her weight gain might have been a side-effect of the Olanzapine. This case example sounds successful in terms of visually measurable effects (weight) and her and/ or husband's report about improved eating and other behavior. However, the written study by Srivivasa et al. does not give much information on whether the researchers, including the therapist over the two years, asked the woman, or persons other than her husband, more about what precipitated her AN. There was no information on anything about her eating or her emotional and social life that pre-dated her marriage or AN, whether the marriage was arranged, and what was her experience of the marriage and in-law household. And had those relationships and her experience of them also improved. After all, the description of her being "dull and inactive most of the time since her marriage" unfortunately sounds possibly pejorative (it might also be a problem of translation) when instead it could be a sign of her displeasure about her marital circumstances that needed further exploration with the woman. Another theme of inquiry with her may have also

58

been about her own goals and ambitions in life, and whether she thought her high school education was cut short to prepare for marriage and housekeeping instead. It is also possible that over time the woman learned to modify her eating behavior to sufficient extent to placate others but may still have continued bulimic strategies secretly. Or she may have just adapted her behavior, but the precipitants remained unresolved. There was no information either sought or reported to examine other possibilities, besides her husband's criticism and her concerns about thinness as attractive.

In another study involving an Amish community, in Pennsylvania, USA, Steinle et al. (2002) of the University of Maryland, were primarily investigating dietary behavior in relation to obesity and diabetes. They appeared to not be focused on EDs nor including the 'cultural-media-thinness' hypothesis. They used an eating behavior questionnaire that reportedly categorized their participants into those who typically use restraint or instead disinhibition around food and eating or eat mostly because of feeling hungry. Their 624 participants, from 28 families, were relatives of a person with obesity but did not have obesity themselves at the start of the study. There were 338 women and 286 men, ranging in age from 30 to 46 years old. The researchers also did genetic testing related to obesity about which we don't need to mention here. The interesting finding for our discussion was that there appeared to be no difference between the women and men in the eating categories when BMI was factored in. But that with BMI aside women showed greater restraint scores than men. Again, these findings are in the absence of exposure to social media and the pressure to be thin to be attractive.

If you wear glasses that see EDs mostly through the lens of the 'Westernized media and social pressure for attractive thinness' interpretation, then you may miss information contrary to that over-reaching and over-simplified notion. From our discussion above we have learned about AN in non-western cultures, case examples not involving socially driven thinness, from older history, from the Amish culture that eschews westernized media and values, and from studies that are not even intentionally researching EDs directly. The story of EDs is complex and cannot be so easily reduced to the 'Western culture-bound' interpretation alone. And as we read about each case example, we began to see emerge some differences in expression of body image, body invasion (possession), bodily conversion, and personal identity, and some actual commonality of possible psychosocial aspects (e.g., cultural expectations of conformity about romance and marriage; educational and career ambition; perceived isolation from family; and conflict within social group). And these examples are of persons coping mostly within their own culture of origin. This is not to infer that fat phobia body image concern is not real. Indeed, it is for many persons. Betty Friedan (1963), Gloria Steinem (1969), Germaine Greer (1970), and other Western feminists have for some time drawn our attention to pressure for cultural conformity and the effect this has had on women in the Western context, some of which is like the case examples we read about in this chapter. And the focus on body image is in part a representation of the cultural pressures involved. But as you continue to read subsequent chapters you will come across other information that suggests there is still more for us to consider about cultural contexts and the persons, who have EDs, themselves. So, our next chapter takes a different angle and looks at what possibly occurs with persons in interaction with a culture not of their own origin. Then whether what we observed on an individual case level, in this chapter just finished, might also occur for groupings of persons within their culture of origin. This too builds the story about EDS and about freedom.

"The liberty protected by the Fifth Amendment's Due Process Clause contains within it the prohibition against denying to any person the equal protection of the laws. While the Fifth Amendment itself withdraws from Government the power to degrade or demean in the way this law does, the equal protection guarantee of the Fourteenth Amendment makes that Fifth Amendment right all the more specific and all the better understood and preserved."

(Majority Opinion [5-4] of The US Supreme Court, written by Justice Anthony Kennedy, on United States v. Windsor, 570 U.S. 744 [2013]; nullifying the Defense of Marriage Act 1996).

"No union is more profound than marriage, for it embodies the highest ideals of love, fidelity, devotion, sacrifice, and family. In forming a marital union, two people become something greater than once they were. As some of the petitioners in these cases demonstrate, marriage embodies a love that may endure even past death. It would misunderstand these men and women to say they

disrespected the idea of marriage. Their plea is that they do respect it, respect it so deeply that they seek to find its fulfillment for themselves. Their hope is not to be condemned to live in loneliness, excluded from one of civilization's oldest institutions. They ask for equal dignity in the eyes of the law. The Constitution grants them that right."

(Majority Opinion [5-4] of The US Supreme Court, written by Justice Anthony Kennedy, on Obergefell v. Hodges, 576 U.S. 644 [2015]).

ACCULTURATION, MINORITIES AND BODY IMAGE

Another related issue is that most of the research literature and media to date on EDs is based upon Western-bound notions and so mostly upon female persons of white ethnicity. Consequently, and even looking just within the bounds of the USA, persons of non-white ethnicity are less likely to seek help for an ED and so are also less represented in research. Coffino et al. (2019), of the University at Albany, State University of New York, and Yale School of Medicine, examined responses from the 2012-2013 (US) National Epidemiologic Survey on Alcohol and Related Conditions-III (N=36,309). The survey included respondents who had answered questions about seeking help or not for ED symptoms and who also met the *DSM-5* criteria for AN (n =275), BN (n=91) and BED (n= 256). The researchers found, after accounting for socio-demographic characteristics, that men and ethnic/racial minorities (non-Hispanic blacks and Hispanics) were significantly less likely to ever seek help for BED than were women or non-Hispanic whites, respectively. Hispanics also were significantly less likely to seek help for AN relative to non-Hispanic whites. Coffino et al. recommended that there is a need for different strategies to encourage help-seeking among individuals with EDs, particularly among men and ethnic/racial minorities.

Rodgers et al. (2018), of Boston (USA) and Montpellier (France), did a review of around 40 research articles pertaining to EDs and ethnicity in the USA. They also found that our understanding is limited because smaller ethnic and racial groups, males, and intersecting minority statuses have been neglected in research into EDs. They further noted that there was a trend in the available research suggesting a relationship between higher levels of ED symptoms and greater expression about body image with acculturation, about which we will explain for you shortly. But that any relationship between ethnic identity alone and eating disorder symptoms is less consistent, although several studies suggest that positive ethnic identity may be protective. It seems then they found something like what we had discussed earlier about EDs in non-western cultures of other countries. EDs without fat phobia already existed and might have been of lower prevalence historically and concurrent until westernizing influences permeated those cultures to a greater extent. But when those influences had effect, persons with EDs caught in the transition from traditional culture to a westernizing culture began expressing fat phobia. So, it seems it may not just be about the direct effect of media and social pressure about thinness, but the social process or stress encountered during acculturation. The following study helps to explain acculturation.

A study not reviewed by Rogers et al but very relevant to this discussion on acculturation was conducted by Davis and Katzman (1999). They reported on the psychological aspects associated with eating problems in 93 female and 104 male Chinese students, between 17 to 28 years of age, in the USA for university study. The participants were given self-report questionnaires that asked about eating disorder aspects, body image, depression, self-esteem, awareness of their own emotions, and self-rating of acculturation (i.e., self-identify as mostly Chinese, bicultural, or mostly American). Davis and Katzman cited Berry (1980) for their definition of acculturation as being the process by which one group asserts its influence over another and what happens is likely to be difficult, reactive, and conflictual: affecting ones physical as well as psychological functioning. So, the inference is that the Chinese students being from a different culture would feel the effects of the host country's much larger Westernized culture. The researchers found that there was no gender difference on acculturation scores, and that 95 vs. 84 participants identified with having low vs. high acculturation, respectively. The authors should have perhaps noted in their paper's title that none of the participants were directly from China itself and so not likely naive to Westernized culture. About 90% of participants were born in HK and less than 10% were born in the USA or Canada. Over half (53%) of the participants resided in the USA for less than 5 years, 36% for 5 - 10 years, and 12% for over 10 years. And the participants were recruited via Chinese student associations, so presumably all had available similar social supports. However, both men and women who identified as highly acculturated reported greater perfectionism. Men who reported feeling ineffective were mostly in the group of men who endorsed low acculturation. While women overall reported greater body dissatisfaction and drive for thinness, it was the women who identified with high acculturation who also endorsed more eating disorder items, bulimia, ineffectiveness and maturity fears. Davis and Katzmen suggested that for those participants who reported having perfectionism this may represent an immigrant's over-correction of real or imagined deficits while attempting to assimilate (fit in). And that women do so via attempts to alter their bodies. The researchers also noted that for women who identified as highly acculturated, their greater fear of maturity and sense of ineffectiveness were at similar levels for that found for highly westernized high school girls in HK who also live between two cultures. The authors found that neither low self-esteem nor depression featured among any of the participant groupings. It is not clear what the researchers thought of how the low acculturated participants had less perfectionism, less maturity fears, and less eating disorder issues. It could be those participants generally did not have such concerns or traits and so coped differently. Alternatively, or additionally, by maintaining a strong cultural allegiance no matter the length of time in the host country may somehow have acted as a protective factor not just for the absence of depression as the authors had noted. And, as discussed above, the possibility of a protective factor from maintaining cultural identity was noted by Rodgers et al. (2018) too.

Soh et al. (2007) had made the opposite argument when they found in their study that Singaporean Chinese participants who had an ED (n= 18) self-reported identifying more within their traditional culture vs. Western culture. Also interesting was that the Singaporean Chinese control participants (n = 33) identified their allegiance to traditional culture, including preferring their 'rigid' family structure, even more. The controls also self-reported having some eating disorder behavior and restraint overeating, so in that sense they may not have been controls at all. And the psychological aspects at play for both groups of participants may have been more to do with other factors, considering the fact they were still in their home country and so not confronted as much with possible barriers to transition into a different culture. For example, their EDs may have been more to do with their transition or not from their traditional family context, or family expectations about marriage, or other local cultural things. Like we read about in the case studies in India. Humphrey and Ricciardelli (2004) found such a distinction in their study of 81 Chinese –Australian women, thirteen of whom were born in Australia and the remaining had each arrived in Australia during their young adulthood. Whatever the explanation, these findings do again inform us that exposure to Western culture's pressure toward thinness is not the defining factor for developing an ED. It instead appears to be more about how people manifest different strategies while faced with opportunity or pressure to acculturate or not into a different culture or transition within a family or other local scale context.

Another minority group for which acculturation might also apply is that of persons whose sexual orientation does not match the Western-bound notion of EDs being mostly about white heterosexual women. Calzo et al. (2018), of San Diego State University, Harvard Medical School, University College London, and University Hospital of Geneva, noted that most of the research on sexual orientation disparities in eating disorder behaviors had been conducted in the USA, Canada, and Australia. Most of which found consistent evidence of eating disorders not only among heterosexual adults but also those persons who identified as being gay, lesbian, or bisexual. So Calzo et al. investigated the possible association of sexual orientation and eating disorder symptoms in the UK. They examined data collected by the Avon Longitudinal study of Parents and Children, for a cohort of children born in the English county in 1991 and 1992 (n= 5048, with 53% women) for whom sexual orientation was assessed at 16 years old and ED symptoms assessed at ages 14 and 16. Twelve percent (around 605) identified as having a sexual orientation that was not or just mostly heterosexual. In their retrospective analyses Calzo et al. controlled for BMI, ethnicity, and socioeconomic status. They found that at age 14, gay and bisexual boys and mostly heterosexual (bisexual) girls had reported greater body dissatisfaction than their same-gender heterosexual peers. All sexual minority boys and mostly heterosexual (bisexual) girls reported greater degree of eating disorder behaviors than their same-gender heterosexual peers. By age 16, gay and bisexual boys had 12.5 times the occurrence than heterosexual boys for binge eating, mostly heterosexual (bisexual) boys had more than 3 times occurrence. Sexual minority girls had over twice the occurrence than heterosexual girls for binge eating and purging. The authors concluded that their findings suggested the need for early prevention efforts for sexual minority youth. The authors didn't refer to acculturation. But one only needs to consider how the stigma society still attaches to homosexuality and

65

how this may be in part an explanation for the much greater occurrence of ED behavior for gay and bisexual boys who likely feel unaccepted as they really are, like some other minority persons seem too.

To illustrate this a little further let's look at a study by Feldman and Meyer (2007) of the National Development and Research Institutes, USA, and Columbia University. They interviewed 126 white heterosexuals and 388 white, black, Latino persons who identified as lesbian, gay, or bisexual men and woman accessed through similar community venues they each attended, such as gyms. The researchers used DSM IV criteria for identifying AN, BN, and BED among the participants. They found that, like we discussed above regarding minority adolescents, gay and bi-sexual men had significantly higher prevalence of EDs than heterosexual men. There was no difference in prevalence for EDs between lesbian and bisexual women and heterosexual women, or across gender or racial groups. Meyer, when interviewed by ScienceDaily in 2007, said that their study also found that "even gay and bisexual men who participate in gay gyms, where body-focus and community values regarding attractiveness would be heightened, did not have higher rates of eating disorders than those gay and bisexual men who participated in non-gay gyms or who did not participate in a gym at all". Adding, "this suggests that factors other than values and norms in the gay community are related to the higher rates of eating disorder among these men."

Worthy to note here is that the DSM system of the American Psychiatric Association (APA) had considered homosexuality, without any good scientific or social evidence, as among "psychopathic disorders" (DSM-1, 1952), and then among "sexual deviations", like fetishism, pedophilia, sadism and masochism (DSM-II, 1968). Following protests by gay rights activists, and the eventual serious consideration of research initiated separately by Alfred Kinsey and Evelyn Hooker in the 1950s, the Australian and New Zealand College of Psychiatry declared homosexuality not an illness in October 1973. The APA dropped homosexuality from the DSM-II in December 1973. But in the DSM-III (1980) homosexuality was still referred to under a new "ego-dystonic homosexuality" category, to mean some persons might have marked and personal distress about one's sexual orientation, rather than the APA consider societal intolerance and stigma being prevalent factors. However, by the DSM-III Revised version (1987) that category was also removed. Almost thirty years later the US Supreme Court in 2015 answered a highly contentious issue about sexual orientation by deciding same-sex marriage qualifies as having equal recognition as opposite-sex marriage under the 1868 14th Amendment of the US Constitution. In 2020 the US Supreme court decided LGBT persons have the same protections from workplace discrimination based on race, color, religion, sex, or national origin. Despite the long overdue recasting of homosexuality as no longer an illness and the protections of personal freedom, the stigma against LGBT persons will still take many decades to disappear, if not be resurrected again and again. Little wonder then that LGBT persons still foresee barriers that in order to pass you must acculturate as though not LGBT. Little wonder then, perhaps, that Calzo et al. (2018) found the 3 to 12.5 times occurrence for ED behaviors for persons from sexual minorities compared to heterosexual same age (16) teenage peers in one English county alone. These societal barriers are another indication of the lack of freedom perhaps playing a part in the manifestation of EDs.

Taken together, the discussion from the recent two chapters suggests there may be more complex interpersonal and/or societal factors involved than just the over-simplified idea of media sponsored/Western-bound ideal about thinness. Perhaps listening better to persons with AN might take us to a place of better understanding. Holmes, Drake and their colleagues (2017), media studies researchers and occupational therapists at the University of East Anglia, developed and ran a 10-week discussion group for women with AN. The participants' ages ranged from 19 to 51 years. The group was called 'Cultural Approaches to Eating Disorders' and included themes on gendered constructions/beliefs about appetite (nutritional and sexual), cultural expectations surrounding female emotion and anger, cultural proscriptions of femininity, and the dynamics of 'healthy' eating/living and fitness cultures' aimed at women. Although the researchers still utilized media depictions the participants were informed to think about and discuss themes represented vs. just whether there was direct effect from the media itself. Holmes and colleagues reported that their participants found the tendency to portray women with anorexia as the passive victims of media influence as both patronizing and simplistic. According to these researchers, their participants found it useful to situate their problem within society rather than being in an individualized framework, like that of the medical perspective. And that an individualized ('illness') framework may encourage self-blame. One of their participants did raise a good point though about if the issue is with society, then how are they as individuals going to be able to change anything about society. Possibly something akin to what the five Amish girls were conveying in the study by Cassady et al. (2005). Although Holmes et al. did not state this, many persons with EDs endorse CBT and IPT over medical interventions. And in the effective facilitation of CBT or IPT a therapist is aware of the issues for a client regarding the 'pendulum' of blame (i.e., the tendency by a person to blame themselves, or to instead blame others in perceived need to defend from being blamed for something or anything), finding self-worth vs. worth defined by others (society included) and supporting interpersonal efficacy. In other words, a good facilitative therapist assists the client to attempt self-efficacy within the sphere of what they can influence, and they widen that sphere when appropriate for them. And in DBT there is the theme of acceptance, including of things that one cannot change and live life as you want despite those things. The approach taken by Holmes, Drake and colleagues might be characterized as being more directive rather than facilitative and that their participants might have reiterated things, they thought the presenters wanted to hear. Nevertheless, the themes Homes et al. identified do seem consistent with what we have discussed above about evidence from multiple sources, other countries, and some of which involved controlled studies. That is, there are possibly other more complex interpersonal and societal factors at play, like acculturation and barriers to participation 'as one is' than just being under the influence of the Western-bound value for thinness. We will revisit these factors further in a later chapter. Meanwhile, we will next review some other areas of relevance to EDs. Those being about genetics, metabolism, temperament, and brain functioning.

FROM BODY IS HOW: MAYBE

THE LONG AND WINDING ROAD OF SEEKING PATHOLOGY:

GENETICS, METABOLISM, BRAIN, MOOD

GENETICS AND METABOLISM

In this chapter you will discover that despite the apparent sophistication of genetic research, and the advances made in other areas of human health and treatment, and some large scale Western international ED genetic studies, the evidence for a specific genetic basis for EDs remains unclear. One of the problems is that person sample sizes in ED genetic studies are small and so renders a low power for meaningful statistical analyses. However, in this chapter you will still read about some interesting observations based on reports by the persons with EDs themselves which add to our overall discussion in this book. Some of those observations come from longitudinal studies that assess behavior in the same persons over many years, which helps to demonstrate continuity of association of some behaviors with others. And there are some other observations too that also throw some light on assumptions made about sexual development and EDs.

Studies of families, in which one member has already been diagnosed as having an ED, indicate that the incidence of there being another close relative also having an ED is 7 to 10 times that found in the general population. However, these persons tend to grow up in the same home or closely similar social environment, which makes it difficult to distinguish between what is genetic versus social environmental influence to an ED. (Berrittine, 2004). In attempt to make this distinction there have also been studies of monozygotic versus dizygotic twins

69

of persons already diagnosed with an ED, or who have self-reported having ED type attitudes and behavior. Monozygotic twins share around 100% of the same genetics and are so considered 'identical', while dizygotic fraternal twins share up to 50% genetically. It is assumed in these studies that ED related attitudes and behaviors found more prevalent among monozygotic vs. dizygotic twins indicates more of a genetic vs. social environmental etiology. Among monozygotic twins there is on average 44% of persons found to have an ED in addition to the co-twin, compared to an average of 12.5% for dizygotic twins. Hence, this evidence hence been used to suggest that genetics may have a greater influence than social environment even for persons of the same family (Kipman et al., 1999). Although most researchers are quick to add that it is likely interactions between a genetic predisposition and the social environment that brings about a person's ED, not genetics alone.

Some studies of twins have looked at the possible influence of sex hormones on the development of EDs. Klump et al. (2010) studied 1624 MZ and 994 DZ twins, all female, and found that weight and shape concerns were more prevalent for MZ versus DZ twins but only for those of age 13 and older. The group of pre-adolescent twins (i.e., 10- to 12-year-olds) did not have a difference between MZ and DZ twins for such concerns, and both MZ and DZ twins tended to endorse social experiences related to weight and shape concerns. Klump et al. attributed this difference between pre-adolescent and adolescent groups to the possible effect of pubertal hormones (a genetically timed developmental event), like estrogen, on the adolescent brain making clearer the concerns about weight and shape having a strong genetic basis. Pubertal hormones were not directly measured in this study. When they were measured by Klump and another group of colleagues (2018) the results (lower estrogen) were confusing in that they contradicted results (higher estrogen) of comparing MZ vs. DZ twins in an earlier study by these same researchers. It is conceivable that some other aspect, such as temperament, may become more salient as adolescence becomes more challenging with greater expectations for independent social participation and achievement, let alone the experience of bodily transformations. Klump et al.'s suggestion, with contradictory evidence, that it is feminizing ovarian hormones behind some of their findings does not fit the fact that we know now that many men can have EDs, and to date there has been no evidence to suggest they have had problems with pubertal masculinization or masculine identity. You will get a good sense of this too when later you read about self-narratives by men who have EDs.

Whether exposure to prenatal female or male sex hormones has an association with EDs in later life was examined by Lydecker et al. (2012). In this study the researchers used information on both male and female, MZ and DZ twins, with and without EDs in later life. The participants were from Norway (N= 2796), Sweden (N= 16,458), and the USA (N= 2607). They found that there was no evidence to support the idea that prenatal exposure to hormones from an opposite-sex twin somehow sets up an individual for an ED. To be clearer, the notion of the exclusiveness of feminizing hormones prenatally or at puberty, as suggested by Klump et al. (2010), seems even more unlikely to be dominantly involved in determining EDs. And while we are discussing about pre- and peri-natal factors, Raevuori et al. (2014) undertook a literature review of clinical evidence and found little evidence, other than a small amount for premature birth, for these factors playing a role in the later manifestation of an ED.

Another possible factor involved in the apparent differences between early and late adolescent twins, other than obvious hormonal and body morphological changes, is the effect of peer-teasing. Fairweather-Schmidt and Wade (2015) compared self-report responses, about negative life events and peer teasing, by 247 pairs of Australian female twins given at ages 12-15 and then again 16-19. These researchers found the same difference as Klump et al. (2010) for early vs. late adolescent MZ vs. DZ twins, but also found the difference was enhanced by a history of weight related teasing from at least early adolescence. Fairweather-Schmidt and Wade (2015) said that the self-reports of other negative life events appeared not to have the same effect. So, while the MZ vs. DZ distinction still seems to suggest genetic predisposition for developing an ED, it appears from this research that it is not necessarily a direct effect of pubertal hormones (at least alone) but rather a social environmental aspect that 'unlocks' or interacts with whatever that disposition is.

Munn-Chernoff et al. (2015) undertook a Missouri, USA, population-based study (i.e., not just of persons already clinically diagnosed and in treatment) to look at the possible co-occurrence of major depression (MDD) with over-eating and

71

binge eating (OE/BE) among twins. Their study involved 3,226 European Amer-ican (EA) and 550 African American (AA) young adult women already recruited via a broader twin study. The researchers said that they found a 44% re-occur-rence of MDD and 40% reoccurrence of OE/BE among twins, similarly for both the EA and AA groups. They reported that this again is a strong indication of one genetic basis (of mood, affect or depression) associated with EDs. In an earlier 2013 study of 5593 Australian same-sex and opposite-sex twins Munn-Chernoff et al. said they had found that between 38 to 53% of (male and female) partici-pants reported they too had alcohol dependence and binge eating, like their co-twin. The researchers for some reason only questioned the female participants about compensatory behavior (over exercising, purging, restricting etc.), but that too was heavily endorsed by respective twins.

Negative urgency, the tendency to act impulsively when experiencing negative emotions, was another possible factor that Racine et al. (2017), from Michi-gan, USA, studied in twins (all female, aged from 11 to 25 years old) especially regarding binge eating. They found many of the participants reported they experience negative urgency preceding their binge eating. Those who identified having a high degree of negative urgency also endorsed having a greater amount of binge eating, and MZ vs. DZ twins did so more. And among the participants who recognized having negative urgency they also tended to endorse a greater degree of appearance pressure, thin-ideal internalization, and body dissatisfac-tion. Interestingly, dietary restraint was not identified as being strongly associ-ated, which makes some sense if one considers restraint seems to be the logical opposite of impulsivity. However, as is known there can be overlap of BN and AN over a person's lifetime, and sometimes restraint of eating follows bingeing and purging in the day-to-day phases of an ED. It could also be that there are other things for us all to understand about restraint, of which we will attempt later to elucidate further.

Suicidality (i.e., ranging from transitory thoughts to actual attempts) has also been identified by Wade et al. (2015) as co-existing with EDs (43%) more so than for twins without EDs (24%), in an Australian study of female only twins (N=1002, age range 28 to 40 years). This difference was more pronounced too among MZ twins and appeared to stand without there also being a high degree of depression (by usual diagnostic criteria). This led Wade et al. to conjecture whether something like emotional dysregulation or other factor of temperament may be associated with both the ED and suicidality.

Bould et al. (2015), in their study of 158,679 Swedish young persons (age range 12 – 24 years old; and not a study of twins), found that among parents of children diagnosed as having an ED there was greater prevalence for parental anxiety, depression, bipolar affective disorder, and personality disorders but not schizophrenia, somatoform disorder or substance misuse. Whether or not one considers this evidence from these family and twin studies to unequivocally support there being a genetic basis to EDs, the observations still tend to show EDs, along with mood and anxiety, and/or aspects of temperament, re-occurring among relatives more frequently than the general population. And for clarification, the evidence from these studies of MZ vs. DZ twins, and with and without signs of EDs respectively, is based a lot upon participants self-report in interview, via clinical check lists and on questionnaires. So not direct comparisons at the actual genetic levels.

Some studies (not twin studies) have attempted to examine for actual gene level differences for persons with an ED vs. persons without an ED (controls). For instance, Ceccarini et al. (2020) say they have replicated findings of structural differences (polymorphisms) in genes for a serotonin receptor (5-HT2AR) and a protein involved in nerve growth and maintenance (brain-derived neurotrophic factor) in their Italian study of 556 persons diagnosed as having an ED vs. 355 controls. Genis-Mendoza et al. (2019) said they found similar structural changes for the serotonin receptor gene in their Mexican study of 168 persons with EDs and 292 controls. Because some medications for depression, anxiety and obsessive-compulsive problems involve the regulation of serotonin it is easy to conjecture here that these findings by Ceccarini et al. (2020) and Genis-Mendoza et al. (2019) strongly suggest that EDs at the brain level are like say depression or anxiety. Especially given the self-report evidence for mood, anxiety and suicidality from persons with EDs, which we also reviewed above for the MZ vs. DZ twin studies. However, there may be other things related to temperament or unknown factors not necessarily representing illness. Also of note, is that the numbers of participants in the Italian and Mexican studies are low and there is a need for further replication of these studies to be sure of their results.

While some studies tend to select which specific gene area they wish to examine, genomic-wide studies instead take a wide sweep of a person's genome to examine for gene variations. If enough of the same variations occur for persons with the same 'illness', then researchers consider those variations as likely suspects in the etiology of the illness.

An international research consortium (Duncan et al. 2017), of 220 researchers and clinicians from a range of mostly Western countries and US states, assessed for a possible genetic association to EDs. Meta analyses were based on a participant group of 3,495 persons with AN, AN-NOS, and BN (diagnoses based on DSM V). A diagnosis of AN-NOS means the person had not shown symptoms of AN all at one once but had sufficient history. Persons with BN were included because there is a lot of cross-over between AN and BN over time. There was a comparative control group of 10,982 persons without AN, AN-NOS or BN. A genome-wide analysis of participants' DNA found variations on chromosomes 12 as more frequent among the ED group compared to controls. Duncan et al. then cross-referenced from other independent genome wide studies, not necessarily or originally specific to EDs, to assess for what other human health and functional factors had already been identified as associated with these same variations on Chromosome 12. They found that other studies had previously identified schizophrenia, neuroticism, educational attainment, body mass index in relation to obesity, some auto-immune disorders, high-density lipoprotein cholesterol, type1 diabetes, insulin, and glucose. The authors did not state they think there is any direct equivalency between schizophrenia (characterized by sensory hallucinations, delusions, thought form disorder, depersonalization, etc.) and ED, but did say the Chromosome 12 correlation seems to support the idea of AN being considered a psychiatric disorder. Neuroticism, psychologically, means a person has the tendency to see the world as threatening and unsafe, and consequently be frequently distressed. The authors suggested that the genetic correlation they found with neuroticism coincides with neuroticism being often clinically described as preceding AN in adolescence. In other research, some of which we will review shortly, neuroticism is referred to as being inhibition. About the correlation with educational attainment the authors posited this probably reflects a person with AN having both "internal and external pressures for academic success in highly educated families". Although not stated by the authors, an alternative interpretation, that could apply to all persons with AN from a range of different educational and economic backgrounds, is that this genetic correlation may reflect other things like personal ambition in many areas of interest, not just academics. Duncan et al though reserved their biggest statement of finding for the correlations with type 1 diabetes, insulin and other biochemical/biophysical markers, saying these suggest AN is also a heritable metabolic disorder not just psychiatric. They added that the correlation with BMI from other studies involving obesity and gene variations on Chromosome 12 is a strong indication of a shared biology underlying the extremes of weight regulation.

However, there are some other things worthwhile mentioning. Duncan et al. (2017) wrote that an earlier, and possibly the first, genomic-wide study about AN by Wang et al. (2011) had "strongly suggested that (genetic) signals for anorexia nervosa would be detected with increased sample sizes" (p. 851). However, close reading of Wang et al. shows that they found no significant findings for single-nucleotide polymorphisms (SNPs) that could clearly distinguish between their AN groups (N=1033) and controls (N= 3733). Only two genes, one relating to an opioid receptor and the other a serotonin receptor, topped the list of weak findings. Which were apparently not replicated by Duncan et al. Wang et al. also found no significant difference in copy number variations (CNVs) between their AN groups and controls. In fact, controls vs. the AN group had the greatest number of CNV deletions (20 vs. 6) and duplications (32 vs. 15) in genes 'hypothesized' to relate to other psychiatric disorders and epilepsy. Only two of the AN group of over 1000 AN participants had a rare CNV relating to chromosome 13. Something again not found by Duncan et al. Some of the authors from the Duncan et al. (2017) group (Yilmaz, Hardaway and Bulik) had already recommended in 2015 that a clinical sample size for genetic related research should be at least 10,000 before any meaningful results could be expected. In their review of genetic and epigenetic studies of EDs they tended to characterize much of the research as lacking sufficient sample sizes and being then also contradicted by attempts of replication. And only a year later, Hubel, Leppa, Breen, and Bulik (2018) said that, compared to family and twin studies, "candidate gene and linkage studies have been less informative". And "(c)ontinued growth of sample sizes is essential for rigorous discovery of actionable variation". Yet, Duncan et al. (2017) published their study with only 3492 clinical participants.

75

In 2019 Watson et al. published a study that this time had 16,992 participants with AN and 55, 525 controls from 17 different countries. There were again over two hundred authors from around six different research consortiums, including the Duncan et al. group (2017). All participants were chosen for also having European ancestry to standardize as much genetic background as possible. Around 97% were female. The researchers said they identified four gene loci variations, on chromosomes 11, 10, 3, and 1, that they think form the metabolic etiology for AN. Some of these variations they say relate to some of the same metabolic indices (e.g., insulin, glucose, and lipids) as reported by Duncan et al. However, the variants on chromosome 12 in this 2019 study "did not reach genomic-wide significance". Which raises the question of whether future studies with even larger samples of persons with AN may not replicate the findings of this 2019 research either. Another interesting outcome was that BMI of participants had only a "mild but statistically non-significant" association with the 'metabolic' genetic variations identified. Which is confusing given how BMI status has for such a long time been presented as core evidence, along with fat-phobia, for defining AN medically for psychiatric diagnosis and weight and metabolic recovery focused treatment. And yet in the following section, about metabolism specifically, you will read how BMI has been used by a sub-group of these same researchers to suggest it represents metabolic influences early in child development and eventual AN.

There are some other things worth highlighting too. Watson et al. noted that for those participants for whom they had information on chromosomal sex (XX female: 14,818 and XY male: 447) there were no differences in the findings of gene variations. In other words, if you accept their interpretation of the four genetic variations having a large influence on the etiology of AN, then that etiology is the same for both females and males. Besides BMI status, the authors seemed to say that for many of the participant sample groups the manifest clinical picture was "inadequately detailed". And they knew of only one sample description that noted some persons binged (2381) and some did not (2262), but those numbers were insufficient for meaningful statistical analyses. So, by not having actual clinical measures, let alone metabolic measures, these researchers are missing a large part of the picture to check their 'genetic' findings against and upon which to base statements about etiology. Another issue is that one can accept at face value that Watson et al. are reporting a greater prevalence of the four genetic variations among the participants with AN vs. controls. But among all the array of tables and figures there was no information on the simple percentages of the persons who had these variations, singularly or up to all four, among the AN group vs. controls. And if indeed there were some among the AN group who had one or none, what was the percentage or raw number, what was their clinical history, and what would be the explanation for not having the variations if they had a known severe clinical history. And what if any of the controls had some of these variations, then did they (say, as post-hoc analyses) at least have any relatives who had an ED. Without this kind of information, it only confirms what the researchers said themselves latterly deep in their text: "Although GWAS (genomic-wide association study) findings are informative genome-wide, identifying strong hypotheses about their connections to specific genes is not straightforward". In other words, just because a loci variation is near a gene does not automatically mean that gene is involved. But the opposite is exactly what can be taken from the titles and abstracts of publications like Duncan et al. and Watson et al. Even more importantly then is the inference about genetic variations being directly linked to things at the human behavioral level, to AN as experienced by the person.

Both the Duncan et al. (2017) and Watson et al. (2019) studies seem to have design limitations as we discussed above, but especially that of sample sizes. Here is a comparison to make this point a little more. A massive study by Vujkovic et al. (2020), mostly of the USA and some from China and Pakistan, started with 1.4 million people from around the world, of which 230,000 were found to have type-2 diabetes. Although the researchers identified 588 genetic variants of interest, 286 of which had not previously been found, ultimately only 12 variants had strong enough association. And this was because the variants already had association with other diseases well known to be related to diabetes, such as coronary heart disease, acute ischemic stroke, retinopathy, chronic kidney disease, and neuropathy. One of the authors, Benjamin Voight, remarked that no one variant was implicated as the "worst" or "most dangerous" .... it is the accumulation of many of these variants that can add up to a considerable increase in risk (for diabetes). (43). In other words, inferring a connection between the variants and diabetes had a lot more certainty because of demonstrable physical ill health effects. But as we discussed about the Duncan et al. and Watson et al. studies there wasn't even any clear association with BMI nor any other sufficient clinical measures to test their inferences against.

From another angle, the studies by Duncan et al. (2017) and Watson et al. (2019) apparently did not find variations thought by Scott-Van Zeeland et al. (2014) to be associated with an estrogen receptor and another with an enzyme involved in cholesterol metabolism for persons who have EDs; nor for the Tachykinin receptor 1 (TACR1) gene as reported by Negraes et al. (2017) in their study of laboratory reproduced neurons from stem cells taken from only 4 adolescents, each of whom had AN. Nor did they apparently find gene variations that have been reported by Ceccarini et al. (2020) and Genis-Mendoza et al. (2019) thought to be related to serotonin, and so presumably to brain neural regulation of mood and anxiety. With genome-wide searches of presumably sufficient sample size wouldn't one expect to see these other genes be also identified? You might expect cross validation of genetic studies.

Because the prevalence of EDs in the world, and as currently diagnosed, appears relatively much lower than things like diabetes it does make it more difficult to have a sufficiently large enough sample size, especially if you are restricting the study to European/Western based populations. So, it remains to be seen what could be discovered with larger numbers of participants with EDs in samples from non-western countries included and compared. And a larger sample allowing for sub-analyses by gender, by AN vs. BN vs. BED, and what interpretations are offered for exceptions if any percentage of participants do not show the main findings of a frequent variation found overall in the 'main' group. What might also be interesting is the MZ twins who reportedly do not have an ED, but whose co-twin does, and looking into if they have the same gene variations as found via a much larger international study. The problem then would be to try and explain why they did not manifest an ED despite having the same genetics. Maybe they and their twins commonly manifest something different instead, which is not yet recognizable to clinical researchers by using current diagnostic understanding or perhaps shouldn't be considered as being 'clinical' or 'pathological'. Genetic research overall likely needs to expand from relying on the idea that one or few individual human genomes can be used as baselines to supposedly 'identify' variations in other persons. Our being able to draw meaningful understanding from genetics may instead require a networking of multiple individual, multinational, multi-grouping baselines. A pangenome of common variation baselines more representative of the 7 billion world population: Western, Eastern, African and many others. (44).

Metabolism

It seems disappointing that in the two decades since the human genome project there have been limited results from genetic studies into EDs. However, Yilmaz et al. (2019), of the Universities of North Carolina and Geneva, looked further into the possible metabolic aspect of AN. They examined for early childhood BMIs and diagnoses of EDs made later in adolescence in data collected by the Avon Longitudinal study of Parents and Children, for children born in the English county in 1991 and 1992. This is the same longitudinal cohort data reviewed by Calzo et al. (2018) that found a much greater occurrence of EDs among gay boys and bisexual girls and boys. In the Avon study BMIs were conducted from birth to 12.5 years of age, and EDs were assessed at ages 14, 16, and 18 years. Yilmaz et al. compared the recorded BMIs for 559 persons diagnosed with EDs (AN = 243; BN = 69; BED = 214; or a purging disorder = 133) with those of a control group (n=966) in which no person had an ED or partial ED symptoms reported. The controls presumably had cultural, educational and home-life similarities with their peers who manifested EDs. The researchers found that the average growth trajectory for individuals with later AN veered significantly below that of the control group before 4 years of age for girls and 2 years for boys. BMI trajectories were higher than the control trajectory for all other ED groups. Specifically, the mean BN trajectory veered significantly above that of controls at 2 years for girls, but boys with later BN did not exhibit higher BMIs. The mean BED and purging disorder trajectories significantly diverged from the control trajectory at no older than 6 years for girls and boys. Yilmaz et al. interpreted these findings to represent how pre-existing metabolic factors could be a large part in the etiology of EDs. According to the researchers, the pre-existing low weight in early childhood could represent a key biological risk factor or early manifestation of AN. However, as we read above, the study by Watson et al. (2019) unexpectedly did not find a statistically significant connection between BMI and the genetic variations they identified as metabolically etiologic for AN. Because the divergent trajectories occurred at such young ages, particularly for boys before age 2 who latterly manifested AN, this is possibly further evidence that the EDs were not primarily caused by exposure to social pressures to be thin or about dieting either. So, with a fair amount of ambiguity of genetic and metabolic evidence what else could be going on? Perhaps temperament, of which we turn to discuss in the next chapter.

TEMPERAMENT

A pre-existing psychological factor like temperament, instead of or in addition to metabolism, might be what puts a child on a different trajectory as well. Temperament refers to a person's pattern of behavior and emotional response style that is present already in infancy and remains consistent throughout their life span. This is sometimes also referred to as traits that a person is born with (e.g., neuroticism, sociability, impulsivity). Evidence of temperament has come from longitudinal studies in which participants are followed from infancy through adulthood. Inhibition is often described in longitudinal research as a commonly inherited temperament/ trait which generally serves to give us all cautious awareness. It helps us in situations that could be threatening to our well-being. In evolutionary terms, having such a trait was probably very useful when we did not have physical structures (houses) and social structures (towns and armies) as protection from predators. However, for some persons still now having too much of this temperament leads to being too fearful around unfamiliar people, objects or situations. This can influence socializing, even with peers around the same age. By adolescence some persons with high inhibition socially withdraw and can manifest anxiety, depression, and substance over-use. Tang et al. (2020), of the University of Maryland, Catholic University of America, and the National Institutes of Mental Health, conducted a longitudinal study following 165 persons for around thirty years from infancy. The researchers had wondered why some persons and not others with high inhibition in infancy went on to manifest social with-drawl and anxiety, etc. Tang et al. first observed each participant at age 14 months in three situations: playing in an unfamiliar playroom, exposure to an adult stranger and a novel toy robot. The researchers assessed the degree of each infants' behavioral inhibition according to their hesitancy to interact with the situations and how long they stuck close to their mothers. When each participant reached age 15 years the researchers then had each person do a letter recognition test in which they were instructed to respond quickly. The researchers weren't as interested in accuracy as much as they were in the participants' response to errors made. While doing the test each person's electrical brain activity was recorded by electroencephalography (EEG). Tang et al. found that some of the participants, but not others also with inhibition identified in infancy, tended to react more to errors. By the time the participants had reached age 26 there were 109 total participants still available for the final stage of the study in which they answered self-report questionnaires about personality styles, mood, anxiety, and social functioning. What the researchers found was that most of the participants, for whom inhibition was identified in infancy, continued in adulthood to feel less inclined to socialize not only with strangers but also with friends and family. They also self-reported feeling less in-tune in intimate relationships. What is also interesting is that despite these temperamental traits most of the participants did have social and intimate relationships, although fewer past relationships. The participants had also attained work and educational goals too. For example, 86% of the participants had attained a bachelor's degree compared to the national average of 35%. The other interesting finding was that of the participants who by adulthood self-reported greater extent of anxiety, social anxiety, and depression, most had shown the greater sensitivity to making errors on the letter recognition test at age 15. So, it seems from this study by Tang et al. that there are multiple temperamental factors that contribute by interaction to what we can usually only observe externally of someone manifesting, by an older age, anxiety or depression. And this likely also applies to persons who manifest an ED or closely related behavior.

An example is Rodgers et al.'s (2020) study of social media use among 681, mostly Australian born, mostly English speaking, participants of approximately equal number of female and male adolescents of mean age 12.76 years. The researchers found that for those girls and boys who had depressive symptoms and/or lower self-esteem they reported more internalization of social media body image ideals. Depressive symptoms were more closely associated with those adolescents who made comparisons with ideals perceived to be higher up in appearance and status, while lower self-esteem was associated more with body dissatisfaction. Although some boys tended to compare themselves against muscular ideals, the researchers say that the two genders were otherwise more similar than different in their responses in this study. So, this study seems to be saying that exposure to social media body images is insufficient to outright cause severe body dissatisfaction, unless those persons exposed already have depression or low self-esteem. Another USA study by Coyne et al. (2020), which followed 500 adolescents over eight years, similarly found that increased time spent on media use was not associated with increase in mental health issues. A 2019 Canadian study, by Heffer et al., supports this idea too that social media use itself does not directly bring about negative psychological effects, but rather persons with depression perhaps show greater use of social media. These researchers surveyed 594 adolescents (mean age = 12.21) annually for two years and 1132 undergraduate students (mean age = 19.06) for six years. They found that for both groups of participants, social media use did not predict depressive symptoms over time for either males or females. Instead, it was greater depressive symptoms that predicted more social-media use among adolescent girls.

Depressive symptoms (negative affect) were also identified by Jackson and Chen (2011) as featuring prominently, along with conversations with peers, in self-reports of appearance pressure and body dissatisfaction by younger (n = 795, mean age = 12.66) and middle adolescent girls (n= 740, mean age =16.14) of Chongqing in mainland China. In contrast, responses by younger adolescent boys (n = 692, mean age = 12.66) indicated they considered their physical appearance based on interactions with friends, peers and mass media information on diets and thinness as attractive. However, middle adolescent boys (n = 682, mean age = 16.14) placed less emphasis on mass media and interactions with peers, but endorsed negative affect like the younger and middle adolescent girls. The middle adolescent boys also placed more emphasis on fear of negative evaluation of appearance than the younger boys and both groups of girls. These results show how adolescents in China respond similarly (whether only recently or have done so prior to 'western' influence) to adolescents in Western countries to aspects relating to peer interactions and media. But also, importantly they show how the presence of negative affect seems to be a universal trait and indicative of the continuation of inhibition from infancy as found by Tang et al. (2020).

Schnepper et al. (2020) may have also demonstrated the importance of negative emotions in connection with appetite response in their study involving 69

Austrian women who ranged in age from 16 to 50 years old (M= 21.9), all of whom were in the normal range for BMI. They were either university students or from the general community. None of them had an ED, other mental health or substance use diagnosis. Participants answered questionnaires on their typical eating styles, their pre-study typical emotional status, and gave information about instances of negative interpersonal (but not traumatic) experiences. The researchers used that information to construct scripts to read back to each respective participant during the study. Neutral scripts were about brushing one's teeth or driving to school or work. The researchers used ECG and EEG to gauge general physiological responsiveness. They used EMG to measure facial responsiveness to pictures of food, as a proxy for appetite response, or just pictures of neutral objects. Facial responsiveness was recorded while each participant heard either a negative emotion script or a neutral script. Schnepper et al. found that there was little or no overlap among the participants who identified themselves prior to the study as being either typically an emotional eater or a restrictive eater. Those who self-identified as an emotional eater showed a stronger appetite response (to the pictures of food) and described the food as more pleasant looking while hearing the negative emotion scripts compared to the neutral scripts. In contrast the self-identified restrictive eaters paid more attention to food pictures during the negative emotion scripts but less overall facial and general responsiveness. The researchers suggested that these differing eating styles in response to negative emotions are themselves also enduring traits, like that we already discussed for negative emotion itself demonstrated by Tang et al.'s (2020) longitudinal study. What was also interesting is that those participants who self-described as having a higher degree of self-restraint also reported having a slightly higher negative emotional state before their participation in the main part of the study. These findings about restraint we will revisit later too.

Another possibly related area of evidence about temperament comes from a review by Hodges et al. (2020) of around 50 nutrition, physiology and psychology studies on caregiver-infant interactions during feeding. Because of the variety of different methods used across the 50 studies it would have been difficult to conduct a reliable statistical meta-analysis. So, the findings by Hodges et al. are instead best described as trend impressions of the observations reported in the studies reviewed, and their explanatory reinterpretations. Their main impression was that feeding was not just about the caregiver accurately recognizing cues from the infant but also how the infant is responsible for the clarity of the cues (i.e., cues intended to communicate hunger and fullness). Another impression was that an infant's temperament and traits, such as enjoyment of eating, responsiveness to fullness, and pace of eating, affect the caregiver-infant interaction. Hodges et al.'s concluding impression was that babies who can communicate clear cues and thereby adjust their food intake to their body's physiologic needs continued to have healthy outcomes. For those babies who had difficulty with clarifying cues, they have a tendency for ongoing difficulty with self-regulation of food intake and so greater chance of developing obesity. The reviewers hypothesized that the vagus nerve may play a part in the transfer of information on the caregiver-infant interaction to the brain and so the programming for future self-regulation. Or, they said, alternatively the caregiver-infant interaction might influence gene expressions regarding ongoing self-regulation and consumption. Again, though, much of their review contains mostly impressions and hypotheses. However, of interest to our discussion is that at least some of the researchers they cite are reporting differences in infants' behaviors around eating that possibly reflect differences in inherited temperament. Although we imagine Yilmaz et al. might say the examples given of temperament, especially responsiveness to fullness and pace of eating, may instead be due to a feedback problem in the infant's metabolic system making the feeding difficult to regulate, uncomfortable and not enjoyable. Therefore, Tang et al.'s research is helpful because it demonstrates other behavior and temperament (inhibition) not confused by interpretations about the basic need of feeding.

Smith et al.'s (2017) study of 1921 sets of UK twins, in relation to food fussiness and food neophobia, possibly adds to this discussion as well. These researchers had parents of 16-month-old twins rate each of their twins for a tendency to be highly selective about which foods they were willing to eat (fussiness) and/or a tendency to reject unfamiliar food (neophobia). Smith et al. found that both fussiness and neophobia about food occurred mostly within the same children. They also found a minimal difference in the presence and proportions of variations in fussiness or neophobias between MZ and DZ twins. This led the researchers to say there appeared to be an equal 'genetic' and social environmental influence for food fussiness and neophobia. Although not distinctly stated by these authors, it could also indicate that fussiness and neophobia may be like other eating, digestive and metabolic things, such as intolerance for some components of food (e.g., lactose intolerance), which possibly have a much broader genetic presence in the general population. And it is also conceivable that food fussiness and neophobia are associated with developmental changes in childhood that are not just food and eating specific, such as emotional processing, that are themselves more broadly represented in the general population.

SO WHERE TO NEXT ON THE ROAD TO FINDING PATHOLOGY

Despite other advances in genetic research and medical treatment in some areas of human health the evidence of actual genetic variations being the basis for EDs is not clear at all. The lack of evidence could be due to studies so far having insufficient number of persons with EDs participating in the research. The lack of evidence could also be due to the dominant assumption that genetic differences, when discovered, will reflect EDs as being 'illnesses' with underlying pathological processes. However, by the time you finish reading this book you might agree about the possibility of positive and other common human traits and experiences having much involvement in EDs too.

For example, while various studies show an increased prevalence of EDs among twins, monozygotic especially, there still is no direct evidence of genetic markers. There is also no evidence that prenatal or pubertal sex hormones, in genetically timed events, are any different for persons with EDs either. However, from the available twin studies what emerged were things like teasing by peers and the tendency (temperament) for negative affect (like depression), alcohol dependence, negative urgency (impulsivity) and suicidality. And before we say, ah ha! some 'pathological' evidence, these negative emotional aspects are not exclusive to persons who have EDs, and some could be broadly present in the general population. And when reported by participants in the twin studies the degree of negative affect, impulsivity, or suicidality, did not necessarily mean these were of high clinical severity either and seemed to be more apparent in later vs. early adolescence.

Also of interest are the three studies, one each from Australia, Canada and China, which independently show how young persons with negative affect (depression) and/or low self-esteem, compared to those without, are more likely to use social media and be drawn to the idealization of body image depicted in that media. Rather than the perennial myth that it is the media itself causing otherwise healthy young people to be depressed and/or take on body image concerns. And while the study on metabolism by Yilmaz et al. (2019) did not account for things like temperament it was still instructive in showing how persons who later manifested AN had differences in BMI trajectory before age 2 for boys and age 4 for girls. So well before any substantively different exposure than peers to social and western commercial media and gendered differences in that media, nor likely differences in social environment generally.

In addition to theories about genetics and metabolism, supposed differences in brain functioning, for persons who have EDs, have also been viewed as possible indicators of 'pathology' underlying the 'illness'. In the next chapter we review a representative range of studies that propose there being deficits in neuro-cognitive functioning and/or neuro-circuitry of the brain that etiologically underlie an eating disorder and/or supposedly will recover when healthy weight and metabolism is restored. We have tried to give some explanation as to what those brain related terms mean before setting off to see how they each apply or not to EDs. You may find, like us, that as you read about these brain research studies many of the authors have arranged their studies and then present their interpretations on the premise of EDs being 'illnesses'. Somewhat of a surprise to us too is that, when you take away the 'viewing lens' of 'illness', some of the evidence hints at persons who have ED related behavior having some notable strengths in brain functioning.

BRAIN FUNCTIONING IN EATING DISORDERS

Neuro-Cognitive Studies

Neuro-cognitive function refers to how a person's style or pattern of thinking (e.g., cognitions as reaction to pictures of food, or to faces of varying emotional states) are generated or processed in particular parts of our brain. Some of the methodology in neuro-cognitive studies includes EEGs that measure electrical activity via electrodes on the scalp, or functional MRIs or PET scans to measure concentrations or absence of energy use in specific areas of the brain. Or the measurements may be just the accuracy or speed of the participant in doing certain tasks. These measures are used while a person participant may be undertaking tasks as instructed by the researchers. The tasks are intended to represent or elicit specific cognitions. So, the inference is that most participants with an ED in a study, while doing the task(s), will have greater or less activity in an area of the brain and/or a different performance compared to say persons without ED (controls) who do the same task(s). And if indeed found and then replicated across different sets of participants and by different researchers then more certainty is attributed to the finding. This type of research is conducted in proscribed fashion and in a controlled setting, so it is not as though participants are going through an hour or a day that would be typical life for each of them.

Research interest in the neuro-cognitive function of persons with EDs has been substantial and it is beyond our scope to present our own comprehensive review. Fortunately, there have been two recent specialist reviews that help us to summarize things. And before we proceed, because these two reviews end up showing that there is still no conclusive evidence about pathological neuro-cognitive brain processes for persons with EDs, we won't here attempt to explain much about their hypothetical interpretations. So please do not feel you have to fully understand and remember the terms they used for specific behavior and areas of the brain. Smith et al. (2018), of Sanford Research (North Dakota), and the Universities of Southern California and California, provided an extensive review of 28 previous studies since 2010, some of which also included statistical meta-analyses across other multiple studies. Smith et al. found there was some consistency across studies for identifying cognitive styles (e.g., "inhibitory control" and "decision making") in persons with EDs compared to controls without EDs. However, they also noted that varying methodology and statistical results across studies still leaves some uncertainty about findings, including those suggesting a relationship of specific behaviors with specific brain areas. Let alone that in this area of research the number of available participants tend to be low and so renders less power for statistical analyses.

Steinglass et al. (2019), of Columbia University and University of California, also undertook a review in this area of research. They provided a schematic model to represent three aspects they thought worthy of further research. That is in addition to an aspect already well researched in humans, generally, regarding "fear learning/generalization" and the "limbic system". Their model suggests that observable ED behavior about food and eating is possibly associated with underlying psychological traits, likely more present in persons with EDs, that are themselves associated with the neuro-cognitive styles of "reward processing", "behavioral and cognitive control", and "habit-learning". Their model then suggests that directly involved in these neuro-cognitive styles are "abnormalities" in the "ventral frontostriatal" and "dorsal frontostriatal" regions of the brain, respectively. However, to reiterate, Steinglass et al. did say that there is need for further research, thus inferring these behavior-brain models remain only hypothetical and not conclusive at all. And did you also notice that their reference to "reward processing" and "habit-learning" sounds borrowed possibly from the addiction and brain theory we wrote about in the earlier chapter on reductionism. We will be mentioning it again shortly. And so, despite all the research since 2010 there really is not much yet certain about persons who have EDs also having underlying differences in neuro-cognitive brain functioning.

Another area of research, which initially also inferred pathological neuro-cognitive function for persons with EDs, has been with what is called Theory of Mind (ToM). ToM refers to the capacity for understanding that others have, each in their own mind, their own beliefs, intentions, aspirations, emotions and knowl-edge, and so perspectives that may or may not differ from our own. Having a well-functioning ToM is supposedly an important basis for relating to other people every day and in every place. Empathy for another person who is grieving is a possible example of ToM, a situation in which most people would readily identify with how the other person 'must be feeling'. Research psychologists have constructed studies in which they design tasks they think resemble ToM and then assess how persons perform on those tasks. As you read the following research examples you will again notice that over just a few years the evidence again seems to lead us away from firstly presuming brain pathology and instead see some signs of possible superior performance in some areas by persons who have an ED.

For example, de Sampaio et al. (2013) of Brazil, conducted a study of 65 women, 22 of whom they diagnosed as having AN, 19 with BN, and 24 "healthy controls" (HC). The three groups of participants reportedly differed in their performance of a task that required them to rate emotions portrayed in sets of human eyes (i.e., as partial faces distinguishable as either female or male looking). The re-searchers said the participants who had AN had poorer performance, than the BN or HC groups, in recognizing emotions (particularly negative emotions and emotions in sets of male eyes). The authors suggested that, because this poorer performance also occurred regardless of clinical or recovery status, it showed that persons who have AN may have a tendency/trait toward ""specific difficulty in social cognition".

The interpretation by de Sampaio et al. was like that in an earlier study by Gal et al. (2011), of Hungary. In the 2011 study the researchers used 20 short stories, half of which included a socially awkward, inappropriate or inconsiderate in-teraction between characters, to test and compare the responses by 20 partic-ipants diagnosed as having AN with those by 20 "healthy controls" (HC). Gal et al said that the participants in the AN group showed "impairment" in attribut-ing affective (emotional) state to characters in the stories. To the researchers these 'impairments' at first seemed associated with just AN itself, but they also inferred that AN in its social manifestation is akin to autism.

Autism is considered a disorder that can first show in early childhood and characterized by difficulties in social interaction and social communication, and by a narrow and repetitive range of behavior. It is as though a child regresses from having initially developed what seem like normal milestones in infancy. In its severe form a person with autism may seem so preoccupied with repetitive behavior they are unable to respond to familiar persons and can be easily distressed by even minor disruption. It is now also recognized that there is a spectrum of severe to milder forms of autism, such that some persons do live otherwise normal lives. Some persons with autism may also have superior skills in other areas of life despite having difficulties in social communication. Presumably Gal et al. (2011) seemed to think that persons who manifest AN and withdraw from previous high level of social interaction is somehow due to regression in social understanding and skills. But one person being preoccupied with something different (e.g., food, weight, physical appearance) from another person (e.g., rocking, or humming a repetitive sound) does not mean the etiology and permanence is the same. Also, severe AN usually does not occur until at least adolescence and in many cases, there is usually no long persisting social withdrawal like occurs in autism and in schizophrenia for that matter.

A more recent study by Sedgewick et al. (2019), of the UK, partly helps to clear up this apparent confused interpretation of 'social skill deficits' by Gal et al. (2011) and de Sampaio et al. (2013). Sedgewick et al. more carefully compared 20 participants who had AN but little or no sign of autistic spectrum behavior, 20 'healthy controls' (HC), and 17 participants who had both AN and higher degree of AS (AN-AS). The participants were all female, of ages ranging from 14 to 25 years old. The BMIs of the AN and the AN-AS group did not differ. The test used by Sedgewick et al. had participants watch animations of two triangles either moving randomly and not interacting or mimicking social interaction (e.g., one triangle encouraging the other to leave an enclosure, or e.g., pushing each other back and forth). Quite possibly this test is useful because it eliminates any distraction by human features of characters and puts more on the participant to be imaginative in their ToM. The researchers asked each participant to narrate what they saw occurring in the animation. Interestingly, it was found that there were no differences in accuracy while describing each animation between the AN, AN-AS or HC groups, nor in terms of BMI, ED behaviors, anxiety or depression, or autistic aspects. However, the researchers described some qualitative differences between the groups. The AN-AS group focused a lot on the geometric positions of the animated objects, while the AN group tended to describe the appearance of the objects. Both the AN and AN-AS groups attributed far more negative connotations to the objects ("crying", "fighting" and "angry") and to animations that were neutral or positively themed. The AN and AN-AS groups also expressed a lot more concern about whether they were performing correctly. The authors took these findings to indicate that persons with AN have no difficulty with ToM but do have a negative interpretation bias. Which is not all that surprising given what we have already read together about persons who have EDs tending to have negative affect and negative urgency (impulsivity), but not necessarily at severe clinical levels; and about other young persons, even without diagnosed EDs, with negative affect being drawn to social media and idealization of body image depicted in media. But to be clear, having negative affect is not the same as lacking social skills or social understanding as inferred by some of the researchers we covered above.

Another study, this time by Benz et al. (2016), a Danish and North Carolina (USA) joint effort, had also previously found that their three groups of participants with AN (first episode N=43; mean age 16.1 years; and recovered N = 28, mean age 18.4 years) and healthy controls (HC, N = 41, mean age 17.7 years) all performed with the same accuracy on same ToM triangle animation test as used by Sedgewick et al. All three groups also performed with the same accuracy on a social inference test that used short movies which contained either sincere, simple sarcastic, or paradoxical sarcastic interactions. However, Benz et al did not emphasize this ('normal') performance by their participants in the AN group and instead attempted to suggest the possibility of other unidentified social deficits ('pathologically') associated with AN. They went on though to describe a somewhat confusing picture, yet still partly interesting. They state that the first episode AN group performed the same and sometimes better than 'healthy' controls on tests that involved recognizing social stimuli and social cognition, but that the AN recovered group did not. Furthermore, these differences in performance had no apparent association with clinical status of BMI, eating behaviors, clinically described depression or anxiety. So really, not much to do with the 'clinical' features of AN at all. It seems that the most that can be deduced from the researchers' discussion points is that the two AN groups may have differed in a way not yet understood. It could be that persons with AN continue to be exclusive about with whom or how much they socially interact rather than they have social skill deficits. Perhaps that exclusivity is partially based upon sensitivity to making errors, and/or an expectation of negative or judgment related social interaction. But again, the participants with AN in the above studies certainly do not seem to have problems with tests based on the researchers view of ToM being about social skills and social cognitions. Maybe ToM is not so much about social skills but instead an ability to hold and understand social constructs. So, let's look at that possibility.

The idea that persons who have AN type eating problems also have social skill type deficits in ToM (as extension of 'pathology' underlying the 'illness') has also been turned on its own head by a small undergraduate honors study by Kuhlman (2017) while at Butler University, Indiana, USA. She recruited 8 male and 17 female undergraduate student volunteers, of average age 20 years old. She had anticipated too that participant with more eating problems (measured with The Eating Attitudes Test: EAT) would have greater difficulty with tests of ToM. However, she found the opposite. Those participants who scored higher on the EAT also performed better on the Eyes Test (the same test used by de Sampaio et al.,2013) and the Story Comprehension Test (SCT: a test some-what akin to that used by Gal et al., 2011). What was also interesting is that although scores for all 25 male and female participants on the Restraint (e.g., from eating) Scale generally did not show the same overall strong correlation with the ToM tests, it did so moderately for the comprehension of vignettes involving metaphors. And when Kuhlman re-analyzed the performance scores by only female participants with the TOM tasks, she found the correlation with understanding metaphors on the SCT increased. Scores on two other sub-tasks ("Literal" and "Sarcasm") of the SCT then also correlated strongly with scores on the Restraint Scale.

It seems in this area of interest in eating disorders and ToM that researchers initially presumed they would find 'deficits' by persons with EDs. The expectation being based on the notion that EDs are mostly about pathology and illness with implications for social functioning. Most of the researchers then seemed to disbelieve the results in front of them and just thought that social skill deficits among persons with AN were just being illusive. However, persons with EDs, including persons with clinically diagnosed first episode AN, sometimes outperformed 'healthy controls'. Benz et al. (2016) understated their surprise at finding that even the long-standing presumption about (pathological) metabolic system status (i.e., BMI, extent of eating behaviors, and degree of depression or anxiety) all had no apparent bearing either. A finding apparently and unintentionally replicated by Sedgewick et al. (2019). From another angle too it is possible that some of the tests used (human eyes test, animated triangles, and inferences in communication) in this research were mostly tapping into distinct aspects of behavioral responses to social cues and not necessarily ToM. Even still persons with EDs performed just as well and sometimes better.

Furthermore, Kulhman's (2017) small independent effort may have discovered something worthy of closer consideration. She found that with analyzing only data from her female participants the correlation of their accurate performance with the Social Comprehension Test (SCT)and their self-report on the Restraint (from eating) Scale widened to include the SCT aspects of 'Literal' understanding and 'Sarcasm'. Again, these aspects could just as easily reflect ability for responding to social communication cues. However, the possibly more interesting finding, understated by her, was that when performance data by the male and female participants were jointly analyzed there was a correlation between high scores on the Restraint Scale and the 'Metaphor' aspect of the SCT. This correlation strengthened when Kuhlman analyzed just data based on performance by female participants. It is conceivable that understanding metaphors is a closer reflection of ToM than other aspects which possibly over-lap more with general communication cues and skills. And that ToM is more conceptual and not so easily broken down into distinct parts that can be behaviorally measured by constructed tests. Another way of expressing this is that ToM may be more about our having innate conceptual representations of things, including other persons mental and emotional inner world, without firstly having to learn from long term exposure to social cuing or teaching. Empathy might be a good example of a conceptual view of ToM. We will revisit ToM and empathy in a later chapter. For now, though, it appears persons with EDs are as good or better at constructed tests purported to measure ToM, and that a better performance correlates well with eating attitudes and restraint on eating.

Brain Neuro-Circuitry

Research into the neuro-circuitry of our human brain is still based upon the idea again that certain locations of the brain are specialized for certain behaviors, in addition to memory, vision, and speech comprehension and production. However, this area of research also studies whether specific brain chemicals (e.g., dopamine, serotonin) work with specific neural pathways and the spaces between them (called synapses) to 'produce' our behavior. There is of course some solid evidence for some human behavior. A good example is motor function and how that becomes impaired in Parkinson's Disease, and how dopamine is used to help restore motor function and coordination.

You will notice from reading the following review of representative studies that about EDs and attempts to draw links with problems in neuro-circuitry, there has been a tendency to borrow the brain-addiction 'dopamine-(pleasure)-reward' model we reviewed earlier in the chapter on reductionism. And as we found then, while the model might have some usefulness, it literally started in the 1950's and probably needs revision and perhaps shouldn't be fully relied upon for conclusive interpretations. Especially now there are other possible explanations for addiction(s) like that we saw in the studies by Augier and Heilig (2018), on an enzyme (GAT3) effect on Gamma aminobutyric acid (GABA) in relation to alcohol use, and by Dorison et al. (2019) on "sadness" in relation to the addiction to smoking nicotine.

However, you will see in this first example how the authors did apply the 'dopamine-reward' model in the actual treatment of a person with AN and the language used makes clear the presumption of a 'pathological' process. Ely et al. (2016), of University of California, proposed that, rather than EDs be just a 'metabolic' disorder of the usually normal feedback between the gut and the hypothalamus (in the lower portion of our brain), there are "higher order corticolimbic pathways" in the brain that play a "pathophysiological" role in EDS. The authors did cite evidence from other researchers who have found differences in activation of brain areas for persons with EDs compared to persons without ED for things like sweet taste processing, with a virtual card number guessing game or another decision task with both using a low monetary reward ostensibly as a substitute for food, and a maze learning task also with rewards. The evidence included differing levels of activation in areas such as the ventral striatum, dorsal caudate, anterior cingulate cortex, anterior hippocampus and the fronto-striatal region. The interpretation given is that these brain areas are thought to be involved in the recognition and processing of rewards from the physical or perhaps even the social environment. That this research shows different levels of activation of these brain areas for persons with EDs compared to persons without EDs has led to the conclusion that persons with EDs either perceive or process rewards differently.

Frank et al. (2016) reported that elevated responses in these brain 'reward' areas by participants with AN seemed to decrease a little after some weight gain via treatment but remained elevated compared to controls without EDs. The researchers further stated how they think these findings show that elevated responses in these brain areas, in persons with AN, seem to override the hypothalamic signaling of a need to eat. And that these differences, from persons without EDS, are probably a result of learned behavior and worsen as the brain is more malnourished. Meaning that having the fear of weight gain and being afraid to eat certain foods could alter the taste-reward processing pathways in the brain. Frank et al. (2016) seem to say the fear of weight gain may be intrinsic but that they predict future research may show these brain pathways return to levels like that for persons without EDs after sufficient nutritional recovery.

However, at this stage of knowledge of the brain, these differences in brain pathways might be found to be intrinsic as well and not just based on 'learning not to eat' and consequential nutritional status. After all, Yilmaz et al. (2019), in using data from the Avon Longitudinal study of Parents and Children, did find that the average growth trajectory for individuals with later AN veered significantly below that of the control group before 4 years of age for girls and even younger at 2 years for boys. And are there possibly other things at play that give the differing responses by persons with EDs, and it not being about 'taste-rewards'? For example, many of the psychological tasks in the above reviewed research require performance with differences between participants and controls measured as errors or speed compared to expected responses, and in some research while also monitoring the brain areas theorized to be involved. As we saw in the research by Tang et al. (2020) there could be another factor, such as concern about making errors, that moderates the responses by participants with EDs. Like it did for persons with inhibition from infancy and eventually anxiety and depression by adulthood. And remember too that in the ToM neuro-cognitive research by Sedgewick et al. (2019), they had observed that their participants who had AN expressed concern about possibly having made errors more than controls, despite the fact those who had AN performed just as well. So, it is just as conceivable that fear of weight gain somehow equates with a person's fear of making an error, or of being seen to make an error, thinking of themselves as though an error, or prior experience of being teased as though an error. And that fear overrides the hypothalamus and pathways usually involved in feedback for the need to eat or regulate eating. For example, Kube et al. (2016), of the Max Planck Institute, found in their study, with participants in Germany, that women with obesity (n = 14) showed slower reaction times than women controls without obesity (n = 14) to social cues more than monetary cues. The participants with obesity relative to the controls showed diminished heart rate especially when presented with scenarios of negative social outcome. This difference of blunted heart rate was more pronounced in participants with obesity who had also reported more emotional pain following real life experiences of teasing.

Another possible factor, hypothetically, is that having an ED preoccupies, at least temporarily, a lot of a person's time and thinking and so how much is attention itself effecting performance. And how much are those processes of error-concern and attention activating or not the brain areas identified, is another question. Another perennial problem is that the number of participants with EDs and controls in these studies cited by Ely et al. (2016), and by Frank et al. (2016), only ranged between 10 to 30 each. Statistically speaking, that is not a lot of power to base conclusions about the development of EDs. And these studies are only for brief periods, whereas the research by Tang et al. (2020) extended over thirty years. DeGuzman et al., with Frank, (2017), repeated the same method as Frank et al. (2016) in studying participants with AN but weeks after weight recovery and found the same elevated responses in the 'reward' pathways of the brain. They interpreted this as suggesting it may take a longer period of recovered nutritional status for the pathways to return to be like that for persons without AN. And that the persisting elevated responses might be to do with dopamine levels having also been moderated by the malnourished status. But still these studies involve participants, many just adolescents, in only brief one-off sessions, whereas the prospective research by Tang et al. (2020) extended over thirty years. Perhaps the studies on 'reward' pathways require retesting a greater number and of the same participants over their life span, at different levels of nutritional recovery, to see whether the findings still hold.

Ely et al. (2016) also make the case for the 'dopamine-reward' models based upon what they consider similarities in research results for persons with alcohol and other substance over-use and persons with EDs. They base this case in part on the reports of alcohol and substance overuse by some persons with BN in contrast to persons with AN, restrictive type particularly, avoiding alcohol or substance use. Ely et al proposed that AN perhaps acts as a protective factor for some persons not developing substance over-use. To be explicit, it is assumed that persons with AN rule out use of alcohol for the same reasons as not taking foods to avoid weight gain. Ely et al also base it upon the reported findings of persons with EDs having different responses in brain pathways thought to process rewards, as discussed above, that also involve dopamine, and that being reported also for persons with alcohol or substance use addictions. However, remember our earlier discussion of the research by Augier and Heilig (2018) and Dorison et al. (2019) in which their results, respectively, possibly demonstrate that the reward/pleasure/dopamine hypothesis is beginning to show some cracks. That the 'pleasure/reward' aspect might only really apply to all persons, not addiction, that rather than five or six brain pathways there seemed to be mostly the amygdale region involved in addiction, rather than dopamine being the predominant neurochemical involved it was the suppression of neuronal activity by gamma aminobutyric acid (GABA), and that in cigarette smokers it was sadness (not a reward) that was more involved in maintenance and relapse into addiction. And again, Schnepper et al. (2020) showed that even among 69 women not diagnosed as having an ED and who rated pictures of food as pleasant, it still involved the interaction of negative emotional conditions to elicit emotional eating. For their participants who self-described as being typically restrictive in eating it was with the negative emotional conditions that they showed more attention to pictures of food while less overall general physiological responsiveness. Furthermore, those who said they had higher restraint over their eating also self-reported having a slightly higher level of negative emotion before the start of the study.

DOWN THE ROAD WITH PATHOLOGY

IN THE REAR-VIEW MIRROR

The story used to be that some girls and young women, white, highly educated, and of high socioeconomic status, would succumb to the social pressure to be thin, in attempt to meet Western standards of attractiveness. They succumbed so much so their lack of eating and poor nutritional status led to cognitive decline, a further spiraling down of metabolism, and then delusions about being fat while actually emaciated and even while in front of a mirror. Restoration of 'normal mind' would follow recovery of nutritional status and normal metabolism. Then, with mounting evidence of persons with AN but without fat-phobia, both in western countries and in other cultures, the APA only as recent as 2013 adjusted the criterion of fat-phobia as necessary for the diagnosis of AN. So, the story seems to have been adapted to say that fear of weight gain is intrinsic and is reflected in a higher-order brain problem in which persons with AN have a different view of food because they generally misperceive/misprocess most rewards. The rejection of rewards, and thus food, overrides the normal feedback of hunger and satiation and so the metabolic spiral, or rather story, continues much the same.

However, from our discussion so far, we can see that this concept of misperception or misprocessing of 'rewards', as borrowed from the field of addiction, is beginning to show some limits. We also previously discussed how extensive Western-international research of the genome for gene variations associated with a purported metabolic disorder in EDs has been disappointingly inconclusive. Then some of the same genetic-metabolism researchers took a different tact and reported they found evidence of a metabolic disorder via unusually low BMIs in very young childhood of English persons who later in adolescence manifested EDs. That evidence, incidentally, further supported how the Western-media/social-thin hypothesis has been an over-simplification. And of note, boys at age 2 showed the low BMI earlier, by about 1 to 2 years, than girls at age 4. That is a large amount of time difference when one considers just how much human development occurs in infancy to early childhood. Milestones are not named as such for no reason.

Then we discussed how other developmental aspects, such as temperament, like inhibition and sensitivity to making errors, might be alternative or accompanying factors associated with the development and continued manifestation of EDs. Those manifestations might include the observations of persons with EDs when doing psychological performance tasks and/or while their brains are being monitored. So, at this stage, the reported brain differences remain interesting and yet to be fully understood as to what they represent, and perhaps may not be necessarily 'disordered or pathological'. And any genetic factors may not be isolated to EDs alone and instead be a compilation of more common variants associated with temperament, such as inhibition and error-sensitivity, that become salient under certain conditions. After all, who would say at this stage that inhibition isn't like introversion and shyness. Which are more common than just in EDs. Similarly, about error-sensitivity possibly being akin to fear of success and to perfectionism. Those aspects are likely also present to varying degrees in persons without AN. Remember too those persons with AN without fat phobia (n = 7), in the study by Korn et al. (2020), endorsed success at school or work as a greater preference and more so than 'shape' and 'weight' related factors. They also endorsed preference for an intimate relationship but not so for other close friendship or family relationships. Just like the participants (n = 109), none identified as having EDs, in Tang et al.'s (2020) longitudinal study at age 26 reporting a disinclination to socialize not only with strangers but also with friends and family. Thus, possibly indicating ongoing inhibition and so an aspect worthy of further consideration. And the performance by persons with AN on Theory of Mind (ToM) tests has actually been found to be as good as and sometimes better than 'healthy controls'. And eating behaviors, BMI, and clinical level depression or anxiety did not have any apparent effect. This, again, being counter-intuitive to the notion that EDs are based mostly on pathological metabolic and/or reward (food) processing systems rendering persons with an ED also cognitively 'weakened'. Except and obviously when a person might have highly compromised electrolytes and low blood gases (e.g., low oxygen level in hypoxemia/an-oxemia), and be in ICU type care, and, like anyone in that level of care, not really be available to do psychological tests.

Another possible factor worth exploring for is cognitive restraint over food intake, of which Sullivan et al. (1998) noted to be still present in women (n = 70) with AN many years after inpatient weight restoration treatment. Of which Sullivan et al. still then thought to be related to ongoing metabolic recovery. But we should also remember what Steinle et al. (2002) found in their study of Amish women (n=338, ranging in age 30 to 46 years), none identified as having an ED for the purpose of the study but were instead relatives of a family member with obesity. The women endorsed having restraint over food intake more than the men (n = 286), when BMI was accounted for. Soh et al. (2007) also found that their Singaporean Chinese control participants (n= 33; mean age = 22.2 years) self-reported having restraint the same as or more so than participants who had AN and lived in Singapore or Australia. And Kulhman (2017) too found some interesting correlations between better performance on a Social Comprehension Test and self-report on attitudes about eating and restraint by a non-clinical small group of undergraduate students. A correlation between restraint and understanding metaphors in a Theory of Mind context, which strengthened when secondary data analysis only included performance by female participants, seems worthy of further consideration. It is conceivable that some cognitive and/or operational restraint over food intake is genetically or epigenetically ancestral among some people, perhaps for purpose of self-sacrifice on behalf of children during food shortage or other crises.

The search for brain pathology, like that for genetic and metabolic deficits, has not necessarily led us to a dead end. There are at least some signs of strengths in performance on some psychological tests by persons with EDs, all the while actual nutritional and metabolic status apparently having no negative effect. And there are also the hints about restraint associated with better processing of metaphor-like information. Perhaps, we have instead come to another fork in the road of pursuing understanding.

It seems a good time now to take that other path to see what else we can learn. To do so we will **briefly explore the use of food and eating as part of self-expression and in context with shared social communication. Then we will** attempt to summarize narratives by persons about their own direct experience, including that of having an ED; and commentaries by persons who have mostly proposed social perspectives, some of whom have also experienced an ED themselves or with that of a relative (s) or friend(s).

SHARING FOOD AND SOCIAL COMMUNICATION

The desire to record and communicate details of our lives is likely to be as old as handwriting itself. In this chapter we briefly discuss examples of social communication, in our modern telecommunications context, to illustrate just how much food still features in our social world; and in addition to what is found across probably all cultures at formal occasions of weddings, birthdays and funerals, and welcoming guests to our homes.

The practice of journaling, keeping a diary, is an ancient tradition that dates to at least tenth-century Japan. Early diaries were mostly kept as public records. The modern diary has its origins in fifteenth-century Italy where diaries were used for accounting of official activities. Gradually, the focus of diaries shifted from that of recording public life to reflecting on the private one. Leonardo da Vinci filled 5,000 pages of journals with ideas for inventions and clever observations. Presidents have maintained them for posterity, and other famous figures for their own purposes. Oscar Wilde, nineteenth-century playwright, said: *"I never travel without my diary. One should always have something sensational to read on the train."*

The therapeutic potential of self-reflective writing did not come into public awareness until the 1960s, when Ira Progoff, an American psychotherapist, began offering workshops and classes in the use of what he called the Intensive Journal method. Progoff had been using a "psychological notebook" with his therapy clients for several years. His Intensive Journal is a three-ring notebook with many color-coded sections for different aspects of the writer's life explora-tion and psychological healing. The Progoff method of journal keeping quickly became popular (Smyth & Lepore 2002).

Journal writing for personal growth and emotional wellness was introduced to a wider audience through the publication of three books. Progoff's (1978) at a Journal Workshop gave instructions on how to set up an Intensive Journal for those who could not attend a journal workshop in person. In 1977 a young writer and teacher from Minneapolis named Christina Baldwin published her first book, One to One: Self- Understanding Through Journal Writing, based on the adult education journal classes she had been teaching. And in Los Angeles, Tristine Rainer (1978) published The New Diary, a comprehensive guidebook that for many years was the most complete and accessible source of information on how to use a journal for self-discovery and self-exploration.

In the 1980s many public-school systems began formally using journals in English classes and across the curricula as well. These journals, often called "dialogue" or "response" journals, offered a way for students to develop independent thinking skills and gave teachers a method for responding directly to students with individual feedback. Although the intention for classroom journals was educational rather than therapeutic, teachers noticed that a simple assignment to reflect on an academic question or problem often revealed important infor-mation about the student's emotional life. Students often reported feeling a relief of pressure and tension when they could write down troubling events or confusing thoughts or feelings.

There is also the notion that journaling has a positive impact on physical well-be-ing. Pennebaker and colleagues (1998), from the University of Texas at Austin, contend that regular journaling strengthens immune cells, called T-lymphocytes. Pennebaker believes that writing about stressful events helps you come to terms with them, acting as a stress management tool. Thus, reducing the impact of these stressors on your physical health. Or, put another way, journaling may at least help a person better organize their self-care with beneficial effects for their health.

For some time, journaling has been of benefit for things such as:

-Clarifying your thoughts and feelings: Do you ever seem all jumbled up inside, unsure of what you want or feel? Taking a few minutes to jot down your thoughts and emotions (no editing!) will quickly get you in touch with your internal world.

-Knowing yourself better: By writing routinely you will get to know what makes you feel happy and confident. You will also become clear about situations and people who are toxic for you - important information for your emotional well-being.

-Reducing stress: Writing about anger, sadness and other painful emotions helps to release the intensity of these feelings. By doing so you will feel calmer and better able to stay in the present.

-Solving problems more effectively: Typically, we problem solve from an analytical perspective. But sometimes the answer can only be found by engaging creativity and intuition. Writing unlocks these other capabilities and affords the opportunity for unexpected solutions to seemingly unsolvable problems.

-Resolving disagreements with others: Writing about misunderstandings rather than stewing over them will help you to understand another's point of view. And you just may come up with a sensible resolution to the conflict. In addition to all these wonderful benefits, keeping a journal allows you to track patterns, trends and improvement and growth over time. When current circumstances appear insurmountable, you will be able to look back on previous dilemmas that you have since resolved.

And now we have digital diarists: bloggers, the Facebook, Twitter, Instagram and Tik Tok users. We have software programs for keeping a diary in cyberspace. In the twenty-first century, the desire to record the intimate details of our lives has increasingly become a public affair. There is an urge to reveal, rather than conceal in a hidden journal. And yet journal keeping has always had a dichotomy: the desire to express and make visible, the urge to keep secret and hidden.

As with writing, whether in old fashion form (hard copies) or in blogging or vlogging, social media has served as both an avenue in self-expression and for affinity by the reader, listener or watcher. An example of this may be found in the proliferation of publications on 'healthy eating' or 'clean eating'; or, in contrast, strangers consuming vast amounts of foods live on television or video recordings. The documenting of eating and self-expression by way of online forums and webpages on the Internet, serves a gateway of demonstrating their food philosophies to others.

Take for example, Orthorexia. This is a condition where an individual is driven to eat in a way they see as perfect or pure, often involving strict and inflexible eating behaviors. The word orthorexia is Greek, with 'orthos', meaning 'correct or right'. Whether or not orthorexia nervosa will be officially recognized by the DSM and ICD diagnostic systems as an eating disorder, some health professionals consider the eating behaviors as being part of the eating disorder spectrum.

Orthorexia likely starts out with the intention to eat healthy foods, but over time, an obsession starts to develop around eating as healthily as possible. The person might strive for a perfectly 'clean' diet, shunning all food they have not made themselves, cutting out food groups, or only eating specific things in the belief they are superior foods. They experience psychological distress when they cannot fulfil the rules they have set around their diet. Many people eat healthily or follow certain diets, making it hard to determine when being 'health obsessed' can cross over into something detrimental.

Conversely, in the last decade, other food lovers have discovered and become strident fans of a new video genre called "Mukbang". It is now widely popular on YouTube and has reportedly made millionaires out of a few people who are willing to consume enormous amounts of food in front of an audience. Televised cooking and baking shows have been around at least since the 1960's. They too likely tapped into a watcher's interest in the sights and sounds of making and eating recognizable and exotic foods, not just simply the learning of a recipe. The French Chef by Julia Child started in the USA in 1963, and The Galloping Gourmet by Graham Kerr in 1968 in the UK. A Cook's Tour by Anthony Bourdain began in 2002, Hell's Kitchen and Ramsay's Kitchen Nightmares by Gordon Ramsay first aired in 2004 and The Great British Bake Off began in 2010. The latter shows have also further emphasized the personalities of presenters and interactions with contestants. Mukbang has taken all these elements to yet another level.

So, what is Mukbang? The word Mukbang is a combination of the Korean words for "eating" (meok da) and "broadcast" (bangsong). Ella Shin (2021), of Best of Korea, reports that this phenomenon originated in South Korea in the late 2000s, where Mukbang videos were generally live streamed on a Korean platform called Afreeca TV. Viewers' participation involved posting comments continuously and urge the host to eat more or mix what they are eating with something else. But Korean Mukbangers have since moved their shows to other video and streaming platforms, such as YouTube. Countless Mukbang channels have flooded the Internet seeking to take advantage of the global obsession to watch and hear people binge eating mass quantities of food. The host's aim is to stand out, please viewers, and gain followers. The freedom to be expressive and creative has resulted in instances where the host cooks the food on camera first and then consumes it. Some videos feature sound effects of eating or cooking food and verbal descriptions of the food. Other videos focus on someone eating, with no sound or speaking at all.

Some Mukbang channels focus on the personalities or visuals of the hosts themselves, while others focus on recognizable, unusual or outrageous food or the range of foods consumed. Whatever the focus, Mukbangers all over the world have uploaded their eating videos to feed the voracious appetite for new and different Mukbang content.

In the United States, Mukbang videos were unheard of until Fine Brothers Entertainment uploaded its video of popular YouTubers' reactions to Korean eating shows. American YouTubers were intrigued, and a new mass of American content creators started their own channels with their own version of Mukbang. Since then, popular American Youtubers, including The Try Guys, PewDiePie, Tana Mongeau, Liza Koshy and Trisha Paytas have hosted their own Mukbang shows.

The Mukbang trend has been criticized for possibly causing people to copy poor eating habits. Some Mukbang videos do particularly well when they show their audience eating a feast that easily surpasses 4000 calories in one sitting. Thus, many Mukbangers consume excessive amounts of saturated fats and calories, potentially wreaking havoc on their health, solely for the sake of pleasing and obtaining viewers. Critics of Mukbang raise concerns about a diet that encourages extensive amounts of junk or unhealthy food, which could lead to health issues including obesity, high blood pressure, and many other ailments. Other critics say Mukbang encourages and normalizes eating disorders such as bulimia. However, many Mukbangers compensate for their excessive intake on-screen by counting their calorie intake and fasting offscreen. Some Mukbangers

exercise intensely - the Mukbang Youtuber "Banzz" has admitted that he consumes so much that he exercises up to 12 hours a day to burn off all of the
extra calories. Despite the criticisms, Mukbang appears to have attracted much
popularity.

You will recall that in an earlier chapter we discussed the research, as recent
as 2011- 2020 and independently from Australia, Canada, USA and China, that
shows how it is young persons with negative affect ('depression') and/or low
self-esteem, compared to those without, who are more likely to use social media
and be drawn to the idealization of body image depicted in that media. This
dispels the perennial myth that it is the media itself causing otherwise healthy
young people to be depressed and/or take on body image concerns. Perhaps it
is premature to ascribe blame to the media about other eating and health
issues. Rather than admonish the media for being a pathological influence on
health, we perhaps instead need to firstly understand it as being both a social
medium for the freedom of self-expression and for affinity by readers, listeners,
and watchers. We can learn more about and use these nuances of social
communication to better our social world. With that in mind, the next chapter
looks at what we can possibly learn from reviewing some self-narratives and
social commentaries specific to eating disorders.

An interesting article to read:

Khosla, M., Murty, N.A.R., Kanwisher, N. (2022). A highly selective
response to food in human visual cortex revealed by hypothesis-free
voxel decomposition. *Current Biology, 32(19): 4159-4171.*
https://doi.org/10.1016/j.cub.2022.08.009

SELF-NARRATIVE AND SOCIAL COMMENTARY

In this chapter we will cover some representative samples of self-narrative and social commentary to further illustrate the evolving perspectives on EDs from the late 20th Century, and to see what themes arise to assist our own discussion. It is not an exhaustive review of the many self- narratives and commentaries about EDs and having selected only some is not a sign of others being considered less important. What one notices is that some of these narrators and commentators reiterate the themes of 'pathology' and 'illness' and of abuse. Much of which we have also discussed up to now. These authors' stories do somewhat reflect the extent of knowledge in the time periods or context in which they were written. However, we reviewed the narratives and commentaries to also get a sense of what other themes are represented when you pull away the reductive lenses of 'pathology'. There is again much detail in this review, but we do also again provide a summary of general themes at the end of this chapter. There are, however, two or three particularly interesting themes that arise so we give each their own chapter.

Colette Dowling's (1988) book 'Perfect Women: Hidden Fears of Inadequacy and The Drive To Perform' provides an overview of the late 20th Century American feminist commentary on social issues that affect women's self-esteem. Dowling states that her young adult daughter's unexpected abandonment of education and career paths and eventual disclosure of an ED stirred in herself a search about their relationship, and so motivated her to write the book. Dowling drew upon contemporary sources like Bruch, Chodorow, Chernin, Orbach, and even Betty Ford. She interviewed many other women, and mostly female psychotherapists, psychologists, and academics. By also including others' commentary and vignettes, Dowling describes how in her view the mother-daughter and then other woman-woman relationships project, transmit, mirror and so perpetuate passive conformity or grandiosity and excessive performances to quell and disguise low self-esteem. That low self-esteem, Dowling cites Harriet Lerner (1980) to say, is "the product(s) of a distorting and constricting feminine socialization process" which leaves mothers "with little but their own children to possess". And Dowling added (pg. 142), "In the process of separating, we must come to see how our mothers have been blocked in their development and caused to feel anxious about the power and success they would have liked for themselves, and now both want—and do not want—for their daughters." Dowling (pg. 246-247) also describes how her letting go of her agenda toward extraordinary achievement for her daughter and accepting her daughter's own decision making has changed their relationship for the better. She states too that for the first time this letting go gave her a sense of well-being through accepting herself and smaller pleasures rather than the pressure of the next high performance. And it seems her daughter, while she remained "still sensitive", became more "flexible in her ability to deal with life." The daughter at book's end was 25 years of age, working a job "with a lot of responsibility", was considering but also nervous about the time involved in further education, and wanted children but not marriage in her future.

Because Dowling's book appeared to rely heavily on White American sources it perhaps inadvertently supported the stereotype of eating disorders being mostly the story of well-off heterosexual white girls. Whereas Becky Thompson's (1998) "A Hunger So Wide And So Deep: A Multiracial View Of Women's Eating Problems", based on interviews with 18 adult women, demonstrated that American women of African American, Latina and White ethnicity and a variety of socioeconomic backgrounds do indeed experience eating problems. She states (pg. 7) that perceptions of the socialization of White Protestant feminine passivity should not be discounted but, on the other hand, cannot be readily generalized to other Americans of different ethnicity and economic backgrounds. And that "as White middle-class women have fought for the right to work outside of the home, many Black and Latina women have been fighting for the opposite." To be home with their children.

112

Eleven of the eighteen interviewees had also either witnessed or been themselves subjected to physical or sexual abuse or other violence. Three of the eighteen interviewees had immigrated to the USA with family when in adolescence or later, and twelve women identified as lesbian. Rather than view their eating problems as an individual's own pathology manifesting eventually as a disorder Thompson instead conceptualized her interviewees' changes in eating as having initially been survival strategies in emotionally and/or physically unsafe circumstances. Those circumstances being the discreet and/or accumulative effects of subtle and overt racism, sexism, homophobia, classism, the stress of acculturation, and emotional, physical, and sexual abuse as influential factors in producing changes in their eating.

Aimee Liu's 'Solitaire: The Compelling Story Of A Young Woman Growing Up In America And Her Triumph Over Anorexia' (1979; republished 2013) may be the first published memoir by a person with lived-experience of an ED. Her second memoir, 'Gaining: The Truth About Life After Eating Disorders' (2007) she wrote to "connect the dots" between her and her friends' early experiences of anorexia and bulimia and those of other men and women of all ages (and) to explore the reasons why these illnesses now are understood and treated as *biologically based mental illnesses* (italics her own emphasis)." And "genes play a large role in determining who is vulnerable to anorexia and bulimia, and who is not. So do brain chemistry and biological temperament—personality". She added, "I wish my friends and I had had access to this understanding and treatment when we were young. Our recoveries would no doubt have been speedier and more complete if such treatment had been available." Of course, Liu, in 2007 and 2013, did not have the more recent research information we have reviewed in this book.

There are, however, some other interesting things in Liu's memoirs that perhaps deserve mention as well. She said, "my original focus in these pages was the existential struggle, (of) which I still believe is the core to eating disorders". Her Chinese father, who was born in Shanghai, and her mother, a white American, were a family working in diplomatic service in India during Liu's early childhood. She was around 5 years of age when they returned to the USA, where she remained for the years preceding her memoirs. She recalled (pg. 19, 2013 Soli-

113

taire) feeling as though leaving India was like leaving her home. That having lived in a protected diplomatic area in India, "I'm pleased to discover that my life was in danger. It makes me feel special that I've been so spared. I must have an important future ahead of me". She fondly recalls having felt both adventurous and generous when playing in the garden in India, as though it were a "jungle she is hunting in" and then spares a turtle of which she said, "I will always consider him a symbol of freedom and bliss". Early on when back in the USA she felt she wanted to announce her "desire to heal the world" (pg. 59, 2013 Solitaire).

Seemingly in contrast, her life thereafter in America was dominated by the development and manifestation of an ED. Her American grandmother reportedly "planted a monster in (her) mind" by calling her "chubby" (pg. 54). That her own mother invested "so much energy in perfect performance" and that "in order to grow up I might have to challenge her sends me into a panic. I would rather remain a model child." And Liu describes how she identifies with the thinking of friends who also have EDs and her own thinking as being like "you don't want anyone to come near you", "you resent compliments......don't like yourself" (pg. 216, 2013 Solitaire), and "take every motion, every word as judgment......" (pg. 265, 2013, Solitaire), and "I'm not strong enough to stand up for myself, (as) if I haven't enough confidence to legislate my own future." Yet by the end of Solitaire, she recalled (pg. 371, 2013) how she had for the "first time in years (begun to) eat regularly without suffering anger or guilt on account of it", which preceded her managing some key relationships quite differently. She allowed herself sexual intimacy with a boyfriend, whereas previously "emaciation (had acted) as a shield against sex, and a release from social responsibility", (pg. 380, 2013). She also came to the realization how her ED had been "a cop out" from the fear of choosing a path and a career. She saw her parents differently too. "They had never been out to dictate my course" in life. (pg. 403, 2013). About recovery from an ED, she also wrote that "gratitude, compassion, and a sense of purpose, I've come to believe, are as essential for health as calories."

Kate Taylor (2008), In 'Going Hungry: Writers on desire, self-denial and overcoming anorexia', noted that many of the eighteen self-narratives contain various accounts about ambition. One writer, Louise Gluck, described her development as a poet and how her ambition intensified as she reached adolescence, but accomplishments never reached the level of her own expectations. "I cared too much about the quality of what I made." (pg. xxxix). Gluck's essay, written originally in 1981, is about growing up and experiencing her own anorexia in the 1950s, well before general societal awareness of anorexia and other eating disorders. If she had been born later when awareness was greater, she noted: "To have a disease so common, so typical, would have obliged me to devise some entirely different gestures to prove my uniqueness." (p xxx). Lisa Halliday says her anorexia began too with recognizing the limitations of her high school environment. With her growing awareness of literature and art, she no longer trusted the judgment of her teachers. Having no way to measure her talents, she sought relief in something she could measure: her weight. (pg. xxxix). Priscilla Becker, in her essay, suggests that youthful ambitions can sometimes be a little grandiose. "My hopes at that time were more like dreams, or fantasies, really, in which I was a famous musician. I had no plan to bring this about, although by high school I was a fairly accomplished violinist." (pg. xi). Latvia Graham sought "greatness" too, starting with wanting to attend a private boarding school which was at first resisted by her parents. "I was too driven to stay in my small town." (pg.99). "I got what I thought I wanted. It was change: I was leaving the people who knew me and going somewhere to excel." (pg.100). Then later when thinking about college (university) "I imagined reinventing myself, leaving behind my body issues". And Taylor said about herself that the hunger she felt from not eating made her "feel alive and creative, emotionally sensitive and intellectually sharp." (pg. xii). And she too "always wanted to produce something brilliant" and so put intensive labor into her studies and writing. She learned through therapy to retain her creativity without having to maintain the rigidity of the anorexia. "In that sense, recovery wasn't just a matter of relinquishing my anorexia, but of finding and reintegrating a part of myself". (pg. xxii). She said that at twenty-eight, the time of writing her essay, she was still learning and had become a newspaper reporter. "I can't obsess, because I have tight deadlines." And "perhaps not coincidentally, as I've gained professional confidence, I have become more comfortable in my body." (pg. xi).

Latvia Graham's story possibly and partially foretells the 2021 memoir "Going There" by Katie Couric, an American television journalist. The Me-Too context of women being constrained and manipulated by male misogyny and control over financial and company management, like in the movie and television news industries, is a substantial backdrop to Couric's professional career. Of particular interest to our own review here though are some of her other self-reports to Stephanie Emma Pfeffer and Kim Hubbard of People magazine, Oct 13, 2021. She related how she experienced BN from teenage for six or seven years into young adulthood. "I think there was an aspect of perfectionism and high achieving that was very much a part of our family, and that contributed to my discontent about my body". "There was so much pressure on women, and dieting was so much a part of that culture." "Like so many women of our generation, I aspired to be thin and lanky and all the things I'm not". "I think back on my formative years when Twiggy was all the rage and that period of time in the '60s. And there seemed to be an ideal body type, which was extremely thin." And she wasn't alone, her older sisters also were into dieting and losing weight. "We all wanted to achieve and do well in school and go to good colleges." "And so I think the perfectionism contributed to sort of...I don't wanna say self-loathing, because that's too strong a word, but my discontent about my body." She said her BN ended when she recognized how bad it was for her health, seeing the effects of disordered eating on other women, and when Karen Carpenter died (heart failure as result of severe ED) in 1983 it "shook me to the core."

Men And Eating Disorders

There has for many years been a preponderance of self-narratives, commentaries, and media coverage about women and their eating disorders. In this section we provide a bit more detail from narratives by or about men. After you have read them, you might decide too that there seems more similarity than difference between men and women who have eating disorders.

John Nolan, a pseudonym the author used in Taylor's (2008) book, wrote that "the experience of anorexia after having emerged from it is like trying to describe a vivid dream upon waking: The disease has its own powerful internal log-ic that can become fragmented at a distance." (pg.72). He had been a "relatively thin boy" beforehand (pg.72), and saw himself by age 10 as "disciplined, healthy and happy" and a high achiever in athletics. (pg.73). From a young age he "had a fierce desire to excel. Even my elementary school years were spent in a heady dash in which I sought to distinguish myself." (pg. 76). However, his "descent into anorexia began" at age 12 years old when a friend said he was "chubby". That one-off criticism coincided with a "lonely period" in which he had transferred to a new middle school in a new state, and he had "turned to food for comfort."

His concern for emotional vulnerability he attributed to having witnessed his brother's excessive weight gain reportedly in response to his girlfriend being killed in an auto accident. While their parents were perhaps unaware of the girl and her death, they instead focused on the brother's need to lose weight. "I was very sensitive to my brother's feelings, and I tended to cover my ears and rush out of the room if the topic came up." (pg. 75). When examining himself in the mirror for any roll of stomach fat became an established routine, he felt his goal of eliminating that roll altogether would make him "less vulnerable" than his brother had been. "I wanted to be unassailable, and to live in a way that left no space for criticism. He also thought his "anorexic drive" came also from his mother's religious beliefs associated with a denomination that considers "Excess of any kind- and particularly bodily excess- was equated with sin." (pg. 79). He witnessed tension between his mother wanting to immerse her and the family deeper into the religion and his father not wanting to follow. "I wanted to put my hands over my ears. I wanted to leave the room (and)I wondered whether the dispute was my fault." (pg. 79). Coinciding with all this was his thinking he needed to be thinner to attract a girl who apparently had anorexia as well.

Nolan's AN became a "punishing discipline (which)was accompanied by a grow-ing pride in my own virtue." (pg. 80). He felt "superior" to other people he saw eating or of greater weight than himself. As he became even thinner, he "began to experience a kind of endorphin haze that I otherwise experienced only when running long distances." (pg. 82). He characterized his anorexic drive as his "desire to be in control" which has persisted in his adult life too. "It has led me to do many of the things I have been most proud of, including gaining entrance to good schools and running marathons. Yet is has also made it difficult for me to have sustaining relationships or to put myself in positions where I feel vulnerable." (pg.87). He did not state whether he attempted any kind of treatment. He reported that upon seeing a photo of himself handed to him after a marathon he realized how emancipated he had become. It shocked him into taking some better care of his health. "I think my good fortune is that, by the time I began to get better- slowly, to be sure, and not without setbacks- I still had some sense of myself separate from the disease." (pg.84).

Rudy Ruiz, the second of the two male authors in Taylor's (2008) book, described his extended Mexican American family as one in which a plump baby was considered a sign of a healthy and perfect baby. When he was 12 years old, his mother admitted to him that she forced-fed him as a baby. She attributed it to her obsessive- compulsive disorder and her unhappiness of being lonely and feeling trapped in a doomed marriage. (pg. 152). His father reportedly preferred his career over family but cared about Ruiz's future. When of high school age Ruiz tried to emulate his grandfather's "Spartan restraint", but "in my fervor to exercise restraint, it turned out I lacked it: I went too far and lost control". (pg.151). He did not have examples of how to eat healthily among other family members either, most of whom regularly ate more than needed. His own concern about his weight came into focus when a nick name given by an older cousin stuck and then used by others at school. He got behind in his academic and athletic grades at school. When classmates and teachers were dismissive of his goal of going to Harvard, he decided to dedicate more effort into study. He also wanted to get away from the tedium of his family life back and forth across the border, and his "dysfunctional home". (pg. 165). He realized after some months of stringent study that he had also become restrictive in his eating and lost large amounts of weight. His parents begged him to eat more, but never asked what he may need or be missing in his life. "They never took me to a counselor or psychologist; despite the fact my behavior was coupled with hypochondria and interminable hand washing". (pg.164).

Ruiz also went on to derive a sense of "power and superiority as I watched others eat". "In my mind, I was above them all." (pg.164). Without intervention by others, Ruiz, and after one occasion of near fainting, came to his own realization of needing to eat better. He gained sufficient weight in his senior year of high school to appear at least healthy. He got into Harvard and his weight continued to "yo-yo". He used jogging and skipping some meals to reduce his weight again to a bare sufficient level. "My feelings about my adolescent eating disorder are also divided. I regret it and yet simultaneously cherish the role it played in shaping me. It coincided with a period of academic success that helped me change my future". (p166).

Nolan reminded readers of how the British physician Richard Morton in 1694 described the stories of a sixteen-year-old boy and an eighteen- year-old girl in which they suffered a "nervous atrophy" and a "wasting of the body without any remarkable fever, cough, or shortness of breath". Morton saw it as a disease brought on by the "cares and passions" of the mind. (pg.85). Even back then the descriptions of anorexia nervosa for girls and boys seemed much the same. Our next review of a narrative on a 15-year-old English boy in 2013 paints a very similar picture.

In 'Please Eat: A Mother's Struggle To Free Her Son From Anorexia', Bev Mattocks (2013) gives a detailed personal account of the lived experience of her only child and son (Ben), husband (Paul) and herself, in their coping with Ben's manifestation of AN from the age of 15 years. Her description of the AN, and the effects on Ben, his father and herself, is also mostly indistinguishable from accounts of girls and women who present with acute AN. Such as intense pre-occupation with food types and calorific values, reorganizing kitchen cupboards, cooking and baking large amounts of food for the family, yet themselves being extremely restrictive in what they eat, a persistent declaration of being "fat" despite being very low weight, excessive exercising of various types and times of day and night, consequential severe weight loss, dropping out of pre-existing friendships and social activities, severe anxiety and sometimes angry behavior when according to them a food routine is breached or when having to leave home to attend activities involving social interaction.

Bev Mattocks describes the AN as "the demon" (pg. 2) that had "transformed (her son) into someone we didn't recognize" (pg. 33). She contrasts the AN with his earlier teenage years in which he had been a standout rugby player with a

119

muscular physique and size well suited for a forward playing position. He had attained a scholarship to her father's old high school, where the grandfather remained "active in the Old Boy's Association" (pg. 188). Ben prior to the AN manifesting had excelled academically, in drama, choir, band music, other sports, and was reportedly very popular socially. His birthday parties had been legendary.

Mattocks did not delve much into social commentary to find explanation for the AN. Except by end of her book she endorsed the view that anorexia is "a biologically based mental illness, not a life-style choice". She added that "families get wrongly labeled at best dysfunctional and at worst abusive", but instead parents are "part of the solution, not the problem". (pg.256). She did not raise the possibility of family and wider social pressures to 'conform and over-perform' as Dowling had emphasized, and Liu mentioned as well. But she wrote that she was "convinced (men's health magazines are) making him over-critical as he compares himself to the impossibly toned models" (pg. 16.). That, he flicked through the magazines "until he comes to the diets and exercises that promise to deliver bodies like the defined muscle men". As for anyone, though, it would have been difficult for the mother to notice whether by that stage the diet fads within the magazines may have had the greater appeal for the AN already underway, which in its course took Ben toward emaciation rather than muscle building.

Also predating Ben's reportedly confident early teenage years and the exposure to the men's health magazines was the "inner critic inside his head that always manages to rob him of his new-found confidence. A legacy from his primary school years." (pg.7). And by his late teenage years his "anorexic voice" sounded like "his inner critic on steroids". (pg. 36). The mother does not make it clear whether this "inner critic" existed prior to Ben having been bullied by one boy who filled the void of a close friend who had moved away in those early childhood years. Rather than Ben, at that time, having multiple friends he and that close friend "were (both) quiet, studious and had vivid imaginations. They'd lose themselves in a fantasy world inhabited by exotic creatures." (pg. 8). A description somewhat like Liu's fond recall of her early childhood fantasy play while living in India.

Ben's first attempts at treatment were through a local child and adolescent

120

mental health service, which included dietary advice. He also saw a private CBT therapist for only a short while. But none of this treatment led to any substantive changes in eating, weight gain, or decrease in his "anorexic voice" and negative mood and behavior at home. His weight remained just enough above the range that might have otherwise triggered inpatient treatment. Both Ben and his mother instead attribute the small gains he made in increased food intake and social reintegration to her persistence in using eating schedules and behavioral contracts which she had obtained from online resources. They were based upon the Maudsley model of family support we discussed earlier on in the chapter on psychological therapies. Ben also acknowledged his exhaustion with meeting the demands of the anorexia eventually made him amenable for going along with his mother's unwavering support.

Ben completed high school, with much of his senior year studies having been done at home. He attempted a first year at university (college) at which he had a mentor (an older student from his same high school) who had a friend with AN, and so "gets it". (pg.228). And the little girl he once insisted he, at age 3, was going to marry was attending a nearby university too. However, despite these additional supports Ben said he didn't "fit in with the other guys in his apartment" and felt lonely. "Feels as though on a different planet...way out of his depth socially...he felt suicidal." (pg.232). So, like Dowling's daughter, he abandoned that first attempt. He instead lived back home and obtained a part-time teaching assistant voluntary job at his old high school. His mood reportedly improved a great deal, to which the mother said: "the contrast between then and now strikes me dramatically." (pg.236). After he considered teaching as a career, he decided on another attempt at attending university. However, the repeat attempt at first year had again been a difficult transition. He had gone home every weekend and it "was a joyless experience getting him back each week." (pg.251). And he had made friends only with boys close to home on those weekends. However, the mother's epilogue, almost two years later, described how Ben in his second year at university was again living in a shared house, was beginning to make new male friends there, and was eating sufficiently.

The lesser awareness about EDs in males, relative to the bias in the media, clinical and educational information, about EDs being a female 'disease', is also pointed out in 'Men Writing Eating Disorders: Autobiographical Writing and Illness Experience In English and German Narratives', edited by Heiki Bartel (2021). Bartel's treatment of the subject is an examination of the language and cultural constructs used in narratives about "illness", including the barriers that men may face in trying to tell their own stories. She states that the opportunity to tell one's own story can be an important strategy in the recovery from illness, including an eating disorder. She makes clear that she sees EDs as "complex psychiatric illnesses often accompanied by other mental health problems" (p 43). Her regular professional career involves working within medical contexts and illnesses.

Her book is organized around using excerpts from each of the previously published 21 writers to explore language and cultural topics as she sees them rather than each narrative being a stand-alone chapter. The earliest autobiographical report cited was published in 1996 by Michael Krasnow, with six others published after 2018. But cover a time period since the 1970's. At publication the youngest writer was 21 and the oldest 52. Eleven of the writers were from the USA, 4 from the UK, 5 from Germany, and 1 from Austria. Bartel says the men lived either as students, accountants, teachers, journalists, a stand-up comedian, a protestant pastor, and one other a successful pop star. None of the writers were black, Asian, disabled, trans-gender, or bisexual men. Some of the writers, like some women with EDs, had also experienced depression, obsessive compulsive disorder, drug addiction or alcohol dependency.

Some examples of barriers to self-narrative Bartel gives (pg. 38) are: "alexithymia": there being insufficient words, in at least European languages, to describe the many types of mood anyone might experience; and less understood variations of eating disorders with no apparent differences in prevalence between men and women, such as "orthorexia nervosa": which represents righteous obsession with eating healthy food that can have similar effects of social isolation, anxiety, and reduced interest in other healthy human activities. Another barrier Bartel discusses is what she calls the "gendering of illness", in which (Western) culture dissuades men from admitting illness, unless it is sport or work-related injury, and so creates the public perception that most other physical and mental health problems are more women's issues. She contends this is part of viewing

masculinity culturally as though narrowly defined (e.g., as brawny, less emotional or sensitive, adventurous and so less involved at home) versus what may
be the actual personal characteristics, behavior and inner emotional world of
each man. Examples she gives (pg. 45-48) are: one of the 21 writers modeled
American men's fashion sportswear whilst hiding his binge eating disorder; a
second man had difficulty getting help for his anorexia in Austria where (in his
perception) an Arnold-Schwarzenegger physique is still held up as the body ideal
for men; and in contrast a third writer obsessed with 'bigging up' his body to a
hyper-masculine physique; another who had anorexia aspired to have androgy-
nous looks; and a fifth writer starved his body to hide his homosexuality from his
hyper-masculine sports-coach father.

While Bartel's comparative focus was on language and socially "gendered"
constructs in writing, and she does cover how men receive the same ED diagnoses as women, she did not actually emphasize any similarities between the
male writers' self-descriptions and those by women. However, many of the 21
narratives described deliberate concealment of weight loss or gain, misrepresen-
tation to doctors, therapists, friends and family about whether they've eaten or
even how much, and hiding their binging and purging (p136), and over-exercising too (pg. 55-56). All behaviors you also find in self-narratives by women with
EDs. There are also examples in which some of the male writers refer to experiencing their ED as having a domineering inner voice directing their ED behavior
with food and toward other persons. This is also often reported by women with
EDs and is the same as Bev Mattocks (2013) described for her son Ben, whose
narrative is not included by Bartel. Some persons with ED even name their inner
voice and seemingly relate to that personification more than other people close
to them. For instance, Kohl (2009) reportedly wrote that his inner voice was female and said things like: "Forget what everyone is telling you" (in Bartel pg. 65).
Noticing this preoccupation his wife reportedly said things like: "You are having
an affair with anorexia" (in Bartel pg. 61). Other things in common with narratives by women with EDs are most of the 21 narratives linked losing weight with
gaining positive recognition and being sexually attractive (Bartel pg. 58); of not
allowing sexual intimacy, or being touched even by close family, like Liu (1979,
2013) and Taylor (2008) mentioned; "sex and food had to be endured" (Wappis,
2005, in Bartel pg. 60). Again, things you also find in self-narratives by women.

123

A latter aspect raised by Bartel was her contrasting two of the narratives, by German authors, against what she cites as the 'bildungsroman' tradition in German literature. The tradition is of telling a story about manly development by the protagonist to educate the reader on successful integration into mainstream society. According to her the narratives by Stuckard-Barre (2016) and Boks (2019) are examples of anti-bildungsroman. Rather than integration or reconciliation, the stories represent a "collision of the individual with the world" (pg. 90- 91). In Stuckard-Barre's 'Panic Heart' (2016) the narrative is about living among a reactionary pop subculture with drug use and ED, while concurrently being aware of the personal and physiological risks: such as the cardiac risks involved with an ED. In 'Room For Less', Bok (2019) describes taking a day's leave with a friend from an ED clinic they both attend to visit the friend's parents. "The breeding ground for Friedrich's illness is very similar to mine: protected childhood, never wanted for anything – good education, suburbia, quiet atmosphere, fresh air. Very very fruitful soil for eating disordered thoughts. You have to break free from this norm – but how? Abstinence means: setting boundaries and being different. Abstinence from food means: losing weight. Losing weight means being skinny. The skinnier the body, the more unique and special is the person. That's the anorexic logic. *It's really very simple, great!* thinks the boy with the eating disorder and believes he has found the pathway to happiness – for a little while. (Bok pg.188; in Bartel pg. 91).

Bartel cites these narratives as though continuing to support the concept that moving away reactively from the 'parental home' norms is at first reactionary but becomes pathological in conjunction with an ED illness. However, although Bartel (pg. 108) briefly quotes Nolan (from Taylor 2008) she did not include his or Ruiz's self-narratives in her book of male authors on ED. Had she included them, and Kate Taylor's own preface as an editor, she again might have needed to more closely consider the similarities between the male authors and the other 16 narratives by women in Taylor's collection. She might have then recognized the similarity between Bok's (2019) description of "breaking free from the norm" and Taylor's point on how the theme of ambition was common among her group of two male and sixteen female writers. Including moving away from their familiar home bases to fulfill those ambitions, and successfully so. Albeit, still sometimes having to manage not relapsing too deeply into an ED again.

Blogging

Some persons who have EDS also blog as a form of self-narrative. Some websites provide an online platform for some bloggers to share their narratives. Yeshua-Katz and Martins (2012), telecommunications researchers of Indiana University, interviewed 'Pro-Ana' bloggers (33 of whom responded to invitations sent out to 300) to get their direct perspective on why they use such a website. The interviewees were all women from seven different countries, about two-thirds from the USA, and ranged in age from 15 to 33 years old. Although one could say by responding the interviewees may represent a more favorable view of things. However, what was reported at least indicates that there is some range of things occurring in this online community and it is not at all just about copy-cat self-harm behavior.

The researchers acknowledged they themselves found aspects of the website perturbing. However, the interviewees generally were attracted to the site for social support that they felt was unconditional. In contrast, they reported feeling stressed by interactions with family and friends, of whom they felt lack understanding of their circumstances. Eight of the bloggers said how they had found friendships with online peers that continued with meeting in person. Most of the respondents also said they found the process of blog writing improved their mood, and six of them stated it provided them with a different reality too. One person said the blogging gave her the skills of self-expression she needed for recovery. While the online community provided support for weight loss and comfort when a member did not reach a lower weight, it also supported members' choices about attempts at reducing self-harm and even entering recovery. About six interviewees were already undertaking recovery. Twenty-seven respondents identified their ED as a mental illness and the remaining six stated their ED was a coping mechanism. Only three of the 33 characterized their ED as a lifestyle, about which the researchers noted contradicts prior perceptions of such websites promoting a singular philosophy.

Summarizing Narrative Themes

Before this chapter, just completed, we had reviewed research which to date mostly comes from Western countries and/or using Western diagnostic classifications, psychological tests, interviews and observations, of mostly female participants, and 'pathology confirming' interpretations by the researchers. However, we have covered here many accounts of personal journeys and commentaries involving EDs, from at least a half century as well. Again, the currently available literature is all Western derived, but there are still some interesting themes for us to think about. Like, the descriptions by Nolan, Ruiz, Kohl, and of Mattock's by his mother, and other self-narratives by men of their ED related behavior, are no different than those by Dowling of her daughter, by Liu, Graham, Taylor, and other female narrators in Taylor's book, and the clinical descriptions of "signs" and "symptoms" that are used in diagnostic classifications.

There are many psychological similarities too, such as the abandonment, by Dowling's daughter and Mattocks' son, of common family and societal expectations of completing schooling, dating, starting a career, and their periods of social inhibition that contrast with previous high degree of educational and social activity. Or the fear of choosing a career path, as expressed by Liu. Also, feeling vulnerable to criticism and being affected by teasing from significant persons, like Liu's grandmother, Nolan's friend during his "lonely period", Ruiz's older cousin that carried on at school, and Mattocks' surrogate friend. The intensity of an inner critic (Mattocks and Kohl) and the "punishing" and "superior" discipline of AN perceived to ward off criticism (Nolan and Ruiz) are just as much part of the experience of an ED for women too.

All 21 male narrators in Bartel, and Nolan, linked losing weight with gaining positive recognition and being romantically or sexually attractive. Almost all of whom identified as heterosexual, which further debunks any persisting myth about men who have EDs all likely having homosexual and effeminate tendencies. Then, for some narrators, not allowing sexual intimacy, or being touched even by close family, like stated by Liu and Taylor, was characterized by Wappis (in Bartel 2021) as though "sex and food had to be endured". Being shy about intimacy seems to have been also the case for the 37 persons who had AN, with only 8 being in a romantic relationship in the study by Korn et al. (2020). Compared to 21 of the 29 control participants without AN. This despite that the 7 persons who had AN, but not fat phobia (AN-NFP), showed a preference for being in a stable intimate relationship, whereas controls gave greater preference to other life interests. And the participants with AN-NFP showed lesser preference for having relationships with friends and family than did the controls without AN. It seems that persons who have AN have wishes to not be too involved with other people. Instead, they envision being in an intimate and romantic relationship but that those desires conflict with their other preferences. Dowling's daughter had reportedly expressed similar sentiments too about her future, in wanting to have children but not marriage. And wanting to further educate herself. We will return to this theme of education again shortly.

Thompson (1998) also reported about the process of acculturation for some of her 18 interviewees. Remember that acculturation is a process in which a person may encounter barriers that they need to pass in order to live freely among the host or 'mainstream' culture. To pass they must change or hide and suppress aspects about themselves and/or the culture from where they came. But of course, some of those aspects are not easily changed, such as skin color and physical features. Latvia Graham's (in Taylor 2008) recall of her experience at Dartmouth College (University), where she felt "the white kids look down on the minorities as affirmative- action admits", is a possible example of how racism prevents some persons from acculturating fully even in their home country. And this despite she is American, had grown up in and "admired" much in her predominantly White South Carolina neighborhood and school peers, had prior to Dartmouth admission reached her own high educational achievements, and took until college to realize the possibility of even subtle racism in American society.

Another observation in Thompson's (1998) commentary was that several of her 18 female interviewees were taught to diet, binge, and purge by older relatives – who had done so for years themselves – and so predated "strictures about size and shape" and "long before Twiggy" in fashion and "Jane Fonda's" exercise regimes. There is little mention by the 2 men and 16 women self-narrators in Taylor's (2008) book about media having a particular influence on them either. So too Bartel (2021) noticed that "pressure from the media, perhaps surprisingly, (is) not particularly fore-grounded in the 21 texts" of her male self-narrators spanning 50 years. This despite the persistence by some people in holding media as a scapegoat of sorts for EDs. It was only really Collette Dowling and Bev Mattocks, the two mothers who each reported about their own child and AN, who alluded to media having a possible direct influence. Which is a reasonable deflection given that we still live in a society where stigma is still directed toward the family for anything not otherwise well understood about the complex etiology of behavior. It is understandable too that Katie Couric as a television journalist thinks that the media had considerable influence on her developing an ED. But she also identified how her, and her family's "high achieving" drive and "perfectionism" probably set her up for discontent with her own body. We will return to high achieving drive shortly in the chapter on ambition.

Sexual, physical and/or emotional abuse, either direct or witnessed, featured among 11 of the 18 life stories collated by Thompson. But did not feature among the other female or male self-narrators in Taylor (2008) and Bartel (2021). And Liu (2007) said that "among the women I interviewed, sexual abuse was the exception." And later also wrote, in part reference to her own one-off experience of molestation, that "a teenager chooses to starve herself not simply because she has been molested, because her mother doesn't understand her, or because she is hypersensitive, or wishes she could look like Cameron Diaz, she punishes herself for all those reasons, but also for being human." All of which seems to reflect what we found from reading the review of research into childhood sexual abuse (CSA) by Smolak and Murnen (2002). CSA may amplify the possibility of a person manifesting an ED, but not every victim develops an ED. And many persons who have an ED do not have a history of CSA.

A lot of the above makes it sound as though understanding EDs is mostly about viewing things as heavily negative psychologically, relationship wise, and via wider social pressures. Heavy too is the viewing of EDs as also based on an individual's genetic, metabolic, and psychological pathologies. However, there are some other aspects that perhaps get over-shadowed, are possibly strengths versus weaknesses, and are worthy of further exploration. So, we felt that each of these aspects deserved their own chapter, to which we go next to discuss ideas on ambition and then empathy. As each chapter proceeds you will read how the story of freedom begins to unfold again. And how, in living each day as we typically would in our respective cultures, we likely do not notice the micro-social subtleties involving questions of freedom. That is of the individual in their own family and surrounding community. In the other forthcoming chapter, you will also read how the theme of empathy possibly plays out in the context of the individual and their wider society. And those contexts involving cross-cultural differences between countries.

AMBITION

For now, we do not know of a better title than ambition, except perhaps 'purpose'. And this is where Taylor (2008) deserves some recognition. As she got to know herself and other people with AN "what emerged from under the layers of anxiety was the intensity of our desires and ambitions—our hunger." And that was a consistent theme that also arose independently in many of the 18 self-narrators in her book. That included the two male writers Nolan and Ruiz, who each reported having intense yearnings to move away from the familiarity of family and home location to achieve things that would distinguish them from an otherwise non-descript career and life. And their pathway to distinction often involved further education. Nolan wrote that he "had a fierce desire to excel. Even my elementary school years were spent in a heady dash in which I sought to distinguish myself." Latvia Graham (also in Taylor 2008) described how in childhood she first recognized a sense of pursuing "greatness", just like Liu (2013) recalled having a sense of "an important future ahead of me". And Couric (2021) related too about her and her family's drive for high achievement. Which she applied successfully in television media despite the dysfunctional barriers encountered by women in the Me-Too context of the television and movie industries.

What is interesting about this theme of 'ambition' is that it is also reported, but understated perhaps, by Adityanjee et al. (1989) in the independent stories of three teenagers (one male, two females) in India who the authors diagnosed as having multiple personality disorder. Family disapproval of each teenager's romantic interest was also a common aspect. However, what is also striking is the description of their longer standing characteristic behavior and identity as being sociable, attention seeking and highly ambitious. And then there are the seven German participants who had AN but not fat phobia (AN-NFP) in the study by Korn et al. (2020). They self-rated 'success at school or work' their highest preference overall compared to those without AN, and even higher than 'shape' and 'weight' and 'family/friend relationships' related factors. Although much has been made of the idea of 'perfectionism' in persons who have EDs, there probably remains more to explore and understand about ambition as well. From how it plays out in each person's life but also keeping in mind how it possibly has ancient roots that motivated us humans to 'educate' ourselves, make things, explore and migrate throughout the world. And to find, or not, romantic or other social bonds as another ambition and/or to support our other ambitions.

Also interesting is the genomic-wide study by Duncan et al. (2017) in which they reportedly 'found' many of their participants who had EDs also had variations on chromosome 12, for which prior genetic-based research had also reportedly shown a (statistical) correlation with "educational attainment". However, remember we did already say how there were likely insufficient participants in their study to draw statistically meaningful conclusions about their 'findings', and that their main expectation was that there would be metabolic and psychiatric signs in the genetic evidence. Also, their interpretation of this 'finding' of 'educational attainment' was possibly rather biased too. Remember they posited that this probably reflects a person with AN having both "internal and external pressures for academic success in highly educated families". But as we have learned from the social commentary by Thompson (1998), self-narrators (in Taylor 2008, & Bartel 2021), and cross-cultural evidence, persons who have AN or other EDs come from a variety of educational, socio-economic, and cultural backgrounds. So, along with what we learned from the review of self-narratives and social commentaries, at least we can say that strength factors like ambition deserve some highlighting in future research into EDs vs. the continual search for pathology.

It may also be difficult for a person to pursue personal ambition when social norms and expectations surround them too. Bok (2019, in Bartel 2021), in his self-narrative, describes 'the breeding ground" for AN as: "protected childhood, never wanted for anything – good education, suburbia, quiet atmosphere, fresh air. Very very fruitful soil for eating disordered thoughts. You have to break free from this norm – but how? Abstinence means: setting boundaries and being different. Abstinence from food means: losing weight. Losing weight means being skinny. The skinnier the body, the more unique and special is the person. That's the anorexic logic. *It's really very simple, great!*, thinks the boy with the eating disorder and believes he has found the pathway to happiness – for a little while."

131

Liu (2013) described how after recovery from AN she realized her parents "had never been out to dictate my course" in life, yet her ED had been "a cop out" from the fear of choosing a path and a career. But latterly found resolution in undertaking a writing career in which she explores not only about eating disorders but also about the experiences of Asian Americans.

That too seems to reflect what Dowling described about her daughter (1988) and Mattocks her son (2013), how they each abandoned the expected and already successful course of education and social passage to a career and independent life to instead reconstruct those for themselves after having experienced the intensity of AN for at least a few years. And so, the point made by Dowling (1988), and in citing Lerner (1980) and other feminist commentators, about biased social restrictions on women having also been a catalyst for EDs, gets further support from the experience by these female and male self-narrators. We saw this too in the cross-cultural evidence in the female and male case stories involving arranged marriages or disapproval of romantic ambitions in India. Although, what we have also possibly learned here is that socially induced low self-esteem is not necessarily always behind ambition and high performance. Keeping in mind too what we learned from Tang et al.'s (2020) study about inhibition, possibly another form of low self-esteem, as a temperament rather than being only socially induced, such as via teasing too. Low self-esteem may be another limitation in carrying out one's ambition, not necessarily a direct motivator behind ambition. And Thompson (1998) pointed out that many of her interviewees wanted to be at home with their children rather having to work away from their home. For them ambition might be differently defined, and this should guide future commentators and researchers to not be presumptuous about how each person sees their ambition.

We have also learned again, from these self-narrators, that pressure from social media about body image is not as significant as once thought. So, the seven participants with AN-NFP who expressed a stronger interest in more education and work over concerns about body shape and weight may in fact be more insightful as to their 'existential' priorities. Which is the reverse of what Korn et al. (2020) interpreted about these participants compared to others with AN but who also had fat phobia. The latter persons possibly were too timid or less insightful to declare the subject of personal ambition vs. social and family norms and expectations. Further research might help clarify whether the interaction of social norms and constraints with personal ambition has a bigger and more direct role in the etiology of an ED. But from what we have already learned here it sounds like the social constraints upon an individual living out their own ambition is another example of limits on personal freedom.

Soh et al. (2007) had made the opposite argument when they found in their study that Singaporean Chinese participants who had an ED (n= 18) self-reported identifying more within their traditional culture vs. Western culture. Also interesting was that the Singaporean Chinese control participants (n = 33) identified their allegiance to traditional culture, including preferring their 'rigid' family structure, even more. The controls also self-reported having some eating disorder behavior and restraint over their eating, so in that sense they may not have been controls at all. And the psychological aspects at play for both groups of participants may have been more to do with their attempts at transition or not from their traditional family context, or family expectations about marriage, or other local cultural things. Like we read about in the case studies in India.

"But your greatest gift was your intuition and it was a gift you used wisely. This is what underpinned all your other wonderful attributes and if we look to analyze what it was about you that had such a wide appeal we find it in your instinctive feel for what was really important in all our lives.

Without your God-given sensitivity we would be immersed in greater ignorance at the anguish of AIDS and H.I.V. sufferers, the plight of the homeless, the isolation of lepers, the random destruction of landmines.

Diana explained to me once that it was her innermost feelings of suffering that made it possible for her to connect with her constituency of the rejected. And here we come to another truth about her. For all the status, the glamour, the applause, Diana remained throughout a very insecure person at heart, almost childlike in her desire to do good for others so she could release herself from deep feelings of unworthiness of which her eating disorders were merely a symptom.

The world sensed this part of her character and cherished her for her vulnerability whilst admiring her for her honesty."

(Excerpt from the eulogy for Princess Diana,

by her younger brother Charles,

the ninth Earl Spencer, Sept. 6, 1997)

WORLD-VIEW EMPATHY

Empathy, the ability to understand and share the feelings of another person. As Liu (1979, 2013) pronounced, empathy can be a "desire to heal the world", of which she first recognized about herself when only a child. And latter in adulthood wrote about her recovery from AN had involved "gratitude, compassion, and a sense of purpose", and these being as "essential for health as calories". Nolan's (in Taylor, 2008) description of himself as having been "very sensitive to (his older) brother's feelings" raised his awareness of his own "emotional vulnerability". Latvia Graham (in Taylor, 2008) described her recovery involved continuing her ambition for creative writing intersecting nicely with becoming a news reporter. Which perhaps means being out among the world of covering other people's stories. And one of Thompson's (1998) interviewees, a Latina woman, described her body as a *"shock absorber"* that attracted the *"world's pain,"* going back as far as she could remember. These personal stories resemble what Charles Spencer eulogized about Princess Diana and her empathic world view being connected to her ED and self-declared "inner most feelings of suffering". The multitudes from across the world who mourned Diana Spencer's death were possibly endorsing not just her fame but her sense of global empathy. And it is not difficult to imagine how her compassionate missions possibly did not fit with the expectations upon her for other more traditional royal duties. Just like Bok (2019, in Bartel 2021) explained happens for other people striving to be different from the social norms of their own family and surrounding society. As we progress through the remaining few chapters you will read of how this theme of world view empathy possibly plays out among many persons who have EDs and deserves more attention in research.

Some researchers have already attempted to dissect empathy to try and explain it in relation to EDs. Fortunately for us, Kerr-Gaffney et al. (2019) of London, England, have provided a systematic review of 14 research studies (from 2000-2018). The main method of each study was the responses by participants on self-report questionnaires. There were 428 participants in total who had AN, nearly all females. Mean age across the studies ranged from 15 to 23 years. Three studies that looked at empathy in relation to BN and BED were not included because of insufficient participant numbers for meta-analysis even when combined. None of the 14 studies were included in our previous discussions in the chapter on brain functioning. Here again though, Kerr-Gaffney et al. and the studies they reviewed started off with the presumption that "social and emotional difficulties as key factors in the development and maintenance of the illness". And they ended up their review with saying there is seems to be a "profile" in persons with AN having a deficit in 'cognitive' empathy vs. an intact 'affective' empathy, "similar to that found in other psychiatric and neurodevelopmental conditions, such as autism spectrum disorder".

By affective empathy the researchers meant: "the ability to share the feelings of others, without any direct emotional stimulation to oneself." Interestingly, what was found is that persons, particularly adults, with AN did not differ significantly from "healthy" controls on answering questions that reflect 'affective' empathy. Only a few differences were found. That was for adolescents in a narrow age band of 12–15-year-olds whose empathy had been rated by their parents. Yes, we imagine you saying what we thought too: but that may not be unexpected given the typical attempts at independence and heightened self-concern in adolescence. Also, in our previous discussion on studies involving adolescents with EDs their responses in interviews or on questionnaires were affected by a history of having been teased. Another difference noted by Kerr-Gaffney et al. was that persons who had both AN and autism spectrum disorder (ASD) did not do as well as controls or persons with AN only.

Cognitive' empathy the reviewers defined as: the ability to recognize and understand another person's mental state. According to their analyses the participants who had AN did worse than controls with cognitive empathy. However, their opinion was only really based on one part of a four-part test, in only two of 6 studies that used the same test and provided subtest data that made comparisons possible. Again, one of the studies involved only adolescents and the other involved a comparison between adults with AN and those with ASD. Four other studies which also involved adolescents or additional aspects of borderline personality disorder and ASD did not find this difference. It appears, Kerr-Gaffney et al. is putting a lot of weight on this really inconclusive finding to maintain the presumption of a similarity between AN and other "psychiatric and neurodevelopmental conditions". Instead, though, and just like we found in reviewing the
136

research on Theory of Mind (ToM), most of the evidence suggests that persons who have EDs do just as well and sometimes better than 'healthy' controls on psychological tests that are purported to research empathy. It is also likely that future research needs to better discern which participants do and do not have other things going on at any end of a spectrum, like ASD, that could involve things unrelated to EDs on their own.

And that four-part test that Kerr-Gaffney et al. weighed in on included aspects called 'perspective taking', 'empathic concern', 'personal distress' as in tense interpersonal situations. Of which participants who have AN did just fine like controls. The part given so much attention by the reviewers was called "fantasy", defined as "the tendency to identify oneself with fictional characters in books, plays and movies". So why was it such a surprise that adolescents might respond to this differently than adults. Or not even consider that some adults 'being into' fantasy or not, like many (Star) Trekkies or Batman movie fans, has no discernible effect upon their otherwise normal daily lives. Even if there is some greater tendency to identify with fictional characters among persons who have EDs, this might be another aspect of taking time out from over-empathizing with the world rather than a deficiency in empathy. Additionally, as we have discussed previously, it is possible that some persons who have an ED also have a negative interpretation bias that is associated with negative affect and negative urgency, let alone confirmation from negative experiences like teasing. Which is conceivably a whole different aspect that might impact empathy positively or negatively but does not mean empathy itself is deficient. And remember too how we discussed that negative affect and negative urgency are not necessarily the prerogative of ED 'illnesses', they may be more present in the general population and be more salient at different ages and stages of life. This may also be a little over-critical, but you could possibly consider whether Kerr-Gaffney et al. (2019), Korn et al. (2020) and many other researchers looking into the psychology of EDs have themselves perpetuated a negative interpretation bias in setting hypotheses and interpretations of results. A form of reductionism. Even more seriously though, as humans striving to be scientists, we all need to be careful in not over-interpreting even statistical findings that are possibly just anomalies that require a lot more research before setting titles and abstracts for our own publishing ambitions. Especially when it potentially informs the understanding and care of other people. It took us some pain, so to speak, to write this book to temper our own ambition and in attempt to present it as more philosophically raising questions rather than stating certainties. Many years passed before even reaching the confidence, let alone time, to even try writing this book. And yes, we agree with what some of you may say: that what we are proposing here might also be biased in an overly positive view about eating disorders. But we feel we needed to at least bring focus to some new questions.

One other interesting observation is that one of the 14 studies reviewed by Kerr-Gaffney et al. also showed there was no influence on responding to psychological questionnaires by BMI, other clinical physical status, or duration of AN. Of which you might remember was also inadvertently found with two separate studies looking at ToM of which we wrote about in the earlier chapter on brain functioning. But the reverse was nearly always presumed, and may still be: i.e., generalized cognitive decline due to metabolic and nutritional status.

Another interesting thing to consider about empathy, and more specifically in relation to body image, comes from some new observations about obsessive-compulsive disorder (OCD). Excessive hand washing to ward off perceived contamination is considered an example of OCD. Jalal (2021) described some studies of persons without OCD (w-OCD) who responded sometimes like persons with hand washing OCD. In the first study the w-OCD participants watched as an experimenter used a paintbrush to stroke a rubber hand and the participants real but hidden hand simultaneously. The w-OCD participants reported that it felt like the rubber hand was their own hand. When the stroking was not synchronized the "illusory" effect did not occur. Jalal said this type of observation illustrates how our brain determines responses based on statistical likelihoods of sensory experiences, given that the synchronized experimental conditions would rarely occur in our normal environment. In other words, the rare conditions created the illusory effect that the participant thought the rubber hand was part of their own body. In a second part of the study participants w-OCD also reported having OCD-type disgust reaction when the rubber hand was 'contaminated' with fake feces shortly following the synchronized stroking. These experiments have also been conducted in Japan, showing some cross-cultural consistency for the observations. What is just as interesting is that the participants who have OCD considered the rubber hand as theirs even if the stroking was not synchronized.

138

Furthermore, OCD participants also responded equally to having their own hand fake-contaminated or watching an experimenter contaminate their own hand. And even more intriguing was that after OCD participants contaminated their own hand, they felt equivalent relief to watching the experimenter wash their own hand. Jalal proposed that this suggests that persons who have OCD kind of over-ride the usual sensory processing, have a malleable body image, construct their self-representation differently, which includes less distinction between self and others.

We are not suggesting that these specific observations and interpretations about body image and self-other, at this stage only in relation to OCD, are already known to exist in persons with EDs. Far from it. But the observations described by Lalal serve as illustration about the possible malleability of body image and self-other and resembles what we are attempting to get across about empathy and EDs. Furthermore, that persons without OCD produced similar responses, albeit in certain 'rare' conditions, also illustrates that these phenomena are on a non-pathological spectrum that everyone of us is on. Just like that for empathy in EDs, most probably. It is possible that a threshold for responding empathically to social conditions is generally higher for some and much lower for others. Which could change if the social conditions themselves change to be more meaningful to us and for which our threshold is lower.

Our takeaway message seems to be that persons who have EDs have many of the same empathic abilities as other people, who do not have EDs. So, what else might there be for us to understand about persons with EDs and empathy. To be clear here, we, the authors are offering ideas for consideration and not making any claims of factual certainty. You might remember the small ToM study involving only 17 undergraduate students by Kulhman (2017). She found that self-report of higher restraint (of eating) was associated with better processing of metaphor-like information. At this stage this finding can only be considered as preliminary. However, it does hint that to understand empathy we may need to think about it also as conceptual rather than just made up of constituent parts that can be separately researched as though social skills. Kind of along similar lines to what Lalal described about the over-riding of usual sensory processing, the malleability of body image and self-other distinction in persons with OCD, but which can also be induced in persons without OCD. Perhaps the world-view expressed by Liu and about Princess Diana, by her brother, is an example of empathy as a concept in our human thoughts. As we progress through the next chapter you will read about some possible other evidence of this concept of world-view empathy among persons with EDs. And we, as the authors, only learned of it when writing a first draft of the cross-cultural information that follows. So, imagine you are wearing sandals or jandals (flip flops), sunnies (sunglasses), and a summer print shirt, skirt or shorts and sunscreen, because we are about to head firstly to some islands in the south pacific.

Samoa (SMA) and American Samoa (AMS) provide another example of regions, like Hong Kong, where some Westernization is intermixed with traditional culture. What is interesting about the traditional Samoan culture is that, like other traditional Polynesian cultures, bigger bodies are valued, and considered to be a sign of well-being and of fertility. Obesity though is still considered a health risk in SMA and AMS. The Western ideal of thinness is also now present in these Pacific regions but not as pronounced as in Western countries (Swami et al. 2007).

There are differences too in the known prevalence rates of EDs in SMA and AMS compared to five Western countries that we think also have close geopolitical and historical ties with each other and the Samoan islands region. Information relating to Canada (CDA) and India (IN) is included in this discussion for further comparison. The rates reported here in this text are combined for females and males, with AN or BN only. The rates were obtained from the Our World in Data website (Roser et al., 2020). Appendix 1. shows a table of the rates also broken out for females and males separately, with males showing much lower prevalence than females for every country. The USA, Germany (GER), United Kingdom (UK), and CDA have similar prevalence rates of persons with EDs per 100,000 population, such that in 1990 their rates were 0.93, 0.92, 0.89, 0.88 respectively. In 2017 the rates for these same countries had similarly increased to be 1.03, 1.05, 1.09, 0.95. New Zealand (NZ) and Australia (AU), both of whom have some of the largest proportions of Polynesian populations outside of the Pacific Island nations themselves, had the highest rates for the same years, 1990 and 2017. They were 1.26 and 1.33 for NZ and 1.40 and 1.88 for AU. How the rates for these two countries became higher than the four other Western countries we will come back to a little later to discuss.

In contrast though, both SMA and AMS had prevalence rates of only 0.22 and 0.38 in 1990, and 0.25 and 0.35 in 2017 respectively. Similarly, IN had rates of 0.21 and 0.32. Vaidyanathan et al. (2019) did point out the lack of research information on eating disorders in IN. So, it is possible that under-reporting too may have given artificially low prevalence rates for IN. However, a lot of information for prevalence rates for EDs in any country is based upon persons who become known through health care systems. In SMA and AMS their hospital, health and psychiatric systems have likely had closer association with systems and resources from the USA, NZ and Australia. IN has had a close exchange with the health care services and training centers of the UK and associations with other Western countries too. All prevalence rates were likely based on the narrower use of DSM IV vs. DSM V diagnostic criteria in identifying persons with AN and BN, during most of the 1990 to 2017 period, so this would have affected all Western and associated countries the same.

At first glimpse of the low rates for SMA and AMS one might reasonably assume it is due to the cultural difference of valuing larger bodies being a protecting factor somehow over the Western value of a thinner body. But as we learned from our discussion about the evidence from Hong Kong (HK), India (IN) and persons with AN but without fat phobia or media exposure in Western countries, this one (bigger) for one (smaller) explanation is pretty superficial. In some way it is fortunate we can have this discussion now and with the lessons of AN and BN before and in case we see an increase in EDs, in places like SMA and AMS, based now also upon the inclusion of BED. It would be easy to assume that any BED, with which there is no weight loss necessarily, would be just an adaptation of the influence and exposure to the Western value of thinness masked by and playing out in the Samoan context. So, what else might there be that distinguishes SMA and AMS from their Western country associates.

A study by Schrimpf et al. (2019), of Germany and the USA, did not directly examine for EDs but instead affective (emotional) and autonomic nervous system responses during social interactions in Samoan (n= 56) verses German (n = 55) volunteer participants with and without obesity, all in their home country. The participants' ages ranged from 18 to 35 years. The German participants and Samoan participants were university and community college students respectively and needed to be fluent in English. So, it was possible that the Samoan participants had greater exposure to the Western-thin body value than the general Samoan population. All participants were given a range of self-report questionnaires, including the Eating Disorder Inventory-2 which is used frequently in

142

clinical assessments and research on EDs. Heart rate and heart rate velocity via EEG were used as measures of baseline sympathetic nervous system (SNS) and parasympathetic nervous system responses (PNS). Each person participated in a virtual ball-tossing game that comprised episodes of social inclusion and social exclusion.

Schrimpf et al. found that it was the Samoan participants who reported having greater social stress before and at the time of the study. The authors interpreted this result about social stress as possibly being related to rapid socio-cultural and economic transitions. They cited Booth (1999) to note that these rapid transitions had been previously associated with an increased suicide rate in Samoa since the 1970's. They also listed economic reality not matching personal expectations learned from Western influences, reoccurring familial conflicts, and the cultural expectation of not expressing anger, as other possible explanations for their Samoan participants reporting higher degree of social stress. However, after the social exclusion periods in the study, the Samoan participants, more than the German participants, had better mood, happiness, and still felt socially accepted. This held true also for Samoan women with obesity and Samoan men with leanness compared to the German participants matched by body size and gender. Also, while there was little difference in the frequency of teasing about obese body size, historically among the German and Samoan participants, it was the German participants who reported more emotional pain and negative body image from having been teased. Schrimpf et al. postulated that the resilience to social exclusion, regardless of body size too, by the Samoan participants was probably due to the cooperative and group nature of their culture. They cited Pfundmair et al. (2015) and Over and Uskel (2016) as having reached a similar conclusion for participants from other non-western traditional cultures. The authors also noted differences in how the German participants showed increased PNS activity during both social inclusion and exclusion periods, but the Samoan participants showed no PNS increase at all but instead PNS withdrawal during social exclusion. Again, the researchers interpreted this to represent the Samoan cultural expectation of controlling emotions in general. It could have also been that the Samoan participants had learned from early on that the emotional safety net of their culture meant there was less need to be reactive, even physiologically.

143

No matter whether you accept or reject the study methodology and interpretations by Schrimpf et al., it is still evident though that the Samoan participants responded more positively, had less emotional pain, and this being regardless of body type, despite self-report of greater social stress, history of being teased, and during periods of social exclusion. So, indicating a greater degree of resilience, personal and/or cultural, despite being a culture in some transition even at home. A likely take away is still that of the protective nature of identifying and participating freely in a culture, while also feeling supported and not expected to function as much on your own as in Western culture.

Pfundmair et al. (2015) had conducted a study like Schrimpf et al., but with comparing participants from India, Turkey, China, Hong Kong and Germany. They too found that the German participants, from the more individualized Western culture, expressed more psychological needs than Indian, Turkish, and Hong Kong Chinese participants during social exclusion periods manipulated in the study. Mainland Chinese participants showed no psychological needs at all. In a second analysis of results, Plundmair et al were able to show that the factor most at play in the social exclusion condition, that gave the culturally related differences, was the German participants associating threat with social exclusion. In another part of the study the researchers also showed that German participants had increased heart rate during social exclusion, but Chinese participants did not.

Over and Uskel (2016) conducted a study also examining social interaction, specifically ostracism, in children aged 4 to 8 years old. The children were shown depictions of children in a variety of social interactions, in groups and sometimes alone. The children rated how they felt after seeing each depiction. The researchers showed a cultural difference, within the same Black Sea region of Turkey, in that children from farming families (n=15 boys & 15 girls) expressed less emotional pain in response to ostracism than did children from herder families (n = same). But there was no difference in how children from either group responded to depictions of a child in physical pain. Over and Uskel interpreted this difference in response to ostracism to be based upon a greater interdependence in farming communities versus independence among herders. The farmers are tea producers who get assistance from extended family and neighbors when harvesting; and they have no direct involvement in selling. The herders move animals for grazing, and produce meat and dairy products, and do directly sell in
144

competitive local markets. Over and Uskel, in a second part of their study, also showed this difference for children (n= around 50 each group) held even among each group (farmers vs. herders) when their parent's (n = around 50 each group) degree of interdependence verses independence was included. In another part of the study (n= around 60 children and 60 parents each group) the researchers found that children from farming communities treated peers who ostracized others less harshly than the children from herder families.

So where have we reached in our discussion on social-cultural conditions? In an earlier chapter we covered how some persons caught in the transition between their culture of origin and the Western 'individualized' culture do, as a result, manifest ED behavior. We have also discussed how stigma, and therefore social exclusion, seems to influence there being a greater incidence of EDs in gay boys and men in particular. We then looked at how the family/group-based tradition-al cultures of Samoa, India, Turkey, and China seem to act as a buffer for when persons, even while feeling under stress, do not react the same as persons in a Western country during periods of social exclusion. We saw too that even when comparing smaller communities in Turkey, based on traditional family/neighbor farmer-based culture versus an independent/herder culture, children in the latter culture indicated more emotional pain in reaction to depictions of social exclusion. And for many of these same countries with still greater degree of fam-ily/neighbor-based traditional culture there is also a lower incidence of EDs.

But what of SMA's and ASM's neighboring Western countries AU and NZ? As dis-cussed earlier, the prevalence rates for AN and BN in AU and NZ from 1990 and 2017 are notably higher than other closely associated Western countries (UK, CDA, USA, & Ger.). So, what has been going on in AU and NZ? When we started writing this book, we had no idea about these differences in prevalence rates and that we ironically would even be mentioning much about AU and NZ. Both AU and NZ would now still be considered highly Westernized cultures, and pretty much alike in some respects. They, like CDA, each have extensive historical ties with the UK, in particular, and with the USA. They both have had mostly English language, legal, educational, health, and local town, city and regional council systems in place before and after gaining independence from the UK in stages from 1900 to around 1950.

Their systems of national parliamentary government are derived from the UK. NZ functions as one national government. The 6 state and 2 internal territorial federated government systems in AU has some structural similarity to the 50 independent state and 5 territorial governments of the USA. All five countries have fought side-by-side in many wars since 1900. They remain together as security partners in what is referred to sometimes as the 'five eyes' alliance. AU and NZ both had soldiers at and protest marchers against the American-Vietnam War; and shared in the grief over the tragic losses of John F Kennedy, Martin Luther King Jr., John Lennon, Princess Diana, the Hillsborough Disaster, Hurricane Katrina, and many other human tragedies. Although Christmas comes during summer in AU and NZ it is celebrated almost the same as in the UK, CDA and the USA. Both AU and NZ play some of the same competitive sports at home, against each other and internationally. Such as rugby, cricket, field hockey, net ball, motor sports, horse racing etc. Although both AU and NZ have produced their own authors, fashion models, explorers, and music, sports, and science stars, they have both for a long time been the cross-roads for both British and American popular culture: such as: Bing Crosby, Vera Lynn, The Andrew Sisters, Elvis Presley, The Beatles, Gone With The Wind, Star Wars, James Bond, Downton Abbey, Dunkirk, Coronation Street, Peyton Place, Real Housewives; and social influencers such as from Twiggy, Bianca Perez-Mora Macias (Bianca Jagger), to the Kardashians; and social commentators such as Susie Orbach, Gloria Steinem and Germaine Greer. All to say, that the exposure to the Western-media-thinness phenomena in AU and NZ had been concurrent with other Western countries for decades and started well before 1990. But as already discussed, this media-thinness phenomena can now be debunked as being a huge over- simplification for explaining the complexity of eating disorders, including etiology.

When we found the prevalence rate data, discussed above, we also came across another set of information from Our World in Data (Roser et al., 2020 ongoing). That information is set out for the countries covered in this discussion in Appendices 2a and 2b. The data is based upon age-standardized Disability-Adjusted Life Years (DALYs) for AN and BN per 100,000 population. According to Roser et al., DALYs represent total burden of illness/disease, based upon years of life lost and years lived with a disability. One DALY represents one lost year of healthy life. We take this to mean it represents a person(s) has not been able to work, study, socially function, and undertake self-care, etc., to their potential level due to the severity of an ED. It possibly also includes time in lengthy inpatient/ residential treatment programs and intensive out-patient follow-up. In the chart in Appendix 2a. you can see that AU's DALYs numbers began diverging even further and markedly upward from NZ and the 4 other Western countries (CDA, USA, UK, Ger.) in the 1990's. We first assumed that the rate of increases in DALYs from the 1990's to the higher rates by 2017 were progressively accumulative and not due to any leaps along the way. At least for NZ and the three other coun- tries, but possibly not AU. However, we decided to look at whether there were any differences from one year to the next for each country. That information we have set out in Appendix 2b. What we found interesting was that there seemed to be some clustering of larger differences for two time periods. For example, for AU, NZ, CAN and Ger. there were bigger differences around the 2002 to 2004 years (AU: 3.64 - 3.99; NZ 0.75 – 1.04; & CAN: 0.63 - 0.81; Ger. 0.63), relative to the 5-preceding year-to-year differences for each country (means: AU: 2.70; NZ: 0.41; CAN: 0.26; & Ger. 0.35). There did not seem to be a clustering for the UK numbers for these years, and the USA numbers seem to show a steady ongoing decline in year-to-year DALYs, with no clustering. We have no idea as to why, for these two countries, but will return to this a little later. However, the clustering for the other four countries for this period seems to suggest common reaction to a world event, such as 9/11 (2001) and in its military and security aftermath as the closest allies to the USA. Thereafter, the year-to-year differences tapper off, so that by 2017 even AU's year-to-year differences is markedly lower and come within a similar low range as do the other countries. There was one other exception though, just for the UK, in which there appears to be a cluster around 2007 to 2009 (0.84, 0.90), not so clearly distinct from the 5-preceding year-to- years (mean = 0.63), but certainly different from the 5 post-cluster year-to-year differences (mean= 0.28). This possible cluster for the UK seems to coincide with the financial crisis of the Great Recession that began in late 2007. Why would this be seen in the UK but no other countries considering the world-wide effect of the Great Recession? It would require a lot more socio-economic investiga- tion than we, the authors, are capable of. But one guess is that because the UK government felt that it had to use up to the equivalent of 20% GDP to bail out the UK based financial institutions, compared to the 6% bailout in the USA, there was a real or perceived view of greater economic impact of the recession in the

UK. And the urgent concern was very much a publicly known crisis about almost everyone's economic survival.

Not shown in Appendix 2a, so not to add confusion, are the DALYs for China, a country that has also featured at times throughout this book. Like prevalence rates, the DALYs remain lower than for the Western countries, including SMA and AMS, we have discussed in this chapter. We did, however, check the year-to-year differences in DALYs for China so as not to overlook any possible clustering for that country. There was a gradual increase in DALYs from 1996 (19.41) through 2017 (32.43), but no apparent clustering. Li et al. (2021) conjectured whether the gradual increase in prevalence and DALYs data for AN and BN in China possibly reflects increased identification and reporting of EDs, and changing socioeconomic conditions (e.g., increased urbanization and increased media exposure) in China. However, these researchers appear to be mostly viewing EDs from a psychiatric, metabolic, media-influenced 'pathology' lens. They did not seem aware of the things we have discussed throughout this book, nor the above about possible clustering and what comes next about AU and NZ.

Returning to AU and NZ. Why do the prevalence rates and year-year differences in DALYs appear higher than for other Western countries? Again, we can only guess and a lot more research needs to be undertaken to try and understand these possible indicators. And that would need to include asking persons who have EDs about their views and reactions to small and major societal events of positive and negative social impact. However, one guess is that because AU and NZ were 'founded' as western countries still in transition around a century later than the USA and Canada there may have been a delay in the peaking of incidence rates for EDs in AU and NZ. And the clearer steady decline in year-year differences in DALYs for the USA since around 2010 is another indicator of this difference. Although another guess is that in the USA, at least, the decrease in the year-year DALYs for EDS since 2010 may be associated with other psychological-cultural manifestations becoming more prevalent and/or taking more of the attention and resources of health and social systems: such as the opioid crisis.

The seemingly marked differences in the increasing rates of incidence and year-year DALYs for AU do also suggest that societal transition factors involved, like acculturation, are somehow more salient there, than say in NZ presently. Again,

148

there is need for things such as surveys asking persons with EDs how they view and respond to societal events before any conclusions can be narrowed down. Otherwise, we are just making guesses. But those guesses may be to do with things such as the public-political discourse and acrimony in Australia more evident in the late 1990's and based upon what has been referred to as 'Hanson-ism' policy on abolishing multiculturalism, redefining Aboriginal reconciliation, and limiting immigration from Asian countries in particular. (45) Again, persons who have EDs probably have their own varying views on whether they pay any attention or agree with such or similar ideas. They conceivably also think like some others about possible impacts on their way of life from persons entering their 'home' country. But it might be the public acrimony itself to which they particularly respond. And New Zealand has not been exempted either of such socio-political polarizing tones in public discourse about race relations in the past and possibly of the future. For instance, in the 1970's and 1980's there was both criticism and support for the 'dawn raids' to apprehend immigrant 'over-stayers', which involved targeting mostly pacific islanders who had earlier been allowed entry to NZ to make up for a shortage of labor. The NZ government has just in 2021 issued an apology for those raids. In 1981, there was sharply divided opinion and street protests over whether to allow the South African Springbok rugby team to tour NZ, its team roster then still based on the apartheid system of SA. Both AU and NZ as western-based countries in transition still have things related to native and other race relations to resolve. But what persons with EDs respond to may also include a whole range of different things. It might also be that some of them might particularly respond to large positive public events too, such as the public's anticipation of the before and aftereffects of the 2000 Olympics in Sydney, AU. So future researchers and surveys need to keep an open mind to different possibilities.

Hart et al. (2018) noted that only four countries (Germany, Netherlands, NZ and the USA) had done national surveys and they called for AU to conduct one as well. It would seem national surveys should include questions based on our discussion here on the AU socio-cultural context and the possibility of world-view empathy. In the interim though, a survey conducted (n= 6052) in just South Australia in 2015 and 2016 by Cheah et al. (2020) found some interesting things. For all first-generation migrants taken together there was less occurrence of

EDs (4.5%) than for AU born persons (6.4%). The researchers interpreted this as representing a 'healthier immigrant' effect. However, for the purpose of our discussion, the greater percentage of AU born persons having an ED may be another reflection of how the socio-cultural conditions were closer to home and not just acculturation experience of immigrants, nor the macro-events of say 9/11 type of things. Among the first-generation immigrants, persons from Asian countries showed an even lower rate of EDs (4%). This difference could presumably have been due to more persons from Asian countries possibly having had more exposure over time to Western cultural influences prior to arriving in AU. Or be based upon there being a longstanding economic relationship between AU and Asian countries, and the survey having been conducted some many years since the late 1990's. A more noticeable presence of Asian persons already in AU might have made available greater access for cultural allegiance that Davis and Katzman (1999) and Rogers et al. (2018) had already suggested was a protective factor against being caught in transition between culture of origin and host country culture. But for immigrants from African countries, Cheah et al. said there was a 11% rate of self-reported ED. So, for those immigrants the process of acculturation may have personally been more acutely difficult and/or they too sensed some unresolved tension about the Western, Aboriginal and multicultural relationships.

A related research group (Burt et al., 2020) used the same 2015-2016 South Australian survey and found that among the 92 respondents who identified as either Aboriginal or Torres Strait Islander, 25 (27%) reported having ED level behavior akin to AN and BN. The researchers said that the ED behavior was not statistically associated with the respondents First Australian status directly or gender, but rather younger age (mean age 36.49 vs. 39.48 for other Australian respondents with ED behavior), BMI, and self-reported lower quality of life. Also interesting was the self-rating (0= not important, 6= very important) of body size as a more important concern by First Australians with EDs (4.43), but also without EDs (3.72) compared even to other Australian respondents with EDs (3.39) and without (2.76). This possibly again demonstrating the relatedness of body image and acculturation causing differences in quality of life vs. the over-simplified notion of influence by the Western thin is attractive theory. The authors said their findings are concerning given that other surveys have shown First Australians experience psychological distress at three times the rate of non-indigenous Australians.

We have taken a long journey into extending our cultural understanding about EDs. From places like Hong Kong, India and Germany, from where we learned about persons who have an ED but not fat phobia. And how, along with many self-narrators and the brief stories of three young persons in India, our attention was instead drawn to the theme of ambition. We visited the story of some American Amish girls, children in Turkey, and ended up in the South Pacific, which drew our attention to the effects of witnessing social disharmony or social exclusion in micro-societies, or the protective nature of social cooperation in places like Samoa. Then to Australia where persons with EDs perhaps demonstrate an empathic worldview in response to not only world events but also nationwide public acrimony over inclusion or exclusion of large groups of people identified by race or origin. And we learned too along the way how acculturation barriers not only affect immigrants but also persons, such as of non-heterosexual orientation, within their own country of origin. When gathered together these socio-cultural conditions of exclusion, ostracism, and acrimony likely also represent loss of freedom for many people to participate in society, in the world. And persons who have EDs empathically draw our attention to these issues about freedom.

We have presented so much information about different places, persons, time periods, and points of view, that even as authors we feel a sense of saturation and the need to next make summary and draw a close to what we have attempted to cover. Our hope is that other persons will take some of the ideas presented and develop them further to inform further understanding of persons who have EDs and how they are not fated as 'pathologically weak' but instead possibly unwitting guardians of freedom for all of us.

LOOKING AHEAD

2062: A reader has this book projecting in holographic form in their 'reading' glasses. Having re-read and reached this same point they wonder whether it's worth continuing with the summary again because they recognize that some of the topics covered have already been taken up by researchers and persons who care for and support people who have EDs. The term ED itself has begun to trickle into disuse and debate for alternative terms is ongoing, including terms reflecting stewardship over freedom.

Now (2022) wouldn't it be great to see that in forty years' time there has been some revision into how EDs are understood. Because as we now know there really has not been much change in our understanding over the past forty years. And before we, the authors, proceed to pull together the themes of this book we have not forgotten that for some persons, for some of their lifetime, their EDs can reach life-threatening levels. That necessitates a great deal of care and attention, fortunately for which there are many caring professional, family and peer supports. But 'illness' does not necessarily define etiology. A bit like how we imagine an illness is derived fully from a virus rather than some people's own immune reactions being out of proportion to the virus when compared to other people. Or sometimes their immune system automatically reacts without the actual threat of a virus being present. But their immune systems are otherwise necessary for a healthy life as for everyone else. Accordingly, we present our summary so that the themes involved might in themselves suggest a reordering of concepts in understanding EDs. And to draw attention to the contribution by persons who have EDs into all of us reaching a better appreciation of our freedom. Also, please do keep in mind that what we propose here are not unassailable conclusions but rather recommendations for further consideration and research.

Ambition: We learned about ambition as an existential priority for persons who have EDs from Amy Liu (1979, 2013), Kate Taylor's (2008) collection of 18 self-narrators, and from the 7 persons who had AN but not fat-phobia and possibly were not understood as being partly insightful by Korn et al. (2020). We saw it too as incidental information in the brief stories of three Indian teenagers who had reportedly manifested personality change (Adityanjee et al., 1989) as another psychological strategy, seemingly in response to similar family and societal constraints on personal, educational, career, and romantic ambitions. Tanja Ahlin (2018) learned too from a young Indian female pharmacist about how eventual insight into her ED revealed her guilt of having uniquely reached educational and career goals that she felt had caused economic burden and less opportunity for others in her family. And while the study by Duncan et al. (2017) had inconclusive findings on genetic evidence of psychiatric and metabolic factors for EDs, they 'found' many of their participants who had EDs also had variations on chromosome 12. According to Duncan et al., prior genetic-based research had shown a (statistical) correlation between variations on chromosome 12 and "educational attainment".

All these strands of observations from self-narrators, self-reporters in research studies, of persons in different cultures, and incidentally from genetic research into EDs, by themselves have remained obscure. But together they suggest we should pay some closer attention. Some of the questions we likely need to ask are: do persons who have EDs have a greater degree of ambition than most of their peers? Does their ambition reflect any ancestral origins that inspired our predecessors and our contemporaries to migrate throughout the world, educate ourselves and invent? Are there specific things about which persons who have EDs are ambitious? Does their ambition become more salient because it interacts with other traits or temperaments? Does it become more salient when confronted by social expectations that conflict with their goals? Does insight into ambitions, conflicts and reaching social resolution with significant others and societal peers lessen fat-phobia?

Empathy: Many psychological researchers, like Kerr-Gaffney et al. (2019), presumed persons with EDs would be deficient in empathy because of their "social
and emotional difficulties".

It turns out though that they have many of the same abilities as people who
do not have EDs, when tested on things such as 'perspective taking', 'empathic
concern', and recognizing 'personal distress' in intense interpersonal situations.
Some other researchers (Benz et al. ,2016) were even surprised by how their
younger clients who had AN outperformed 'healthy controls' on a test of 'social
inference'.

Those presumptions about deficiencies were also based upon thinking that
empathy can be tested as though made up of distinct types of social skills. May
be so. But from our own review we have read of different strands of information that together suggest we might need to additionally consider empathy as
a more conceptual 'world-view' rather than just discreet social skills. And this
'world-view' perhaps not only means empathy for groups of other people but
almost any other individual. These strands are what Liu (1979, 2013) recognized
in childhood about her "desire to heal the world", Princess Diana's brother
(1997) exclaiming her "greatest gift was (her) intuition" for her "constituency of
the rejected", and of what we observed of the extraordinary higher incidence
rate for EDs in Australia compared to other Western countries. As though on
a larger scale reflecting what the 5 Amish girls in the report by Cassady et al.
(2005) were demonstrating in their retreat to their beds, 'conversion' behavior,
and food intake restriction in response to some social conflict in their small tight
community. Then possibly also, but again only tentative evidence, the deepening
of response by persons with EDs across many of the Western countries around
the time of 9/11 and its aftermath of social debate over security vs. citizens'
freedom, and radical ideology vs. religious freedom. These suggest we need to
learn a lot more from persons with EDs about how they see themselves and
their place in their family, community, country and the world. Do they have ambitious goals to "heal the world" like Liu and Princess Diana? Or even report the
news from the world of other people, like Latvia Graham? Of what they identify
as events or circumstances that get their attention and concern. Of how they
describe their reactions to such things. Is it a case of them projecting their own
emotional vulnerability and sense of rejection onto others? Or is it that their

154

empathy leaves them open and sensitive to incoming negative messaging from or about others? Or both, as though a sensitivity channel that works both ways? Is their ED a way of taking 'time-out' from the possible sense of being over-whelmed by both a sense of responsibility for others, the world, and their own vulnerability? Does the Maudsley model of family-based care, in which parents relieve the 'child' from assuming too much self and family care responsibility, indirectly discern a sense of world-view responsibility in persons who have EDs? And does the special relationship between twins somehow also include a special kind of empathy that research to date has not adequately defined or observed? Does that empathy between twins include a 'world-view' as well? And is that any less or more concentrated among twins, especially monozygotic twins? And we read early on about Ethan Weiss' (2020) story on how he, a medical scientist, and his family embraced their daughter, who had a form of albinism (OCA), and so began to see a new perspective on how differences are not just about one person but can be lessons for a better and more considerate humane world. This too is a lesson we need to embrace from persons who have so-called eating disorders.

Restraint: We, probably like you, hadn't previously thought much about re-straint from eating other than it being another obvious descriptor of restrictive behavior that supposedly is a persistent or reoccurring 'pathologic' marker of AN. Presumably, that is what Sullivan et al. (1998) meant when they noted their surprise that restraint was still present in women with AN many years after in-patient weight restoration treatment. They thought it was a sign that metabolic recovery took longer than was expected. However, there is also some evidence that restraint from eating may be represented more generally among people who themselves do not have EDs. For instance, Steinle et al. (2002) reported on how American Amish women, relatives of persons who had obesity, endorsed having restraint from eating more than the men in their study. Soh et al. (2007) also found that their Singaporean Chinese female control participants self-re-ported having restraint the same as or more so than participants who actually had AN and lived in Singapore or Australia.

Kulhman (2017) too found some interesting correlations between better performance on a Social Comprehension Test and self-report on attitudes about eating and restraint by a non-clinical small group of undergraduate students. Of particular interest to us was a correlation between restraint and understanding metaphors in a Theory of Mind context, which strengthened when secondary data analysis only included the performance by female participants. Schnepper et al. (2020) found that some participants who did not have EDs self-described having a higher degree of restraint and having a slightly higher negative emotional state before participation in the main part of their research. Both studies hint at the possibility that the tendency for manifesting restraint is associated with states of conceptual empathy and mood, even among persons assessed as not having EDs per se.

Yilmaz et al. (2019) found that the average growth trajectory for a study group of English individuals, who later in teenage had AN, veered significantly below that of the control group before 4 years of age for girls and 2 years for boys. Of which the researchers attributed to metabolic factors. But, as we've already discussed, this could be related to temperament as well. And possibly negative affect and/ or empathic temperament. Yet it is still an indication that things related to later AN could be inheritable, and this could apply to restraint too. So, this raises an interesting question about whether restraint from eating is genetically or epigenetically ancestral among some people, perhaps for eventual purpose of self-sacrifice on behalf of children or other people during food shortage or other crises. And so, is it somehow closely affiliated with world-view empathy? And to conjecture further, if restraint is on a spectrum of related behavior, could over-eating be also a response to not only personal circumstances but also 'world-view' crises by some people or even including the people who also restrain but at varying times of their lives. That, ancestrally, there likely were times when food had to be fully consumed, despite earlier satiation, before it quickly spoiled and/or when people had to be more mobile.

Teasing: It is not difficult to imagine that if a person has both empathy and a sense of vulnerability that experiencing teasing as criticism could make it difficult to be out in the world realizing their ambitions. While genetic based research has only given inconclusive results about genes themselves, what has emerged is that teasing by peers, rather than other negative life events (Fair-weather-Schmidt et al., 2015), seems to distinguish between twins who in later adolescence have EDs and those who do not. Kube et al (2016) also found that a history of real-life teasing seemed to differentiate between women partici-pants with obesity compared to women without obesity and no experience of being teased when presented with scenarios of negative social outcome while being tested for reaction times to social cues. Vaidyanathan, Kuppili, and Menon (2019) noted how among persons who had EDs in India there was generally a lack of concern about body fat or shape. In contrast though, most females of Indian descent, who had EDs, but lived in the United Kingdom, attributed body weight and shape concerns to having been teased by peers about the same things. And many of the self-narratives we reviewed identified feeling vulner-able to criticism and being affected by teasing from known persons, like Liu's grandmother, Nolan's friend during his "lonely period", Ruiz's older cousin that carried on at school, and Mattock's surrogate friend. The narratives about males with EDs noted for us that they have their own intense inner critic (Mattocks and Kohl) and that the "punishing" and "superior" discipline of AN is perceived to ward off criticism (Nolan and Ruiz) as is the case for women who have EDs too. Like Thompson (1998) cited a Latina woman interviewee to say about her body as a *"shock absorber"* that attracted the *"world's pain,"* going back as far as she can remember. She had experienced emotional abuse and her relatives' con-stant criticism of her weight, she had little chance to understand either her body or her appetite as trustworthy or safe.

Temperament: The tendencies (temperament) to have negative affect and shyness probably also confound a person's attempts at venturing out ambitious-ly and empathically in the world. Again, among twins, those who identified as over-eaters or binge eaters also reported having depression (Munn-Chernoff et al., 2015), alcohol dependence (Munn-Chernoff et al., 2013), negative urgency (Racine et al., 2017), and suicidality (Wade et al., 2015). Wade et al. pointed out that the suicidality ranged from transitory thoughts to actual attempts and was more pronounced among monozygotic twins and appeared to stand without there also being a high degree of depression (by usual diagnostic criteria). This led Wade et al to conjecture whether something like emotional dysregulation or other factor of temperament may be associated with both the ED and suicidality. This idea that negative affect does not necessarily have to be the same and severe like major depression to be a pervasive factor in significant human behavior is akin to what Perez, Joiner and Lewinshon (2004) noted about dysthymia. And Dorison et al. (2019) found with "sadness", in relation to the addiction of smoking nicotine. Their findings were based on a complex three stage study involving a large population survey and subsidiary psychological explorations of actual cigarette use and emotional experience.

Schnepper et al. (2020) showed that even among women not diagnosed as having an ED, and who rated pictures of food as pleasant, it still involved the interaction of negative emotional conditions to elicit emotional eating. And the three studies, one each from Australia, Canada and China (Rogers et al., 2020; Heffer et al., 2019; Jackson and Chen, 2011) independently show how young persons with negative affect ('depression'), compared to those without, are more likely to use social media, be affected by conversations with peers, and be drawn to the idealization of body image depicted in that media. Rather than the perennial myth that it is the media itself causing otherwise healthy young people to be depressed and/or take on body image concerns.

Sedgewick et al. (2019) observed that their participants who had AN expressed concern about possibly having made errors more than controls, despite the fact those who had AN performed just as well. Which brings us back to the thirty-year study by Tang et al. (2020). Although they did not specifically look at EDs many of the same elements, we have just discussed so far in this summary, were found in their study. Of their participants who by young adulthood had difficulties with depressed mood, anxiety or social anxiety, not only had inhibition previously been identified in their infancy but they tended by adolescence to react more to the thought of possibly making errors on a test. Even though they made no more errors than other persons.

Most of the participants in Tang et al.'s study, for whom inhibition was identified in infancy, continued in adulthood to feel less inclined to socialize not only with strangers but also with friends and family. They also self-reported feeling less in-tune in intimate relationships. Like the self-narrators Liu (1979, 2013) and

158

Taylor (2008) wrote about not allowing sexual intimacy, or being touched even by close family, and how Wappis (in Bartel 2021) also equated "sex and food had to be endured". But despite these temperamental traits most of the participants in Tang et al. did have social and intimate relationships, although fewer past relationships. The participants had also attained work and educational goals too. For example, 86% of the participants had attained a bachelor's degree compared to the national average of 35%. Again, we see the elements of ambition, such as via educational attainment, and the disinclination to be heavily involved in relationships like that demonstrated by participants with AN in Korn et al. (2020) and Mattocks' (2013) son and Dowling's (1988) daughter.

It seems that for our better understanding of EDs there has been a missed opportunity over the past 40 years in not conducting longitudinal research like that done by Tang et al. (2020) and Dorison et al. (2019). So, it remains for It to be studied further whether fear of weight gain somehow equates with a person's fear of making an error, or of being seen to make an error, thinking of themselves as though an error, and/or prior experience of being teased as though an error. And is inhibition as a temperament in EDs based, at least in part, upon a self-perception of 'error' from early childhood. Or also created or exacerbated by social stigma, such as suggested in the study by Calzo et al., 2018 which showed that by age 16, and compared to heterosexual peers, gay and bisexual boys had up to 12.5 times the occurrence for binge eating, and bi-sexual girls had over twice the occurrence for binge eating and purging.

Pathology In Perspective: To reiterate, there is of course some people for whom their circumstances from not eating and/or frequent purging can reach life threatening levels. And while their blood gases and electrolytes, for example, may be at risky low levels their cognitive abilities are only temporarily impaired. But illness levels do not necessarily define etiology. It could also be those other under-recognized factors, like Autism Spectrum Disorder, Borderline Personality Disorder, Obsessive-Compulsive Disorder, and substance use addiction, as we currently understand and label them, complicate the diagnosis and long-term outcome for some people who also have EDs. And any of those factors themselves may have their own spectrum, as do probably ambition, world-view empathy, restraint, negative affect, social inhibition, and self-view of vulnerability and error.

The need to render the notion of EDs being of mostly pathological origin to a less superior perspective comes from evidence in studies that had themselves made the presumption of pathology. For instance, and again, the distinguishing factor in twin studies has not been genes themselves but instead self-report of negative affect, negative urgency, and teasing. Which could be a lot more present in the general population than currently understood. Additionally, there have been no conclusive results from genomic-wide studies either that presumed EDs would be identified as serious psychiatric disorders at a similar level to schizophrenia, and as though also originating from metabolic pathology. And none of those studies examined the positive human aspects of ambition, worldview empathy and restraint of possibly ancient self-sacrificial origin. Perhaps genetic research into EDs also needs to consider these positive aspects over presumptions of pathology, and include not just Western but also Eastern, African and other participants.

The search for brain pathology and deficits in social and empathic understanding, like that for genetic and metabolic deficits, has not necessarily led us to a dead end either. Some of that research borrowed a potentially outdated narrow explanation for addiction, difficulty in processing rewards (Frank et al., 2016; Ely et al., 2016; DeGuzman et al., with Frank, 2017) and did not account for some participants' concerns about making errors when they know their performance of reaction time or accuracy in particular is being measured (Sedgewick et al., 2019; Tang et al., 2020), or having a history of being teased (Kube et al., 2016). And other research has unintentionally found that persons with EDs did just as well and sometimes better on some psychological self-reports and tests of social understanding and empathy when compared to persons who do not have EDs (Benz et al., 2016; Kerr-Gaffney et al., 2019; Sedgewick et al., 2019), all the while actual nutritional and metabolic clinical status apparently had no negative impact (Calderoni et al., 2013; Benz et al., 2016; Sedgewick et al., 2019).

Media and Western Focus on Thin Body: Thompson's (1998) commentary spoke of how several of her 18 female interviewees were taught to diet, binge, and purge by older relatives – who had done so for years themselves – and so predated "strictures about size and shape" and "long before Twiggy" in fashion and "Jane Fonda's" exercise regimes. There is little mention by the 2 men and 16 women self-narrators in Taylor's (2008) book about media having a particular influence on them either. So too Bartel (2021) noticed that "pressure from the media, perhaps surprisingly, (is) not particularly fore-grounded in the 21 texts" of her male self-narrators spanning 50 years. This despite the persistence by some people in holding media as a scapegoat of sorts for EDs. It was only really Collette Dowling and Bev Mattocks, the two mothers who each reported about their own child and AN, who alluded to media having a possible direct influence. And although Katie Couric (2021) as a television journalist thinks that the media had considerable influence on her developing an ED, she also identified how her, and her family's "high achieving" drive and "perfectionism" probably set her up for discontent with her own body. Again, research that addresses these issues about media has actually shown that it is a person's negative affect (depression like), compared to those without, which makes them more likely to use social media, be affected by conversations with peers, and be drawn to the idealization of body image depicted in that media (Rogers et al., 2020; Heffer et al., 2019; Jackson and Chen, 2011). Then of course, with persons who had AN but not fat phobia, like initially reported in Hong Kong in the 1990's, there was a clue that it is a myth of sorts that the social pathology of exposure to Western media itself causing otherwise healthy young people to be depressed and/or take on body image concerns that manifest as EDs. While many persons follow the trends of dieting and body shape, that general interest appears to not determine an ED. Because we, as in most people, tend to be reductionistic, it is difficult to understand this distinction.

Reductionism (Our Own Admissions): We, the authors, have learned of at least two possible but fundamental reductionism errors on our part and of some professional systems we have functioned in. This despite of us also having family therapy and social-community psychology experience. The first is more about our clinical lens and especially that related to CBT, IPT, and DBT. We have occasionally put more weight on the negative affect/self-negative cognitions lens upon which to view individuals who have EDs. Even to the extent of extrapolating to the possibility that persons who have EDs, with their inner critical 'voices', are also greatly affected by their presumption above that of actual degree of criticism coming from other persons. May be. The second reductive error, we think, is perhaps our and others over reliance on thinking persons who manifest EDs are somehow and mostly affected by the forces of patriarchal social culture and associated media being the predominant instigators. But after learning more about blending of ambition, world-view empathy, and the possible ancestry of restraint, then it appears these qualities are insufficiently understood and appreciated for what and how they can enhance our societies, advance all our freedoms. That they are not just reactions to an otherwise constraining society.

Freedom: From the outset of our extensive journey through reviewing a lot about EDs we saw signs about the significance of freedom interwoven in the story. At the smaller interpersonal scale, persons with EDs endorse psychological therapies of the type which show successful outcomes when the therapist is facilitative rather than when other treatment processes more directly control food intake and weight gain. We also learned to peel away the misleading primacy given to physical and mental pathology and/or social pathology portrayed as a prevailing body image influence of the media. After which we instead could see more clearly the issue of personal freedom of realizing ambitions sometimes conflicting with expectations coming from family and community. The better-known history for which has so far been that for women. Obviously, it is a fair question to ask how is that any different than for most adolescents in relation to their families. However, we saw too the themes of world-view empathy and restraint that seem to increasingly respond when there is public rancor involving freedoms of other people stigmatized within their own community or about people perceived mostly as though of different origin and of possible threat to freedom of people in their own nation. As though it is about the freedom of participation and ambition via migration and self-actualization that is really an ancient human story. As much as having to protect the freedom and things one already has at 'home'. No wonder then that from what was once probably an adaptive response to lack of food and other crises, restraint continues as a way of coping with an overwhelming sense of responsibility for the world too. Even to the extent it can involve risk to one's own life. And so much ambitious responsibility that would be extremely difficult for any mortal to achieve by the time of eulogies about any one of us. Has the time now come that we need to change the conversation from firstly and primarily 'seeing' and 'treating' an individual's pathology to instead mutually engaging others as though heroic in their own way and possibly on behalf of us all too? To heed their discernment about the state of our tempestuous public relationships, give permission for them to not have to carry so much responsibility for the world. For us all to seek better ways to mutually support and facilitate each other's personal differences and so our many freedoms.

ADDITIONAL NOTES

1. 'Candle in the Wind 1997' ('Goodbye England's Rose') was performed by Elton John at the funeral service for Diana, Princess of Wales, on September 6, 1997. The song was adapted from the original song 'Candle in the Wind-Goodbye Norma Jean' (1973), by Elton John and Bernie Taupin. Recording of the 1997 version was produced by George Martin who is also known as the "Fifth Beatle".

2. From the Record of Penninghame Kirk Session, February 1711.

3. John Campion's 1983 translation of *EL SUEÑO* (The Dream), by Sor Juana Inés de la Cruz (1651-1695), is no longer in print but available online. SUENO UC PRESS (worldatuningfork.com)

4. Reference: Thompson, A. (2019). *Popular Mechanics*.

5. See for example Robert McGehee of UC Berkeley & Gilly Elor of University of Washington, https://newscenter.ibl.gov/2020/05/04/study-could-dark-matter-be-hiding-in-existing-data/ Scienmag May 3, 2020

6. Reference: Pomeroy, R. (2017). *Live Science. Yahoo News*.

7. Reference: Eckstein, M. (2019). *U.S. Naval Institute News*.

8. In addition to genes themselves there are other inherited genetic processes (i.e., epigenetic) with variations that do not require a change in the underlying nucleotide sequence of DNA. Epigenetic processes involve things like the timing of when genes and chromosomes are activated and control over how they are expressed in the cell life of a person or animal. Variations in epigenetics can come about by a person's interaction with the environment some of which can be passed on to subsequent generations. The activation of puberty and at younger age than previous generations is a good example of epigenetics at work regulating the timing of gene expression.

9. CRISPR: an acronym for clustered regularly interspaced short palindromic repeats. These repeats are a family of DNA sequences found in the genome of bacteria that are engineered not to be infectious but still can enter human cells and carry 'healthy' human DNA to replace 'unhealthy' DNA.

10. Reference: Stein, R. (2020). *National Public Radio (NPR: USA)*.

11. Reference: Huerta-Sánchez, E., et al. (2014). *Nature*.

12. Reference: Gouy, A., Excoffier, L. (2020). *Molecular Biology and Evolution*.

13. Reference: Lin, Y-L., et al. (2015). *Molecular Biology and Evolution*.

14. Reference : Skov, L., et al. (2020). *Nature*.

15. Reference: Kolobova, K., et al. (2020). *Inverse*.

16. Reference: Hardy, B. L., et al. (2020). *Scientific Reports*.

17. Reference: Rodríguez-Vidal, J., et al. (2014). *Proceedings of National Academy of Sciences*.

18. Reference: Leder, D., et al. (2021). *Nature Ecology and Evolution*.

19. Reference: Pomeroy, E., et al. (2020). *Antiquity*.

20. Reference: Greshko, M. (2018). *National Geographic. Science News*.

21. Reference : Potter, B. A., et al. (2014). *Proceedings of National Academy of Sciences USA*.

22. Reference: Atwood, R. (2011). *Archaeology*.

23. References: Nakatsuka, A., et al. (2020). *Cell*; Feinman, G. M., Carballo, D. M. (2018); Nicholas, L.M., Feinman, G.M. (2022).

24. Reference : Courel, B., et al. (2020). *Royal Society Open Science.*

25. Spinal Muscular Atrophy is a genetic disorder caused by insufficient spinal motor neuron (SMN) protein. Without enough SMN protein, nerve cells in the brain stem and spinal cord degenerate which affect muscles that control breathing, speaking, walking, and swallowing.

26. For more discussion on ethics of genomic testing see Reference: Biesecker, L. G., et al. (2021). *British Medical Journal*.

27. References: Koob, G. F. (2015). *European Journal of Pharmacology*; Koob, G. F., Le Moal, M. (1997). *Science*; Koob, G. F., Volkow, N. D. (2016). *Lancet Psychiatry*.

28. References: American Psychiatric Association.2013. and World Health Organization. 1993 & 2015.See also Goyal S. et al. (2012). *Indian Journal of Psychological Medicine*; and Gaebel, W., et al. (2020). *Dialogues in Clinical Neuroscience*.

29. Herpetz, S., et al. (2011). *Deutsches Arzteblatt International*.

30. Reference: Soh, N. L-W., et al. (2007). *Australian and New Zealand Journal of Psychiatry*.

31. There happen to be some recent dramatic representations and documentaries that convey some of the societal denial and collusion, and the powerlessness, personal reactions and impact on victims, because of abuse. Here are some examples based on true accounts: 'Antwone Fisher' (based on autobiography 'Finding Fish' by Antwone Fisher; directed by Denzel Washington,

165

EULOGISTS FOR FREEDOM

2002); 'Family Affair' (written and directed by Chico Colvard, 2010) 'Spotlight' (written by Tom McCarthy & Josh Singer, 2015); Unbelievable (based on 'An Unbelievable Story of Rape' by T. Christian Miller & Ken Armstrong; and on 'Anatomy of Doubt' by This American Life [Ira Glass]; Netflix 2019); 'Tell Me Who I Am' (based on book of same title by Alex Lewis, Marcus Lewis, and Joanna Hodgkin; Netflix 2019); Athlete A (directed by Bonni Cohen and Jon Shenk, Netflix 2020.

32. See 29 & Reference: American Psychiatric Association.2010.

33. Reference: Reas, D. L., & Grilo, C. M. (2021). *Clinical Therapeutics*

34. See 29.

35. Reference : Redgrave, G. W., et al. (2015). *International Journal of Eating Disorders*.

36. References: Douzenis, A., Michopoulos, I. (2015). *International Journal of Law and Psychiatry*; and Latzer, Y., Zohr-Beja, A. (2015). *International Journal of Clinical Psychiatry and Mental Health*; and Túry, F., et al. (2019). Journal of Clinical Psychology.

37. See 29. and Reference: American Psychiatric Association 2010.

38. References: Linehan, M. M., et al. (1991); & Linehan, M. (1993).

39. Reference: American Psychiatric Association 2013 and World Health Organization 1993 & 2015.

40. Reference: Shuo, C., et al. (2018) *Studies in Literature and Language*.

41. Reference: Zeitlin, J. T. (1994). *Harvard Journal of Asiatic Studies*.

42. Reference: Pandey, G. (2021). *BBC News, Delhi*.

43. Reference: Gardner, A. (2020). ScienMag.

44. Reference: Kiefer, P. (2021). *Popular Science*.

45. Reference: Koleth E. (2010). Multiculturalism: a review of Australian policy statements and recent debates in Australia and overseas. Research Paper no. 6 2010–11. *Parliamentary Library. Parliament of Australia*.

REFERENCES

Adityanjee, R., Khandelwal, S. K. (1989). Current status of multiple personality disorder in India. *American Journal of Psychiatry, 146*(12),1607-10. https://doi.org/10.1176/ajp.146.12.1607

Agras, W. S., Telch, C. F., Arnow, B., Eldredge, K., Wilfley, D. E., Raeburn, S. D., Henderson, J., Marnell, M. (1994). Weight loss, cognitive-behavioral, and desipramine treatments in binge eating disorder: An additive design. *Behavior Therapy, 25*:225–238. https://doi.org/10.1016/S0005-7894(05)80285-0

Agras, W. S., Walsh, B. T., Fairburn, C. G., Wilson, G. T., Kraemer, H. C. (2000). A multi-center comparison of cognitive-behavioral therapy and interpersonal psychotherapy for bulimia nervosa. *Archives of General Psychiatry, 57*(5):459–466. doi:10.1001/archpsyc.57.5.459

Ahlin, T. (2018). What keeps Maya from eating? A case study of disordered eating from North India. *Transcultural Psychiatry, 55*(4), 551–571. https://doi.org/10.1177/1363461518762275

American Psychiatric Association. (1952). *Diagnostic and statistical manual of mental disorders.* 1st ed. https://ia800701.us.archive.org/10/items/dsm-1/dsm-1952.pdf (1968): 2nd ed.)https://www.madinamerica.com/wp-content/uploads/2015/08/DSM-II.pdf. (1980): 3rd ed. https://drive.google.com/file/d/16_tLsL38MIyHPHOv3gf-djaCFBSUQzQok/view. (1987): 3rd ed. Revised. https://drive.google.com/file/d/1EO-AVlLd-HclIdbiLjXWcKwczo1P9NEPJ/view. (2013): 5th ed.. https://doi.org/10.1176/appi.books.9780890425596

American Psychiatric Association. (2010). *Practice guideline for the treatment of patients with eating disorders,* (3rd ed.) https://www.psychiatryonline.org/pb/assets/raw/site-wide/practice_guidelines/guidelines/eatingdisorders.pdf

Ashhad S., Feldman, J.L. (2020). Emergent elements of inspiratory rhythmogenesis: Network synchronization and synchrony propagation. *Neuron, 106*(3): 482-497. doi: 10.1016/j.neuron.2020.02.005

Atwood, R. (2011). The Nok of Nigeria. *Archaeology, 64*(4): 34-38. https://archive.archaeology.org/1107/features/nok_nigeria_africa_terracotta.html

Augier, E., Barbier, E., Dulman, R. S., & 9 others. (2018). A molecular mechanism for choosing alcohol over an alternative reward. *Science, (6395)*: 1321-1326. https://www.science.org/doi/epdf/10.1126/science.aao1157

Bartel, H. (2021). *Men writing eating disorders: Autobiographical writing and illness experience in English and German narratives.* Emerald Publishing Limited.

Bentz, M., Jepsen, J.R.M., Pedersen, **T.,** Bulik, C., Pedersen, L., Pagsberg, A.K., von Plessen, K.J. (2017). Impairment of social function in young females with recent-onset anorexia nervosa and recovered individuals. *Journal of Adolescent Health*, *60*: 23e32. https://www.researchgate.net/publication/309521822

Berrettini, W. (2004). The genetics of eating disorders. *Psychiatry (Edgmont)*, *1*(3):18-25. PMID: 21191522; PMCID: PMC3010958.

Biesecker, L. G., Green, E. D., Manolio, T., Solomon, B. D., Curtis, D. (2021). Should all babies have their genome sequenced at birth? *British Medical Journal,* *18*:375: n2679. https://doi.org/10.1136/bmj.n2679

Bould, H., Sovio, U., Koupil, I., Dalman, C., Micali, N., Lewis, G., Magnusson, C. (2015). Do eating disorders in parents predict eating disorders in children? Evidence from a Swedish cohort. Acta Psychiatrica Scandinavica, *132*(1):51-9. doi: 10.1111/acps.12389. PMID: 25572654.

Burt, A., Mannan, H., Touyz, S., Hay, P. (2020). Prevalence of DSM-5 diagnostic threshold eating disorders and features amongst Aboriginal and Torres Strait islander peoples (First Australians). *BioMedCentral Psychiatry,20*(449): 1-8. https://bmcpsychiatry.biomedcentral.com/track/pdf/10.1186/s12888-020-02852-1.pdf

Calzo, J.P., Austin, S.B, Micali, N. (2018). Sexual orientation disparities in eating disorder symptoms among adolescent boys and girls in the UK. *European Child and Adolescent Psychiatry, 27*(11):1483-1490. doi: 10.1007/s00787-018-1145-9. PMID: 29550905; PMCID: PMC6141356.

Cassady, J. D., Kirschke, D. L.., Jones, T. F., Craig, A. S., Bermudez, O. B., Schaffner, W. (2005). Case series: Outbreak of conversion disorder among Amish adolescent girls. *Journal of the American Academy of Child and Adolescent Psychiatry, 44*(3): 291-298. https://eric.ed.gov/?id=EJ696951

Ceccarini, M.R., Tasegian, A., Franzago, M., & 8 others. (2020). 5-HT2AR and BDNF gene variants in eating disorders susceptibility. *American Journal of Medical Genetics Part B: Neuropsychiatric Genetics*, *183*(3), 155-163. doi: 10.1002/ajmg.b.32771.

Cheah, S.L., Jackson, E., Touyz, S., Hay, P. (2020). Prevalence of eating disorder is lower in migrants than in the Australian-born population. *Eating Behaviors*, *37*:101370. doi: 10.1016/j.eatbeh.2020.101370. PMID: 32087555.

Coffino, J.A., Udo, T., Grilo, C.M. (2019). Rates of help-seeking in US adults with lifetime DSM-5 eating disorders: Prevalence across diagnoses and differences by sex and ethnicity/race. *Mayo Clinic Proceedings, 94*(8): 1415-1426. https://www.mayoclinicproceedings.org/article/S0025-6196(19)30352-0/fulltext.

Columbia University's Mailman School of Public Health. (2007). Gay men have higher prevalence of eating disorders. *ScienceDaily*. April 14. www.sciencedaily.com/releases/2007/04/070413160923.htm

Courel, B., Robson, H. K., Lucquin, A., & 24 others. (2020). Organic residue analysis shows sub-regional patterns in the use of pottery by Northern European hunter–gatherers. *Royal Society Open Science, 7*(4): 192016 http://doi.org/10.1098/rsos.192016

Couric, K. (2021). *Going there*. Little, Brown and Company.

Coyne, S.M., Rogers, A.A., Zurcher, J.D., Stockdale, L., Booth, M. (2020). Does time spent using social media impact mental health? An eight-year longitudinal study. *Computers in Human Behavior, 104*: 106160. https://scholarsarchive.byu.edu/cgi/viewcontent.cgi?article=5103&context=facpub

Davis, A.A., Nguyen, M. (2014). A case study of Anorexia Nervosa driven by religious sacrifice. *Case Reports in Psychiatry,* 512764. https://doi.org/10.1155/2014/512764

Davis, C., Katzman, M. (1999). Perfection as acculturation: psychological correlates of eating problems in Chinese male and female students living in the United States. *International Journal of Eating Disorders, 25*(1): 65-70 doi: 10.1002/(sici)1098-108x(199901)25:1<65::aid-eat8>3.0.co;2-w

DeGuzman, M., Shott, M. E., Yang, T. T., Riederer, J., Frank, G. (2017). Association of elevated reward prediction error response with weight gain in adolescent anorexia nervosa. *The American Journal of Psychiatry, 174*(6), 557–565. https://doi.org/10.1176/appi.ajp.2016.16060671

de Sampaio, F.T.P., Soneira, S., Aulicino, A., Allegri, R.F. (2013). Theory of mind in eating disorders and their relationship to clinical profile. *European Eating Disorders Review, 21*(6):479-87. PMID: 23893460.

Dorison, C. A., Wang, K., Rees, V.W., Kawachi, I., Ericson, K. M. M., Lerner, J.S. (2019). Sadness, but not all negative emotions, heightens addictive substance use. *Proceedings of the National Academy of Sciences, 117 (2): 943-949.* doi.org/10.1073/PNAS.1909888116. https://pubmed.ncbi.nlm.nih.gov/31888990/

Douzenis, A., Michopoulos, I. (2015). Involuntary admission: The case of anorexia nervosa. *International Journal of Law and Psychiatry,* 39: 31-35. https://www.sciencedirect.com/science/article/abs/pii/S0160252715000199

Dowling, C. (1988). *Perfect women: Hidden fears of inadequacy and the drive to perform*. Summit Books.

Duncan, L., Yilmaz, Z., Gaspar, H., Eating Disorders Working Group of the Psychiatric Genomics Consortium, & 12 others. (2017). Significant locus and metabolic genetic correlations revealed in genome-wide association study of anorexia nervosa. *The American Journal of Psychiatry, 174*(9), 850–858. https://doi.org/10.1176/appi.ajp.2017.16121402

Dunn, R.R., Amato, K.R., Archie, E.A., Arandjelovic, M., Crittenden, A.N., Nichols, L.M. (2020). The internal, external and extended microbiomes of hominins. *Frontiers in Ecology and Evolution, February 19.* https://doi.org/10.3389/fevo.2020.00025

Eckstein, M. (2019). Navy reverting DDGs back to physical throttles, after fleet rejects touchscreen controls. *U.S. Naval Institute News*. (August 9). https://news.usni.org/2019/08/09/navy-reverting-ddgs-back-to-physical-throttles-after-fleet-rejects-touchscreen-controls

Eisler, I., Dare, C., Russell, G. F., Szmukler, G., le Grange, D., Dodge, E. (1997). Family and individual therapy in anorexia nervosa. A 5-year follow-up. *Archives of General Psychiatry*, *54*(11):1025-30. doi: 10.1001/archpsyc.1997.01830230063008. PMID: 9366659.

Ely, A., Berner, L, A., Wierenga, C.E., Kaye, W.H. (2016). Neurobiology of eating disorders: Clinical implications. *Psychiatric Times,33*(4). https://www.psychiatrictimes.com/view/neurobiology-eating-disorders-clinical-implications

Fairburn, C.G., Jones, R., Peveler, R. C., Hope, R. A., O'Connor, M. (1993). Psychotherapy and bulimia nervosa. Longer-term effects of interpersonal psychotherapy, behavior therapy, and cognitive behavior therapy. *Archives of General Psychiatry, 50*(6):419-28. doi: 10.1001/archpsyc.1993.01820180009001.

Fairweather-Schmidt, A.K, Wade, T.D. (2015). Changes in genetic and environmental influences on disordered eating between early and late adolescence: a longitudinal twin study. *Psychological Medicine*, *45*(15):3249-58. doi: 10.1017/S0033291715001257. PMID: 26134758.

Feinman, G. M., Carballo, D. M. (2018). Collaborative and competitive strategies in the variability and resilience of large-scale societies in Mesoamerica. *Economic Anthropology, *(5): 7–19. doi: 10.1002/sea2.12098

Feldman, M. B., Meyer, I.H. (2007). Eating disorders in diverse lesbian, gay, and bisexual populations. *International Journal of Eating Disorders, 40*(3): 218-226. https://doi.org/10.1002/eat.20360

Frank, G.K.W., Shott, M.E., Riederer, J., Pryor, T.L. (2016). Altered structural and effective connectivity in anorexia and bulimia nervosa in circuits that regulate energy and reward homeostasis**.** *Translational Psychiatry*, *6*(11): e932. https://doi.org/10.1038/tp.2016.199

Friedan, B. (1963). *The feminine mystique*. W. W. Norton.

Gaebel, W., Stricker, J., Kerst A. (2020). Changes from ICD-10 to ICD-11 and future directions in psychiatric classification. *Dialogues in Clinical Neuroscience, 22*(1):7–15 https://www.ncbi.nlm.nih.gov/pmc/articles/PMC7365296/

Gál,Z., Egyed, K., Pászthy, B., Németh, D. (2011). Impaired theory of mind in anorexia nervosa. *Psychiatria Hungarica*, *26*(1):12-25. https://pubmed.ncbi.nlm.nih.gov/21502668/

Gardner, A. (2020). Researchers identify novel genetic variants linked to type-2 diabetes. ScienMag. June 23, https://scienmag.com/researchers-identify-novel-genetic-variants-linked-to-type-2-diabetes/

Genis-Mendoza, A. D., Ruiz-Ramos, D., López-Narvaez, M. L., & 7 others. (2019). Genetic association analysis of 5-HTR2A gene variants in eating disorders in a Mexican population. *Brain and Behavior*, *9*(7), e01286. https://doi.org/10.1002/brb3.1286

Goldstein, L.H., Robinson, E.J., Mellers, CODES study group, & 14 others. (2020). Cognitive behavioural therapy for adults with dissociative seizures (CODES): a pragmatic, multicentre, randomised controlled trial. *Lancet Psychiatry*. 7(6):491-505. https://www.ncbi.nlm.nih.gov/pmc/articles/PMC7242906/

Gouy, A., Excoffier, L. (2020). Polygenic patterns of adaptive introgression in modern humans are mainly shaped by response to pathogens. *Molecular Biology and Evolution*, *37: 1420-1433*.doi:10.1093/molbev/msz306

Goyal, S., Balhara, Y.P.S., Khandelwal, S. K. (2012). Revisiting classification of eating disorders-toward Diagnostic and Statistical Manual of Mental Disorders-5 and International Statistical Classification of Diseases and Related Health Problems-11. *Indian Journal of Psychological Medicine*, *34*(3): 290-296. https://www.researchgate.net/publication/235730049;doi:10.4103/0253-7176.106041

Green, M. A., Willis, M., Fernandez-Kong, K., & 7 others. (2017). Dissonance-based eating disorder program reduces cardiac risk: A preliminary trial. *Health Psychology*. *36*(4):346-355. doi: 10.1037/hea0000438. PMID: 27808527.

Greer, G. (1970). *The female eunuch*. MacGibbon & Kee.

Greshko, M. (2018). Ancient DNA reveals complex migrations of the first Americans. *National Geographic. Science News,* November 8. https://www.nationalgeographic.com/science/article/ancient-dna-reveals-complex-migrations-first-americans

Grubbs, J.B., Lee, B.N., Hoagland, K.C., Kraus, S.W., Perry, S.L. (2020). Addiction or transgression? Moral incongruence and self-reported problematic pornography use in a nationally representative sample. *Clinical Psychological Science*, (5), 936–946. https://journals.sagepub.com/doi/10.1177/2167702620922966

Hardy, B. L., Moncel, M.H., Kerfant, C., Lebon, M., et al.(2020). Direct evidence of Neanderthal fibre technology and its cognitive and behavioral implications. *Scientific Reports,* April 9: 10 (4889). https://doi.org/10.1038/s41598-020-61839-w

Hart, L.M., Mitchison, D., Hay, P.J. (2018). The case for a national survey of eating disorders in Australia. *Journal of Eating Disorders, 6*(30). https://doi.org/10.1186/s40337-018-0221-3

Heffer, T., Good, M., Daly, O., MacDonell, E., Willoughby, T. (2019). The longitudinal association between social-media use and depressive symptoms among adolescents and young adults: An empirical reply to Twenge et al. (2018). *Clinical Psychological Science*, 7(3), 462–470. https://doi.org/10.1177/2167702618812727

Herpetz, S., Hageman, U., Vocks, S., von Wietersheim, J., Cuntz, U., Zeeck, A. (2011). The diagnosis and treatment of eating disorders. *Deutsches Arzteblatt International*, *108*(40): 678-685.https://www.ncbi.nlm.nih.gov/pmc/articles/PMC3221424/

Hodges, E.A., Propper, C.B., Estrem, H., Schultz, M.B. (2020). Feeding During Infancy: Interpersonal Behavior, Physiology, and Obesity Risk. *Child Development Perspectives,14(3):185-191.* https://doi.org/10.1111/cdep.12376

Holmes, S., Drake, S., Odgers, K., Wilson, J. (2017). Feminist approaches to anorexia nervosa: A qualitative study of a treatment group. *Journal of Eating Disorders*, 5(36): 1-15. DOI 10.1186/s40337-017-0166-y

Hübel, C., Leppä, V., Breen, G., Bulik, C.M. (2018). Rigor and reproducibility in genetic research on eating disorders. *International Journal of Eating Disorders*, 51(7):593-607. doi: 10.1002/eat.22896.

Huerta-Sánchez, E., Jin, X., Asan, Bianba, Z., & 23 others. (2014). Altitude adaptation in Tibetans caused by introgression of Denisovan-like DNA. *Nature,* (512) : 194-197. https://pubmed.ncbi.nlm.nih.gov/25043035/

Humphry, T.A., Ricciardelli, L.A. (2004). The development of eating pathology in Chinese-Australian women: acculturation versus culture clash. *International Journal of Eating Disorders*, 35(4):579-88. doi: 10.1002/eat.10269.

Jackson, T., Chen, H. (2011). Risk factors for disordered eating during early and middle adolescence: Prospective evidence from mainland Chinese boys and girls. *Journal of Abnormal Psychology, 120*(2), 454–464. https://doi.org/10.1037/a0022122

Jalal, B. (2021). A new way to understand – and possibly treat – OCD. *Scientific American,* September 7. https://www.scientificamerican.com/article/a-new-way-to-understand-and-possibly-treat-ocd/

Jha, B. K., Awadhia, N. P. (1967). Anorexia nervosa-Review of the syndrome with a case report. *Indian Journal of Psychiatry*, 9(2), 172-180.

Kan, C., Eid, L., Treasure, J., Himmerich, H. (2020). A meta-analysis of dropout and metabolic effects of antipsychotics in anorexia nervosa. *Frontiers in Psychiatry, 11*(208). doi: 10.3389/fpsyt.2020.00208

Kerr-Gaffney, J., Harrison, A., Tchanturia, K. (2019). Cognitive and affective empathy in eating disorders: A systematic review and meta-analysis. *Frontiers in Psychiatry, 10*(102). https://www.ncbi.nlm.nih.gov/pmc/articles/PMC6410675/

Keshavan, M.S., Narayanan, H.S., Gangadhar, B.N. (1989). 'Bhanamati' sorcery and psychopathology in south India. A clinical study. *British Journal of Psychiatry, 154*:218-220. doi: 10.1192/bjp.154.2.218. PMID: 2635890.

Kiefer, P. (2021). The benchmark for human diversity is based on one man's genome. A new tool could change that. *Popular Science*, Dec 16. https://www.popsci.com/science/human-genome-blueprint/

Kipman, A., Gorwood, P., Mouren-Siméoni, M.C., Adès, J. (1999). Genetic factors in anorexia nervosa. *European Psychiatry*, 14(4):189-98. doi: 10.1016/s0924-9338(99)80741-x. PMID: 10572347.

REFERENCES

Klump, K. L., Burt, S. A., Spanos, A., McGue, M., Iacono, W. G., Wade, T. D. (2010). Age differences in genetic and environmental influences on weight and shape concerns. *The International Journal of Eating Disorders*, *43*(8): 679–688. https://doi.org/10.1002/eat.20772

Klump, K.L., Fowler, N., Mayhall, L., Culbert, K.M., Sisk, C.L., Burt, S.A. (2018). Estrogen moderates genetic influences on binge eating during puberty: Disruption of normative processes? *Journal of Abnormal Psychology*, *127*(5): 458 – 470. https://www.apa.org/pubs/journals/releases/abn-abn0000352.pdf

Klump, K. L., Keel, P. K., Sisk, C., Burt, S. A. (2010). Preliminary evidence that estra-diol moderates genetic influences on disordered eating attitudes and behaviors during puberty. *Psychological Medicine, 40*(10): 1745–1753. https://doi.org/10.1017/S0033291709992236

Koleth, E. (2010). Multiculturalism: a review of Australian policy statements and recent debates in Australia and overseas. Research Paper no. 6 2010–11. *Parliamentary Library. Parliament of Australia.* October 8.

Koob, G. F. (2015). The dark side of emotion: the addiction perspective**.** *European Journal of Pharmacology,* (753): 73-87. https://www.ncbi.nlm.nih.gov/pmc/articles/PMC4380644/

Koob, G. F., Le Moal, M. (1997). Drug abuse: hedonic homeostatic dysregulation. *Science,* (5335): 52-58. https://pubmed.ncbi.nlm.nih.gov/9311926/

Koob, G. F., Volkow, N.D. (2016). Neurobiology of addiction: a neurocircuitry analysis. *Lancet Psychiatry,* 8: 760-773. https://pubmed.ncbi.nlm.nih.gov/27475769/

Kolobova, K., Krajcarz, M. T., Roberts, R. B. (2020). Ancient stone tools tell an eplc new story about Neanderthals. *Inverse*, March 12. https://www.inverse.com/science/stone-tools-reveal-epic-trek-of-nomadic-neanderthals

Korn, J., Vocks, S., Rollins, L. H., Thomas, J. J., Hartmann, A. S. (2020). Fat-phobic and non-fat-phobic anorexia nervosa: A conjoint analysis on the importance of shape and weight. *Frontiers in Psychology*, *11*(90). https://doi.org/10.3389/fpsyg.2020.00090

Kube, J., Schrimpf, A., García-García, I., Villringer, A., Neumann, J., Horstmann, A. (2016). Differential heart rate responses to social and monetary reinforcement in women with obesity. *Psychophysiology, 53*(6)**:** 868-879. https://doi.org/10.1111/psyp.12624

Kuhlman, S. (2017). "Disordered Eating Habits and Theory of Mind in Undergraduate Students" *Undergraduate Honors Thesis Collection*. 410. https://digitalcommons.butler.edu/ugtheses/410

Kuhn, T. S. (1962). *The structure of scientific revolutions*. University of Chicago Press.

Latzer,Y., Zohr-Beja, A. (2015). Involuntary hospitalization of patients with anorexia nervosa in extreme situations can save their lives. *International Journal of Clinical Psychiatry and Mental Health*, 2:131-140. http://dx.doi.org/10.12970/2310-8231.2014.02.02.6

Leder, D., Hermann, R., Hüls, M., & 10 others. (2021). A 51,000-year-old engraved bone reveals Neanderthals' capacity for symbolic behaviour. *Nature Ecology and Evolution*, (5): 1273–1282. https://doi.org/10.1038/s41559-021-01487-z

Lee, S. (1991). Anorexia nervosa in Hong Kong: A Chinese perspective. *Psychological Medicine, 21*(3): 703-711. doi:10.1017/S0033291700022340

Lee, S., Ho, T., Hsu, L. (1993). Fat phobic and non-fat phobic anorexia nervosa: A comparative study of 70 Chinese patients in Hong Kong. *Psychological Medicine, 23*(4): 999-1017. doi:10.1017/S0033291700026465

Lenz, A. S., Taylor, R., Fleming, M., Serman, N. (2014). Effectiveness of dialectical behavior therapy for treating eating disorders. *Journal of Counseling & Development*, *92*(1): 26-35. https://www.researchgate.net/publication/260305850

Li, Z., Wang, L., Guan, H., Han, C., Cui, P., Liu, A., Li, Y. (2021). Burden of eating disorders in China, 1990-2019: An updated systematic analysis of the Global Burden of Disease Study 2019. *Frontiers in Psychiatry,* 12: 632418. https://www.ncbi.nlm.nih.gov/pmc/articles/PMC8175855/

Lin, Y-L., Pavlidis, P., Karakoc, E., Ajay, J., Gokcumen, O. (2015). The evolution and functional impact of human deletion variants shared with archaic hominin genomes. *Molecular Biology and Evolution, 32(4): 1008-1019.* https://www.ncbi.nlm.nih.gov/pmc/articles/PMC4379406/

Linehan, M. (1993). *Skills training manual for treating Borderline Personality Disorder.* Guilford Press.

Linehan, M. M., Armstrong, H. E., Suarez, A., Allmon, D., Heard, H.L. (1991). Cognitive-behavioral treatment of chronically parasuicidal borderline patients. *Archives of General Psychiatry, 48*(12), 1060-1064. doi: 10.1001/archpsyc.1991.01810360024003

Liu, A. (2007). *Gaining: The truth about life after eating disorders*. Warner Books.

Liu, A. (1979/2013). *Solitaire: The compelling story of a young woman growing up in America and her triumph over anorexia.* Harper and Row.

Lydecker, J., Pisetsky, E., Mitchell, K., & 6 others. (2012). Association between co-twin sex and eating disorders in opposite sex twin pairs: Evaluations in North American, Norwegian, and Swedish samples. *Journal of Psychosomatic Research, 72*(1): 73-77. doi-10.1016/j.jpsychores.2011.05.014

Marzola, E., Desedime, N., Giovannone, C., Amianto, F., Fassino, S., Abbate-Daga, G. (2015). Atypical antipsychotics as augmentation therapy in anorexia nervosa. *PLoS ONE 10(4)*: e0125569. https://doi.org/10.1371/journal.pone.0125569

Mathisen, T. F., Rosenvinge, J. H., Friborg, O., Vrabel, K. R. (2020). Is physical exercise and dietary therapy a feasible alternative to cognitive behavior therapy in treatment of eating disorders? A randomized controlled trial of two group therapies. *International Journal of Eating Disorders*, 53(5): 1-12. https://www.researchgate.net/publication/338624069

Mattocks, B. (2013/2014). *Please eat: A mother's struggle to free her son from anorexia.* Creative Copy.

Munn-Chernoff, M. A., Grant, J. D., Agrawal, A., & 6 others. (2015). Are there common familial influences for major depressive disorder and an overeating-binge eating dimension in both European American and African American female twins? *The International Journal of Eating Disorders*, 48(4), 375–382. https://doi.org/10.1002/eat.22280

Munn-Chernoff, M. A., Duncan, A. E., Grant, J. D., & 6 others. (2013). A twin study of alcohol dependence, binge eating, and compensatory behaviors. *Journal of Studies on Alcohol and Drugs,* 74(5): 664-673. https://www.jsad.com/doi/10.15288/jsad.2013.74.664

Nakatsuka, A., Lazarudis, L., Barbieri, C. & 47 others. (2020). A paleogenomic reconstruction of the deep population history of the Andes. *Cell, 181*(5): 131-1145. https://www.cell.com/cell/fulltext/S0092-8674(20)30477-3?

Negraes, P., Cugola, F., Herai, R., & 5 others. (2017). Modeling anorexia nervosa: transcriptional insights from human iPSC-derived neurons. *Translational Psychiatry*, 7, e1060. https://doi.org/10.1038/tp.2017.37

Nicholas, L.M., Feinman, G.M. (2022). The foundation of Monte Albán, intensification, and growth: coactive processes and joint production. *Frontiers in Political Science,* 4:805047. doi: 10.3389/fpos.2022.805047

Obata,Y, Castaño, A., Boeing, S., & 15 others. (2020). Neuronal programming by microbiota regulates intestinal physiology. Nature, 578 (7794): 284-289. doi: 10.1038/s41586-020-1975-8.

Olds, J., Milner, P. (1954). Positive reinforcement produced by electrical stimulation of the septal area and other regions of rat brain. *Journal of Comparative and Physiological Psychology,* 47:419–427. https://pubmed.ncbi.nlm.nih.gov/13233369/

Over, H., Uskul, A.K. (2016). Culture moderates children's responses to ostracism situations. *Journal of Personality and Social Psychology, 110*(5):710-724. doi: 10.1037/pspi0000050. http://eprints.whiterose.ac.uk/94490/1/....pdf

Pandey, G. (2021) What's behind suicides by thousands of Indian housewives? *BBC News, Delhi.* Dec 16. https://www.bbc.com/news/world-asia-india-59634393

Pennebaker, J.W. (1997). Writing about emotional experiences as a therapeutic process. *Psychological Science*, 8(3) 162- 166. http: Writing about Emotional Experiences as a Therapeutic Process (gruberpeplab.com)

Perez, M., Joiner, T.E., Lewinshon, P. M. (2004). Is major depressive disorder or dysthymia more strongly associated with bulimia nervosa? *The International Journal of Eating Disorders, 36*(1):55-61. doi:10.1002/eat.20020

Petrie, K.J., Booth, R.J., & Pennebaker, J.W. (1998). The immunological effects of thought suppression. *Journal of Personality and Social Psychology*, 75(5) 1261- 1272.http://spider.apa.org/ftdocs/psp/1998/november/psp7551264.html (utoronto.ca)

Pfeffer, S.E., Hubbard, K. (2021). Katie Couric suffered from bulimia in '80s: 'When Karen Carpenter died, it shook me to the core'. *People.* October 13. https://people.com/health/katie-couric-suffered-from-bulimia-in-the-1980s-when-karen-carpenter-died-it-shook-me-to-the-core/

Pfundmair, M., Aydin, N., Du, H., Yeung, S., Frey, D., Graupmann, V. (2015). Exclude me if you can: Cultural effects on the outcomes of social exclusion. *Journal of Cross-Cultural Psychology, 46*(4), 579–596. https://doi.org/10.1177/0022022115571203

Platte, P., Zelten, J. F., Stunkard, A. J. (2000). Body image in the old order Amish: A people separate from "The World". *International Journal of Eating Disorders, 28* (4): 408-414. doi/abs/10.1002/1098-108X%28200012%2928%3A4%3C408%3A%3AAID-EAT8%3E3.0.CO%3B2-U

Pomeroy, E., Bennett, P., Hunt, C. O, & 7 others. 2020). New Neanderthal remains associated with the 'flower burial' at Shanidar Cave. *Antiquity, 94* (373): 11-26. https://doi.org/10.15184/aqy.2019.207

Pomeroy, R. (2017). Why Georges Lemaître should be as famous as Einstein. *Live Science. Yahoo News.* March 10. https://news.yahoo.com/why-georges-lema-tre-famous-132100330.

Potter, B. A., Irish, J. D., Reuther, J. D., McKinney, H. J. (2014). New insights into Eastern Beringian mortuary behavior: A terminal Pleistocene double infant burial at Upward Sun River. *Proceedings of National Academy of Sciences USA, 111*(48): 17060-17065. https://www.ncbi.nlm.nih.gov/pmc/articles/PMC4260572/

Quinn, R. A., Melnik, A. V., Dorrestein, P. C., & 58 others. (2020). Global chemical effects of the microbiome include new bile-acid conjugations. *Nature,* (579): 123-129. https://www.nature.com/articles/s41586-020-2047-9

Racine, S. E., VanHuysse, J. L., Keel, P. K., Burt, S. A., Neale, M. C., Boker, S., Klump, K. L. (2017). Eating disorder-specific risk factors moderate the relationship between negative urgency and binge eating: A behavioral genetic investigation. *Journal of Abnormal Psychology, 126*(5), 481–494. https://doi.org/10.1037/abn0000204

Raevuori, A., Linna, M.S., Keski-Rahkonen, A. (2014). Prenatal and perinatal factors in eating disorders: a descriptive review. *International Journal of Eating Disorders, 47*(7):676-85. doi: 10.1002/eat.22323. PMID: 24946313.

Reas, D. L., Grilo, C. M. (2021). Psychotherapy and medications for eating disorders: Better together? *Clinical Therapeutics, 43*(1), 17–39. https://doi.org/10.1016/j.clin-thera.2020.10.006

Redfield J. (1993). *The Celestine Prophecy.* Warner Books.

Redgrave, G. W., Coughlin, J. W., Schreyer, C. C., & 6 others. (2015). Refeeding and weight restoration outcomes in anorexia nervosa: Challenging current guidelines. *International Journal of Eating Disorders, 48*(7): 866-873. https://pubmed.ncbi.nlm.nih.gov/25625572/

Rienecke, R. D. (2017). Family-based treatment of eating disorders in adolescents: current insights. *Adolescent Health Medicine and Therapeutics, 8*:69-79. doi: 10.2147/AHMT.S115775. PMID: 28615982; PMCID: PMC5459462.

Rodgers, R.F., Berry, R., Franko, D.L. (2018). Eating Disorders in ethnic minorities: an update. Current Psychiatry Reports, 20(90). https://doi.org/10.1007/s11920-018-0938-3

Rodgers, R.F., Slater, A., Gordon, C.S., McLean, S.A., Jarman, H.K., Paxton, S.J. (2020). A biopsychosocial model of social media use and body image concerns, disordered eating, and muscle-building behaviors among adolescent girls and boys. *Journal of Youth and Adolescence*, 49:399–409. https://doi.org/10.1007/s10964-019-01190-0

Rodríguez-Vidal, J., d'Errico, F., Pacheco, F.G., & 14 others. (2014). A rock engraving made by Neanderthals in Gibraltar. *Proceedings of National Academy of Sciences, 1111* (37): 13301-13306. https://doi.org/10.1073/pnas.1411529111

Roser, M., Ritchie, H. (2016, ongoing) - "Burden of Disease". *Published online at OurWorldInData.org.* Retrieved from: 'https://ourworldindata.org/burden-of-disease'. Online resource. Global Change Data Lab. England and Wales charity # 1186433. https://ourworldindata.org/grapher/eating-disorder-dalys-rate.

Safer, D.L., Robinson, A.H., Jo, B. (2010). Outcome from a randomized controlled trial of group therapy for binge eating disorder: comparing dialectical behavior therapy adapted for binge eating to an active comparison group therapy. *Behavior Therapy, 41*(1):106-20. doi:10.1016/j.beth.2009.01.006

Saini, A. (2019). *Superior: The return of race science.* Beacon Press.

Saini, A. (2019). The disturbing return of scientific racism. *Wired,* December 6. https://www.wired.co.uk/article/superior-the-return-of-race-science-angela-saini?utm_medium=apple-news&utm_source=applenews

Schnepper, R., Georgii, C., Eichin, K., & 6 others. (2020). Fight, flight, – or grab a bite! Trait emotional and restrained eating style predicts food cue responding under negative emotions. *Frontiers in Behavioral Neuroscience,* June 03. 03, https://doi.org/10.3389/fnbeh.2020.00091

Schrimpf, A., McGarvey, S., Haun, D., Kube, J., Villringer A., Gaebler, M. (2019). Socio-cultural norms of body size in Westerners and Polynesians affect heart rate variability and emotion during social interactions. *Culture and Brain,* 7: 26-56. https://doi.org/10.1007/s40167-018-0071-5.

Scott-Van Zeeland, A.A., Bloss, C.S., Tewhey, R., & 44 others. (2014). Evidence for the role of EPHX2 gene variants in anorexia nervosa. *Molecular Psychiatry, 19*(6): 724-732. doi: 10.1038/mp.2013.91. https://www.ncbi.nlm.nih.gov/pmc/articles/PMC3852189/

Sedgewick, F., Leppanen, J., Goh, F., Hayward, H., Happé, F., Tchanturia, K. (2019). Similarities and differences in Theory of Mind responses of patients with anorexia nervosa with and without autistic features. *Frontiers in Psychiatry, 10*(318). doi.org/10.3389/fpsyt.2019.00318

Shin, E. (2021). What is Mukbang? Another massive Korean phenomena explained. *Best of Korea.* March 7. https://bestofkorea.com/what-is-mukbang-another-massive-korean-phenomena-explained

Shuo, C., Jingyang, G., Ying, J. (2018). On Wang Rongpei's drama translation strategy: A case study of *The Peony Pavilion. Studies in Literature and Language. Canadian Academy of Oriental and Occidental Culture,17*(3): 28-34. doi:10.3968/10688 http://cscanada.net/index.php/sll/article/view/10688/11015

Sipilä, P., Harrasova, G., Mustelin, L., Rose, R.J., Kaprio, J., Keski-Rahkonen, A. (2017). "Holy anorexia"-relevant or relic? Religiosity and anorexia nervosa among Finnish women. *International Journal of Eating Disorders*, *50*(4): 406-414. doi.org/10.1002/eat.22698

Six, T., Koster, E. (2014). *Characteristics of highly effective therapists.* Master's thesis submitted to Faculty of Psychology and Educational Sciences, Universiteit of Gent.

Skov, L., Macià, M.C., Sveinbjörnsson, G., & 9 others. (2020). The nature of Neanderthal introgression revealed by 27,566 Icelandic genomes. *Nature,* (582): 78-83. doi: 10.1038/s41586-020-2225-9

Smith, A.D., Herle, M., Fildes, A., Cooke, L., Steinsbekk, S., Llewellyn, C.H. (2017). Food fussiness and food neophobia share a common etiology in early childhood. *Journal of Child Psychology and Psychiatry, and Allied Disciplines*, *58*(2):189-196. https://www.ncbi.nlm.nih.gov/pmc/articles/PMC5298015/

Smith, K.E., Mason, T.B., Johnson, J.S., Lavender, J.M., Wonderlich, S.A. (2018). A systematic review of reviews of neurocognitive functioning in eating disorders: The state-of-the-literature and future directions. *International Journal of Eating Disorders*, *51*(8):798-821. doi: 10.1002/eat.22929. https://www.ncbi.nlm.nih.gov/pmc/articles/PMC6594106/

Smolak, L., Murnen, S K. (2002). A meta-analytic examination of the relationship between childhood sexual abuse and eating disorders. *The International Journal of Eating Disorders, 31*(2): 135-150. doi: 10.1002/eat.10008

Smyth, J., & Lepore, S.J. (2002). *The writing cure: How expressive writing promotes health and emotional well-being.* Washington, D.C.: American Psychological Association. https:// psycnet.apa.org/record/2002-01516-000

Soh, N. L-W., Touyz, S., Dobbins, T.A., & 8 others. (2007). Restraint and eating concern in North European and East Asian women with and without eating disorders in Australia and Singapore. *Australian and New Zealand Journal of Psychiatry*, 41:536-545. https:// openresearch-repository.anu.edu.au/bitstream/1885/17417/2/01_Soh_Restraint_and_ eating_concern_2007.pdf

Spencer, C. (1997). Full text of Earl Spencer's Funeral Oration. https://www.bbc.co.uk/ news/special/politics97/diana/spencerfull.html

Srinivasa, P., Chandrashekar, M., Harish, N., Gowda, M. R., Durgoji, S. (2015). Case report on anorexia nervosa. *Indian Journal of Psychological Medicine*, *37*(2), 236–238. https:// doi.org/10.4103/0253-7176.155655

Steiger, V. R., Brühl, A.B., Weidt, S., Delsignore, A., Rufer, M., Jäncke, L., Herwig, U., Häng-gi, J. (2017). Pattern of structural brain changes in social anxiety disorder after cognitive behavioral group therapy: a longitudinal multimodal MRI study. *Molecular Psychiatry*, *22*(8):1164-1171. doi: 10.1038/mp.2016.217. PMID: 27922605.

Stein, R. (2020). 1st patients to get CRISPR gene-editing treatment continue to thrive. *Morning Addition. NPR. (National Public Radio: USA).* December 15. https://www.npr. org/sections/health-shots/2020/12/15/944184405/1st-patients-to-get-crispr-gene-editing-treatment-continue-to-thrive

Steinem, G. (1969). After Black Power, women's liberation. *New York Magazine.* April 7.

Steinglass, J.E., Berner, L.A., Attia, E. (2019). Cognitive neuroscience of eating disorders. *The Psychiatric Clinics of North America, 42*(1):75-91. doi: 10.1016/j.psc.2018.10.008. https://www.ncbi.nlm.nih.gov/pmc/articles/PMC6601331/

Steinle, N.I., Hsueh, W-C., Snitker, S., & 6 others. (2002). Eating behavior in the Old Order Amish: heritability analysis and a genome-wide linkage analysis. *The American Journal of Clinical Nutrition*, *75*(6):1098– 1106. doi.org/10.1093/ajcn/75.6.1098

Sullivan, P.F., Bulik, C.M., Fear, J.L., Pickering, A. (1998). Outcome of anorexia nervo-sa: a case-control study. *American Journal of Psychiatry*, *155*(7):939-46. doi: 10.1176/ ajp.155.7.939. PMID: 9659861.

Swami, V., Knight, D., Tovée, M.J., Davies, P., Furnham, A. (2007). Preferences for female body size in Britain and the South Pacific. *Body Image, 4*(2): 219-223. doi.org/10.1016/j. bodyim.2007.01.002

Tang, A., Crawford, H., Morales, S., Degnan, K. A., Pine, D. S., Fox, N. A. (2020). Infant behavioral inhibition predicts personality and social outcomes three decades later. *Pro-ceedings of the National Academy of Sciences of the United States of America, 117*(18), 9800–9807. https://www.ncbi.nlm.nih.gov/pmc/articles/PMC7211953/

Taylor, K. (2008). *Going hungry: Writers on desire, self-denial, and overcoming anorexia.* Anchor Books.

Thompson, A. (2019). Scientists say they've ruled out Stephen Hawking's theory about dark matter. *Popular Mechanics*, April 04. https://www.popularmechanics.com/space/deep-space/a27048233/scientists-dismiss-hawking-theory-source-dark-matter/

Thompson, B. (1994). *A hunger so wide and so deep: A multiracial view of women's eating problems.* University of Minnesota Press.

Tong, J., Miao, J., Wang, J., Zhang, J.J., Wu, H.M., Li, T., Hsu, G. (2005). Five cases of male eating disorders in Central China. *International Journal of Eating Disorders, 37*(1) 72-75. doi/abs/10.1002/eat.20061

Túry, F., Szalai, T.D., Szumska, I. (2019). Compulsory treatment in eating disorders: Control, provocation, and the coercion paradox. *Journal of Clinical Psychology*, *75*(8) 1-11. doi:10.1002/jclp.22783

United States Congress. (1868). Constitution of the United States. Fourteenth Amendment. July 9, 1868. https://constitution.congress.gov/browse/amendment-14/

United States Supreme Court. (2020). *Bostock vs. Clayton County.* 17-1618, June 15, 2020. https://www.scotusblog.com/case-files/cases/bostock-v-clayton-county-georgia/

United States Supreme Court. (2015). *Obergefell v. Hodges,* 14-556, June 26, 2015. https://www.scotusblog.com/case-files/cases/obergefell-v-hodges/

United States Supreme Court. (2013). *United States v. Windsor,* 12-307, June 26, 2013. https://www.scotusblog.com/case-files/cases/windsor-v-united-states-2/

Vaidyanathan, S., Kuppili, P.P., Menon, V. (2019). Eating disorders: An overview of Indian research. *Indian Journal of Psychological Medicine*, *41*(4):311-317. doi: 10.4103/IJPSYM. IJPSYM_461_18. PMID: 31391662; PMC6657488

Vujkovic, M., Keaton, J. M., Lynch, & 45 others. (2020). Discovery of 318 new risk loci for type 2 diabetes and related vascular outcomes among 1.4 million participants in a multi-ancestry meta-analysis. *Nature Genetics*, *52*(7), 680–691. https://www.ncbi.nlm.nih.gov/pmc/articles/PMC7343592/

Wade, T. D., Fairweather-Schmidt, A. K., Zhu, G., Martin, N. G. (2015). Does shared genetic risk contribute to the co-occurrence of eating disorders and suicidality? International Journal of Eating Disorders, *48*(6), 684-691. https://doi.org/10.1002/eat.22421

Waldrop, M.A., Karingada, C., Storey, M.A., & 15 others. (2020). Gene therapy for spinal muscular atrophy: Safety and early outcomes. *Pediatrics, 146*(3). https://pubmed.ncbi.nlm.nih.gov/32843442

Wang, K., Zhang, H., Bloss, C.S., Duvvuri, V., Kaye, W., Schork, N.J., Berrettini, W., Hakonarson, H. (2011). A genome-wide association study on common SNPs and rare CNVs in anorexia nervosa. *Molecular Psychiatry*, 16: 949–959. doi.org/10.1038/mp.2010.107

Warren, J.R., Marshall, B. (1983). Unidentified curved bacilli on gastric epithelium in active chronic gastritis. *Lancet,1(8336): 1273-1275.* https://pubmed.ncbi.nlm.nih.gov/6134060/

Watson, H.J., Yilmaz, Z., Thornton, L.M., Hübel, C., Coleman, J.R.I., Gaspar, H.A., & 204 others. (2019). Genome-wide association study identifies eight risk loci and implicates metabo-psychiatric origins for anorexia nervosa. *Nature Genetics,* 51:1207–1214. doi: 10.1038/s41588-019-0439-2. https://www.ncbi.nlm.nih.gov/pmc/articles/PMC6779477/

Weiss, E. J. (2020). Should broken genes be fixed? My daughter changed my thinking. *Center for Genetics and Society. STAT,* Feb 21. https://www.geneticsandsociety.org/article/should-broken-genes-be-fixed-my-daughter-changed-way-i-think-about-question.

World Health Organization (WHO). (1993). *The ICD-10 classification of mental and behavioural disorders.* World Health Organization. https://www.who.int/classifications/icd/en/bluebook.pdf

Yau, E. (2020). Chinese TV shows with strong women characters strike a chord with contemporary female audiences. *South China Morning Post.* June 23. https://www.scmp.com/lifestyle/entertainment/article/3089791/chinese-tv-shows-strong-women-characters-strike-chord

Yeshua-Katz, D., Martins, N. (2013). Communicating stigma: the pro-ana paradox. *Health Communication,* 28(5):499-508. doi: 10.1080/10410236.2012.699889.

Yilmaz, Z., Gottfredson, N., Zerwas, S., Bulik, C. and Micali, N. (2019). Developmental premorbid Body Mass Index trajectories of adolescents with eating disorders in a longitudinal population cohort. *Journal of the American Academy of Child & Adolescent Psychiatry,* 58(2):191-199. https://cdr.lib.unc.edu/downloads/0v838852r?locale=en

Yilmaz, Z., Hardaway, J.A., Bulik, C.M. (2015). Genetics and epigenetics of eating disorders. *Advanced Genomics and Genetics,* 5:131-150. https://www.ncbi.nlm.nih.gov/pmc/articles/PMC4803116/

Zeberg, H., Kelso, J., Pääbo, S. (2020). The Neandertal progesterone receptor. *Molecular Biology and Evolution, (37): 2655-2660.* https://academic.oup.com/mbe/article/37/9/2655/5841671

Zeitlin, J.T. (1994). Shared dreams: The story of The Three Wives' Commentary on *The Peony Pavilion. Harvard Journal of Asiatic Studies,* 54(1): 127-179. https://moodle2.sscnet.ucla.edu/pluginfile.php/616730/course/section/10273785/Zeitlin.pdf

Appendix 1.

Prevalence Rates: Data Checked on https://ourworldindata.org/grapher/prevalence-of-eating-disorders-in-males-vs-females?tab=table&time=1990..

COUNTRY	YEAR	FEMALES	MALES	COMBINED
American Samoa	1990	0.26	0.12	0.38
	2017	0.24	0.11	0.35
Samoa	1990	0.15	0.07	0.22
	2017	0.17	0.08	0.25
India	1990	0.14	0.07	0.21
	2017	0.21	0.11	0.32
Canada	1990	0.63	0.25	0.88
	2017	0.68	0.27	0.95
USA	1990	0.66	0.27	0.93
	2017	0.73	0.3	1.03
UK	1990	0.66	0.23	0.89
	2017	0.81	0.28	1.09
Germany	1990	0.69	0.23	0.92
	2017	0.79	0.26	1.05
Australia	1990	1	0.4	1.4
	2017	1.38	0.5	1.88
New Zealand	1990	0.91	0.35	1.26
	2017	0.95	0.38	1.33

Appendix 2a.

Eating Disorder Disability-Adjusted Life Years.

https://ourworldindata.org/grapher/eating-disorder-dalys-rate?tab=chart&country=ASM~AUS~NZL~DEU~GBR~USA~CAN~WSM

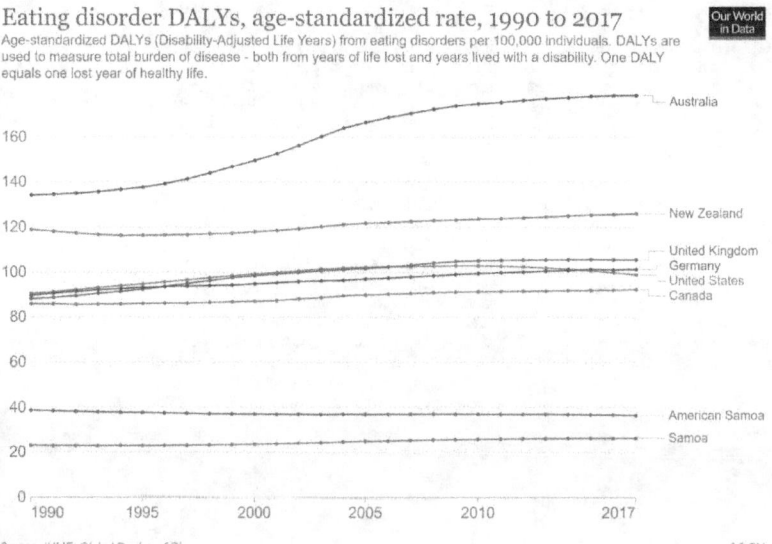

Eating disorder DALYs, age-standardized rate, 1990 to 2017

Age-standardized DALYs (Disability-Adjusted Life Years) from eating disorders per 100,000 individuals. DALYs are used to measure total burden of disease - both from years of life lost and years lived with a disability. One DALY equals one lost year of healthy life.

Appendix 2b.

Year to Prior Year Differences in Disability-Adjusted Life Years (DALYs) by Country

YEAR	AUS.	diff.	NZ.	diff.	USA.	diff.	CAN.	diff.	UK.	diff.	GER.	diff.
1996	139.14		116.45		95.67		86.16		93.63		93.58	
1997	141.32	2.18	116.65	0.2	96.62	0.95	86.23	0.07	95.05	1.42	93.9	0.32
1998	143.93	2.61	117.03	0.38	97.58	0.96	86.61	0.38	96.3	1.25	94.17	0.27
1999	146.88	2.95	117.29	0.26	98.5	0.92	86.96	0.35	97.67	1.37	94.39	0.22
2000	149.67	2.79	117.93	0.64	99.22	0.72	87.14	0.18	98.53	0.86	94.9	0.51
2001	152.67	3	118.5	0.57	99.88	0.66	87.47	0.33	99.24	0.71	95.35	0.45
2002	156.31	3.64	119.25	0.75	100.66	0.78	88.21	0.74	99.97	0.73	95.98	0.63
2003	160.3	3.99	120.29	1.04	101.41	0.75	88.84	0.63	100.7	0.73	96.23	0.25
2004	164	3.7	121.18	0.89	101.98	0.57	89.65	0.81	101.24	0.54	96.52	0.29
2005	166.53	2.53	121.75	0.57	102.29	0.31	90.03	0.38	101.72	0.48	97.09	0.57
2006	168.79	2.26	122.01	0.26	102.49	0.2	90.3	0.27	102.4	0.68	97.48	0.39
2007	170.61	1.82	122.59	0.58	102.69	0.2	90.67	0.37	103.24	0.84	98.03	0.55
2008	172.38	1.77	122.96	0.37	102.84	0.15	91.07	0.4	104.14	0.9	98.5	0.47
2009	173.95	1.57	123.14	0.18	102.94	0.1	91.32	0.25	104.82	0.68	99.06	0.56
2010	174.8	0.85	123.61	0.47	102.96	0.02	91.47	0.15	105.19	0.37	99.52	0.46
2011	175.43	0.63	123.82	0.21	102.8	-0.16	91.56	0.09	105.32	0.13	99.87	0.35
2012	176.32	0.89	124.13	0.31	102.49	-0.31	91.69	0.13	105.49	0.17	100.19	0.32
2013	177.07	0.75	124.57	0.44	101.99	-0.5	91.76	0.07	105.55	0.06	100.6	0.41
2014	177.61	0.54	125.06	0.49	101.46	-0.53	91.94	0.18	105.61	0.06	100.9	0.3
2015	178.18	0.57	125.43	0.37	100.72	-0.74	92.07	0.13	105.68	0.07	101.32	0.42
2016	178.55	0.37	125.76	0.33	99.9	-0.82	92.24	0.17	105.66	-0.02	101.14	-0.18
2017	178.58	0.03	126.09	0.33	98.88	-1.02	92.48	0.24	105.62	-0.04	101.41	0.27

ADDENDUM: SADNESS, ANXIETY, and ASPIRATIONS of

U.S. TEENS

Outcome data from two recent surveys of teenagers in the USA show some of the same trends we have discussed in this book.

A 2021 mid-year survey of 7705 US high school teens at 128 public and private schools, by the Centers For Disease Control And Prevention (CDC), found 44% (3390) reported they had felt sad or hopeless for at least two weeks in the preceding year. Among this same sub-group, 57% of girls vs. 31% of boys and 76% of LGB teens vs. 37% of straight heterosexual students identified having experienced sadness or hopelessness. Over half of the total respondents reported they had received emotional abuse in the home, while 10% (770) said they were physically abused. Twenty percent of LGB vs 10% of heterosexual students reported having been physically abused by a parent or other adult in their home. Hunger was reported by more and nearly a third of Black students.

It is easy to attribute the above reported levels of sadness or hopelessness all to the social and economic disruptive effects of the Covid pandemic, and the pressures felt by and between household members during extended confinement at home. However, the disproportionate results found for girls and LGB students suggest other already existing factors, like acculturation (barriers to pass before full social participation and less alternative opportunities), become more salient when whole communities are under stress.

An earlier (Sept. – Nov. 2018) Pew Research Center study of 920 high school age teens also suggests some trends were already occurring before the pandemic. Some factors reported as more frequent among peers of lower household incomes were bullying (55%), drug addiction (51%), alcohol use (45%), poverty (40%), teen pregnancy (34%), and gangs (33%). However, anxiety and depression were seen as prevalent by 70% of respondents across all income levels. The teens in this study said they personally felt the greatest pressure was to get good grades (61%), more so than to look good (29%), fit in socially (28%), participate in religious activities (8%), be sexually active (8%), use alcohol (6%), or drugs (4%). Aspirations for having an enjoyable job or career (95%) and helping others in need (80%) outweighed other life goals of having a lot of money (51%), getting married (44%), having children (38%), and becoming famous (12%).

In these survey results we see similarities with the themes that we have covered about personal ambition, empathic world view, and sadness being possibly more salient than concerns about body image and settling into close relationships. Which reminds us that persons who have EDs exemplify these themes even more so. That any search to understand the genetics involved needs to consider more 'normal' genes on a spectrum perhaps, and how such persons bring to our attention that socio-cultural barriers limit the freedom still for some people and the effect of society-wide discord. Teenagers are our future and among them are beacons that show us a more empathic world-wide free society is still yet to unfold.

Rico, A., Brener, N.D., Thorton, J., (& 12 others). Overview and methodology of the Adolescent Behaviors and Experiences Survey – United States, January-June 2021. *Morbidity And Mortality Weekly Report,* Supplement 2022; 71(Suppl.-3):1-7. Center For Disease Control And Prevention. doi: http://dx.doi.org/10.15585/mmwr.su7103a

Horowitz, J.M., Graf, N. Most U.S. teens see anxiety and depression as a major problem among their peers. *Pew Research Center Report,* February 2019. 1-15. https://www.pewresearch.org/social-trends/2019/02/20

Another interesting article to read:

Winter, J. (2022). Why more and more girls are hitting puberty early. A pandemic-era rise in early puberty may help physicians to better understand its causes. *The New Yorker*, October 27.

https://www.newyorker.com/science/annals-of-medicine/why-more-and-more-girls-are-hitting-puberty-early

ABOUT THE AUTHORS

We share over 70 years of independent career paths as psychologists from New Zealand and Singapore to the United States and Australia, respectively. Changes in places of living and working for each of us were for family reasons rather than intentional career moves. We even lost contact for many years. During a video catch-up between our families three years ago, we decided to attempt creating this book. Here is some brief history on how each of us arrived at this.

Bernard: During 1984 to 1988, while as junior faculty at the Johns Hopkins School of Medicine (JH), USA, I occasionally attended psychiatric rounds. At the end of one such rounds, the chief psychiatrist gave his synopsis about anorexia nervosa (AN). He emphasized that some of his 'patients' even declined taking the thin wafer used in holy communion because they wanted to avoid the physical discomfort of any food in their stomach. He attributed this to a disruption in the hormonal and metabolic feedback system between the brain and stomach. At the time I didn't know enough to question his metabolic theory. But what struck me even then was how he hadn't presented any other possible explanations. Also known as the differential decision process for making diagnoses and interpretations of clinical observations. I wondered whether he had even asked the clients what else they may have felt about holy communion or even their other religious practices. And it didn't escape me that the chief psychiatrist himself was a practicing Catholic, like I was at the time. I left JH, in part, to get broader vs. specialist experience to help me understand more about people and their psychological health. And to this day I still think about how that chief psychiatrist set off in me a quest to also understand some more about AN. And how AN, when better understood, possibly debunks the commonly theorized separation between every person's mind and body, let alone the person from their social-cultural context.

It was during my time (1992-2002) as the lead clinician at an eating disorders community service in New Zealand (NZ) when I met many persons with AN, some of whom also had Catholic beliefs. They taught me they were wary of taking the wafer at communion, the shaking of hands to exchange a sign of peace and felt self- conflict when even avoiding church attendance. These had nothing to do with stomach discomfort, or obsessive concerns about cleanliness, but instead the person's own sense of unworthiness. During this time, I had frequent collaboration with the Palmerston North Women's Health Collective, where some of my clients also attended support groups. The lesson learned by me was of the effectiveness of focused friendship supports, not just individualized treatment, for successful navigation of life in our wide social world.

In my high school years (early 1970's) in NZ I was fortunate to have been exposed to one of the first trials of intermixing English and social studies. This included more in-depth curriculum on Māori culture and a visit to the Kai Iwi Pā to learn marae (scared and communal place) protocol. Little did I know then how it prepared me for working with one of NZ's first Māori mental health advisors, shortly after my return to NZ in 1988. That was part of broader bi-cultural (Māori and European) changes happening in NZ's health, education, child-welfare and other social and national systems. I seemed to have caught a ride on an experiential conveyer-belt. I became part of a program to prepare nurses and other professionals for working in smaller forensic inpatient units to be newly located in various cities. My six years of participation, in teaching, assignments, and examinations, included a close partnership with Kaumatua (Māori elders) of Ngāti Parewahawaha, and accompanying students on marae immersive experiences. Increasing my own sensitivity to another culture and lessening my expert demeanor and instead embrace greater partnership with all clients, and their families, I felt gave me more information and understanding. And another lens from which to also view AN, about which you would have read that for quite some time it been considered mostly a 'white' girls' issue of being thin as fashionable.

Despite my career being already underway nothing had prepared me for the painful and prolonged personal losses of two very close relatives via acute psychological ill-health. One involved the onset of severe schizophrenia in their forties which eventually overwhelmed their qualities of exceptional considerateness and craftsmanship and their physical health. They died from pneumonia at age 68. The other had been a great athlete, compassionate health worker, and thoughtful parent and spouse. In their mid-thirties they overcame a relapse in severity of long-standing OCD and AN to return to their professional career. But shortly after, and without any prior history, alcoholism began to erode that career and all significant friend and family relationships, and involved many ongoing phases of treatment, AA, Al-Anon, and homelessness. These losses laid bare my own powerlessness over many things. But in the end, I kept up my quest for understanding and came to better recognize my own re-occurring grief and how moving from being stuck in empathy to empathic distance helped me cope and kept alive my interest to write this book and do many other things.

I since spent the latter phase of my career (2002-2022), as a director and consultant in community mental health, in a rural and mountainous region of Vermont (VT), USA. And it has been fortuitous how those personal losses and subsequent lessons from VT have collectively given me better understanding about the shifting balance between need for professionalized treatment, support in the community, and a person's own resilience and abilities. Alcoholics Anonymous (AA) and the Recovery (mental health) movement, now world-wide phenomena, each begun in VT. The 'Vermont way' also includes the state-legislated principle of 'least restrictive' treatment. This VT experience has for me confirmed earlier lessons about distinguishing a person from illness, help people remain in their own home and community, while helping others tolerate behavior they're not used to, being non-judgmental but use good judgment, and use hospitalization and legal processes sparingly.

Lucy: I was a rare and petite sight as the first overseas Chinese student in the School of Psychology, at the University of Aberdeen, Scotland, in the 1980s. Novelty both ways! You see psychology is a very foreign concept in Asia – it is not medicine, law, engineering or accountancy. Indeed, it was not a "hard" science - what career will come of it? Nonetheless, my parents were supportive, and I was determined to commit to a program of study that I am interested in.

My brief experience with distinctive eating occurred in the last Winter in Aberdeen where I would devour a whole 250g packet of Chocolate coated Digestives every night in one sitting. I did not feel sick or disgust, but on the contrary, total satisfaction. It was both addictive and pleasurable. Does this constitute disordered eating? I certainly did not see it as an eating disorder. The real problem was friends' irritating comments and envy of my "petiteness" - that I could eat without any restraint and not be fat. When I returned home in summer, I recalled my mother was rather pleased that I had put on weight and not looking "scrawny".

I was first employed as a psychologist in child guidance services, back in Singapore. I was dissatisfied with the lack of psycho-therapeutic focus in the mental health landscape, and aware that the practice of psychology was more than just being the handmaiden of medical specialists and administration of psychometric tests. Frustrated by this limited scope, I quit the job, packed my bags and left for New Zealand where I first crossed paths with Bernard in 1990. He insisted, once settled into work and country, I should undertake formal applied clinical training. Having only recently completed a master's degree, the thought of returning to study was met with mild resistance. As it is now, it was then - a competitive process to be accepted into the clinical psychology program. I completed the formal clinical psychology training in early 1990s and have dedicated my career in both public and private mental health services ever since.

I have consulted across the age and life span and am passionate in all things psychology, approaching challenges with curiosity. Never one to rest on my laurels, I spent the next two decades juggling family and parenting duties, managed a busy clinical practice, teaching postgraduate clinical trainees, junior staff and provided clinical supervision. Adding to an already full plate, in 2010, I undertook a research Ph.D. in psychological medicine. Several factors led me down the research path. My thirst for knowledge, my frustrations with the lack of clinical translations of Third-wave acceptance-based psychotherapies for adolescents, and the need to be a helicopter mother!! One might ask how would studying enable one to be a helicopter mother? Well, under the guise of research and study, the long after-office hours spent cooped up with my then teenage children in the family's study room would fulfill this need - ensuring that the teens were studying and not gaming online. Post Ph.D., I have been fortunate to have won several prestigious awards for my research, including The Australian Prime Minister Endeavour Overseas Award.

My diverse appetite for psychology matters is rich and commits me to bridge research and translation to practice. In co-writing this book on eating behaviors and culture, this lends itself for both Bernard and I to be curious, expressive, and

190

reflective. In our reminiscence of old times, we share similar principles in our approach to human psychology. That is our conceptualization of things like EDs having historical and social meaning, not just implications for individuals. In our professional service we needed to work within contemporary guidelines while devoting attention to persons who experience things at a clinical level. But now in the later stage of our careers we have returned to exploring more widely how persons with distinctive eating may have lessons for us all.

ACKNOWLEDGMENTS

Karen, Dane, Paden, Kyle, Troy and Bailey.

Al, Aaron and Nicholas.

The unwavering support of our respective families has kept us resilient

during our careers and the labor of writing this book.

Our great appreciation too for the steady guidance by
Pierre Camy and Samantha Pierman of Chapbook Press,
in the publication of this book.

www.ingramcontent.com/pod-product-compliance
Lightning Source LLC
Chambersburg PA
CBHW071328120626
46546CB00002B/485

ADVANCE PRAISE

"*The ChairLeader* is a powerful story about true leadership, heart, and the courage to lift others higher. Chris Malleo and Frankie Kineavy show us that real strength isn't measured by titles, trophies, or physical ability—it's measured by love, resilience, and the way we empower those around us. This book will make you think, feel, and lead differently. It's an inspiring reminder that the greatest leaders aren't the ones who sit the tallest, they're the ones who lift others the highest.

Read it. Live it. Share it."

JON GORDON
17x bestselling author of *The Energy Bus* and
The Power of Positive Leadership

"Championship teams and championship lives are built on the kind of leadership you'll find in *The ChairLeader.* It's about conviction, courage, serving others, and doing the hard things that real leadership demands. Chris and Frankie's story is a reminder that true leaders make everyone around them better both on and off the field."

DABO SWINNEY
Head Coach, Clemson Football, 2x National Champion

"*The ChairLeader* is a rare book. It's about leadership, yes, but it's really about people. Chris and Frankie remind us that the heart of leadership is connection, trust, and lifting others up. Every coach, business leader, and team builder should read this."

PETE CANCRO
Founder and CEO, Jersey Mike's Subs

"This is more than a book on leadership, it's a blueprint for impact. Chris and Frankie show you how connection, courage, and conviction can transform not only teams, but lives. Every leader should read this."

JAKE HERBERT
2012 Olympic Wrestler, 9x US Wrestling National Champion, 3x World Medalist, Big Ten Athlete of the Year, Hodge Trophy Winner